THE INSTRUCTION MYTH

THE INSTRUCTION MYTH

Why Higher Education Is Hard to Change, and How to Change It

JOHN TAGG

RUTGERS UNIVERSITY PRESS

New Brunswick, Camden, and Newark, New Jersey, and London

Library of Congress Cataloging-in-Publication Data

Names: Tagg, John, author.
Title: The instruction myth : why higher education is hard to change, and how
    to change it / John Tagg.
Description: New Brunswick, New Jersey : Rutgers University Press, [2019] |
    Includes bibliographical references and index.
Identifiers: LCCN 2018031144 | ISBN 9781978804456 (hardcover)
Subjects: LCSH: Education, Higher–Aims and objectives–United States. |
    Universities and colleges–United States–Administration. | Educational
    change–United States.
Classification: LCC LA227.4 .T38 2019 | DDC 378.01–dc23
LC record available at https://lccn.loc.gov/2018031144

A British Cataloging-in-Publication record for this book is available from the
British Library.

♾ The paper used in this publication meets the requirements of the American
National Standard for Information Sciences—Permanence of Paper for Printed
Library Materials, ANSI Z39.48-1992.

www.rutgersuniversitypress.org

Manufactured in the United States of America

This book is dedicated with gratitude to my great teachers:

William Lewis
Ron Tabor
George Schell
William Fitzgerald

Far deeper, then, than any question of curriculum or teaching method or determining conditions is the problem of restoring the courage of Americans, academic or non-academic, to face the essential issues of life. How can it be brought about that the teachers in our colleges and universities shall see themselves, not only as the servants of scholarship, but also, in a far deeper sense, as the creators of the national intelligence? If they lose courage in that endeavor, in whom may we expect to find it? Intelligence, wisdom, sensitiveness, generosity—these cannot be set aside from our planning, to be, as it were, by-products of the scholarly pursuits. They are the ends which all of our scholarship and our teaching serve.

—Alexander Meiklejohn, *The Experimental College*, 1932

CONTENTS

THE INSTRUCTION MYTH

INTRODUCTION

Higher education is broken, and we haven't been able to fix it. And in the face of great and growing dysfunctions, it seems resistant to fundamental change. Many claim that colleges and universities as we have known them are on the way out, to be replaced, disrupted, or destroyed by technology and alternative modes of schooling. On the question of why these ancient and established institutions, even in the face of imminent decline, refuse to budge, the tendency has been to leave it at that, to treat the problem as unresolvable, or to proceed to blame various parties for their intransigence. And that just won't do anymore. This book seeks to explain both how colleges and universities are broken and why they have so far successfully resisted real reform. If we can answer those questions, then we can begin to see how to change and renew them.

You should care about this. I won't regale you with the countless reasons why higher education is central to the prospects of the nation and its people. You've heard all of that. And most of it is true. Everybody from national leaders to the teachers in your local high school will tell you that college is increasingly the key to success in the modern world and that the futures of your country, your state, your city, your business, and your children depend in large measure on the work of higher education. What I am telling you here is that higher education, as our designated tool for preparing students for competent and responsible life and work, is not working very well. The emphasis on college completion, which has drawn great public attention of late, is fine as far as it goes. But where it doesn't go at all is to the underlying value of completing college.

The fact is that colleges do not know what they are doing. And I do not mean this just in the idiomatic sense that they are incompetent or fail to execute their tasks well—though that is certainly true in some cases. I mean it in the literal sense: they are unaware of what results they produce; they do not realize what the consequences of their actions are. They literally do not know what they are doing when it comes to undergraduate education.

The fundamental governing principle of colleges and universities today, as my colleague Robert Barr and I argued over twenty years ago, is the Instruction Paradigm.[1] That is to say, colleges are fundamentally in the business of doing instruction, of teaching classes. We refer to it as a paradigm because it is a systematic set of assumptions and ideas that guide action throughout higher education. A paradigm creates a culture and a set of rules. It also gives rise to a set of doctrines or stories that determine what actions are acceptable.

I refer to these ideas as *myths* because that term captures the double nature of the Instruction Paradigm doctrines. They are myths in both the common meaning of the term and the somewhat more technical sense. A myth, in common usage, is a falsehood, a misleading story, or untrue statement. The myths that emerge from the Instruction Paradigm certainly meet this standard. But a myth also serves an important organizing function in the culture that accepts it. The great scholar of comparative religions Mircea Eliade defined it this way: "'Myth' means a 'true story' and, beyond that, a story that is a most precious possession because it is sacred, exemplary, significant."[2] A myth has power in our lives and shapes our perceptions and actions in ways we may not be aware of. A myth is also the organizing story of a culture, a sacred "truth" that serves to structure and explain life. Thus the stories of the Greek or the Egyptian gods served to explain the organization of society and the constraints of daily life to the ancient people who accepted those stories. From our more informed perspective, those stories are also transparent falsehoods. Yet for us today, and even the best informed and most sophisticated of us, our ways of thinking and acting are often shaped by foundational stories and ideas that may, upon examination, prove to be no more credible than Zeus or Horus.

In this book, I identify a series of myths that organize and often define the work of higher education and that derive from the Instruction Paradigm. The central and defining myth, the keystone of the Instruction Paradigm, is the *instruction myth*. The basic story is simple: a student takes a class and learns important things, thus becoming more capable and competent for some future tasks and challenges. The story becomes a foundation for a paradigm or way of thinking when it comes to be generalized universally, as the belief that education consists of exposing students to instruction—to taking classes—and that as long as students are instructed in a systematic way, all is well. As long as the classes are full and students are moving through the system, it is successful by prevailing standards.

The instruction myth is the practical habit of higher education, never explicitly advocated but assumed in almost all policy making—assumed, for example, in most discussion of the completion agenda. What it fails to take much account of is whether the students learn anything, what they learn, how long they remember it, and what they can do with it. Thus the instruction myth creates a veneer of competence around a process that nobody really understands. It lets people act as if they knew what they were doing when they really didn't.

I advocate a different way of thinking, much closer to what most educators and nearly all parents believe about education: the Learning Paradigm, which tells us that what matters about an educational institution is what and how well the students learn. Because, frankly, everybody who has ever gone to school knows that there is no inherent value to sitting in a classroom. It can be useful, it can be a waste of time, or it can be a punishment with no reward. Taking classes is not in itself a good thing. It depends. If students don't learn anything, they have wasted their time no matter how many classes they took and no matter how many degrees they earned. What really matters is what students know and what they can do *as a result of an educational experience*. So if a hundred students have gotten As on their multiple-choice final exam but six months later can't remember the answers to any of the questions, they have wasted their time. If we refigured schools and colleges in the Learning Paradigm, we would evaluate every activity in terms of its learning value. We would ask people to find out what the real and significant consequences of their actions were. We would put a priority on people knowing what they are doing: understanding the results of what they do. And if we did that, we would do many things differently. That was the core argument of my earlier book, *The Learning Paradigm College*.

Nobody advocates the Instruction Paradigm, and hardly anybody really believes the instruction myth is true, but nearly every college or university follows it. Why is this? Because the myth organizes the work of the institution and determines what counts as relevant information.

What does the college as an institution pay attention to on a regular basis? Any administrator at any college can answer these questions: How many students take how many classes? What grades do they receive? Have they taken the requisite number and distribution of classes to receive a degree? The job of faculty members, as far as teaching is concerned, is to teach classes—that is, meet regularly with groups of students—and assign evaluative grades. The institution attends to these things: Did the teacher show up for the classes? Did she assign a grade to each student? If a teacher doesn't show up for class, if a teacher doesn't assign grades, attention will be paid. These are part of the job, prerequisites for continuing employment. Monitoring and maintaining the *processes* of the institution is the priority.

What does the college as an institution pay no attention to? No administrator, at most colleges, can give answers above the level of guesswork to these questions: What did the students learn? Did they remember it? Can they use it?

If the teacher fails to assign grades, she will hear about it quickly and efficiently and be required to comply with the requirement of assigning grades. If students in a teacher's class forget everything they "learned" within a month after the class, neither the teacher nor the college itself will be aware of the fact, much less do anything about it. When colleges as institutions rely on the instruction myth, it camouflages their failures and makes their dysfunctions invisible and therefore impossible to correct. By focusing on the processes and ignoring the results of those processes, institutions can continue for years (as we will see, hundreds of years) without ever really knowing what they are doing, yet with confidence that their job has been done.

It is, of course, assumed that each individual faculty member will teach in such a way as to maximize learning. We call this the *myth of teacher professionalism*. The problem with this—as with many assumptions—is that even the people who assume it do not believe it. And even if they do believe it—which seems very unlikely—they do not test it. It is a rule of thumb, an organizational habit, in the Instruction Paradigm College that everyone trusts every teacher to, individually, take full responsibility for what the students learn in his or her classes. If we accept the instruction myth and the myth of teacher professionalism, we will also adopt a corollary routine assumption: *the privacy of teaching*. Colleges and universities rarely inquire into what actually goes on in classes, and in fact an unwritten rule makes it inappropriate to do so. In the Instruction Paradigm College, we simply assume that every teacher is always doing the right thing in every class. But no one in his or her right mind believes this, least of all the teachers themselves.

Of course, it is certainly true that many students learn a lot in college. I did. You probably did. But if colleges had any conscious control of this process, they would have gotten better at it, and they could tell you how they had gotten better. For the most part, they haven't and they can't. The Instruction Paradigm substitutes form for function, process for product, and thus makes institutions blind to, or at least confused about, what they are in fact accomplishing.

Because of the persistence of the Instruction Paradigm and its complete lack of any reasonable quality control, it is fair to say that as the cost of a college education has gone up, the value of a college education has gone down. The fixation on cost in much of the public discussion is understandable, certainly from the perspective of those who will be paying the bills. (And as I write this my son is a sophomore in college, so I get it!) But fundamentally the conversation about cost is beside the point. The real conversation, the important one we should be having first, is about value. The dismal fact is that for many students, if attending college were much cheaper than it is, it would still be seriously overpriced, because it isn't worth much.

Many books and articles have appeared in the past few years about the failures of higher education. The pace of research about higher education grows, and public interest in colleges and universities rises, roughly in sync with tuition. Yet I have been surprised, given the large output of critique, at how little of what is being said and written today goes directly to the issue that drives this book: *Why* is it so hard for colleges and universities to change, and how can we address the causes of this dysfunction? One of the striking things about many of the issues raised in the following chapters is how little discussed they have been in higher education circles. While there has long been a "national conversation," as the politicians like to say, about the quality of higher education, it has been in many ways a stunted and odd conversation. For example, many people have commented on the resistance of faculty to change. Very few have seriously probed the reasons for that resistance, the nature and the sources of the biases that affect faculty. We have at least thirty years of research that points to the failure of the standard model. But we don't have an open discussion of the persistence of that failure or the underlying causes. We have decades of experience that tells us that the "system" in higher education deflects and avoids even well-designed change with an amazing consistency. But many of the explanations of this process are little more than well-intended guesswork.

The idea that colleges should adopt the Learning Paradigm, that they should begin to observe and record what students learn and to change their standard practices to increase the amount of learning that goes on, is a popular one in colleges and universities. Indeed, generating learning in their students is the chief purpose for which most college faculty became college faculty. I have spoken to hundreds of college and university teachers in the last twenty years about the way their institutions operate, and I am convinced that the vast majority of them value learning and want it to be the touchstone of their work. Many of them enthusiastically endorse the critique of the way their institutions are currently structured. Anonymous surveys, as we shall see, support the same conclusion.

We change all the time, of course. All is flux, as Heraclitus had it, and nothing endures but change. But now I am thinking not about the kind of change that just happens—as the river flows—but the kind of change that we design, as when we resolve to alter our habits. Heraclitus might have said we never step on the same scale twice, but did Heraclitus ever try to lose weight? Designed change, in which we don't just go with the flow but alter the direction of the flow, poses a particular challenge. We must learn how to change by discovering what is preserving the patterns we want to alter. If we don't understand this, we will find ourselves living an ongoing paradox, pushing like Sisyphus and ending up right where we started.

So the largest portion of this book is devoted to explaining how the system of higher education works to keep us in existing patterns. Having described some of the characteristics of the system, we can see how it might be changed. Perhaps a warning is in order. About halfway through this book, readers may be close to concluding that it counsels despair and fatalism, that the system is hermetically sealed against improvement. If I believed that, I would not have written these pages. No, quite to the contrary, I believe that we are today poised to bring about great and powerful improvements in higher education. We have, really for the first time, the understanding of the task and the tools to address it. But in order to address it effectively, we must first understand what has so far kept us from doing so. We must fully face up to the limitations and faults of the system before we can reform it. But reforming it is the whole purpose of this book. So if the news seems unduly harsh, bear with me. There is light at the end of the tunnel.

The book is divided into three main parts. The first asks "Where Are We and How Did We Get Here?" In chapter 1 I will expand on the point I made earlier: that higher education is not performing well in terms of producing student learning. What will be surprising to many is how long we have known this and how consistent the evidence has been over several decades. A summary of some of that evidence will make it clear that the concerns I have expressed about the performance of today's colleges and universities are well grounded.

If higher education is beset with difficulties, how did it get that way? In chapter 2 we will consider the history of change in higher education, especially in the United States. The history is important for a couple of reasons. First, it dispels the easy assumption that current practices are "natural" or "normal." In fact, almost everything about the way higher education functions today is the product of a long process of change and adaptation. Many of the things we take for granted emerged as quite radical innovations, developed to address the challenges of another time. Second, even a brief survey helps us to see how colleges and universities have adapted to their times and how they have maintained some consistent practices, how they have persisted in some things and changed in others. An understanding of the way colleges have changed grounds us in a sense of the radical contingency of the whole process.

Given the way higher education has developed, why is it hard for the system to change today? The second part will address the core question "Why Is Change So Hard?" in seven chapters, first at a very general level, next specifically in terms of today's colleges and universities. In chapter 3 we address the core question in its most general form: Why is change hard? I will argue that most people in most organizations have a bias—*the status quo bias*—against designed change and that this bias is embedded in our basic human psychology. In part it is rooted in loss aversion, a very widespread human tendency of which most of us are completely unaware. But the status quo bias also has roots in our tendency to value what we already have over what we don't have yet, and in the fear of contradicting ourselves.

In chapter 4 we will look at how the status quo bias defends itself in organizations, at the kind of organizational strategies and maneuvers that conceal the bias and protect it from disruption. This applies not just to higher education but to many kinds of organizations.

In chapter 5 we will explore the status quo bias specifically as it applies to colleges and universities. We will look at the structures of our educational institutions—the constant features of their operations that create the framework in which people do their work—and find that the structure of faculty roles creates a system that reinforces the status quo bias in many ways, especially when it comes to the core educational operations of the institutions. We will find that educational institutions protect their existing structures by promulgating mythic beliefs—myths both as foundational beliefs used to interpret the world and as objectively false beliefs—that protect existing structures and reinforce the status quo bias. I have already mentioned the instruction myth—the fundamental Instruction Paradigm assumption that if the students are taking classes, all must be well. The instruction myth inspires and supports other myths that define and limit the work of teaching and learning. Prominent among these are the *myth of quality* and the *myth of academic freedom*. We will discuss defensive routines that systematically deflect attention from the evidence that would lead to change.

We will then examine (chapter 6) how the way universities train and prepare future faculty instills the foundational Instruction Paradigm mythology. We will examine how the structure of colleges frames the work of faculty and see that the organization of faculty work into research-based departments has done much to sustain these myths. We will see that the way the work of teachers is structured and rewarded encourages groupthink and discourages real academic freedom.

In chapter 7 we will turn to another belief that powerfully insulates institutions from change and makes the mythic structure that supports the status quo bias possible: the *myth of the unity of research and teaching*. The myth of unity, which is widely accepted throughout higher education, holds that teaching and research are complementary activities, two sides of the same coin, and successful performance in one tends to predict successful performance in the other. We will examine the evidence for this claim. We will find that the conflict between research and teaching for faculty time results in a peculiar paradox that reinforces many of the myths we have already discussed.

We will then (chapter 8) consider the nature of expertise and find that many of the kinds of preparation and support structures that are available to faculty as researchers are missing in terms of their work as teachers. There is widespread confusion about the nature of real expertise, and what appears to be expertise can be illusory. The real qualities of expertise can help us to find some clues as to how change might be nurtured.

In chapter 9 we will consider one of the major efforts in recent years to address the core issues in reform that we have identified: the Degree Qualifications Profile. We will find scholars who have carefully studied the deficiencies of existing practice and designed programs of change that seem likely to raise the quality of learning in college. And we will find, again, that even in the face of nearly overwhelming evidence that new practices would improve student learning, the factors that we have discussed previously have severely limited the degree of change at many institutions. We will see that in many cases great improvements have been made, but that even clear and demonstrated successes have not been easy to scale up.

By the end of chapter 9 I hope to have made the case that the structural barriers to change in higher education continue to inhibit every effort to shift the paradigm, even well-funded efforts that are supported by solid evidence of effectiveness. If this is the case, we need to ask how change is possible, how individuals and organizations ever change. We need to explicitly address the question of how people and organizations learn to change. In Part III, "Learning to Change, Changing to Learn," we will look at ways of breaking the logjam, of moving institutions toward learning goals that have been closed to them so far.

In chapter 10 we will examine how individuals change ingrained habits. We will begin by discussing the motivations of college and university teachers. We will look at anonymous surveys and interviews to see whether they are happy with the current state of things and will find—and this will be a surprise to some—that many of the changes in the allocation of faculty time over recent decades go against the preferences of individual faculty members but are driven almost entirely by organizational structures and reward systems. Most college and university teachers are motivated to become more effective teachers and personally place a very high priority on teaching. At the same time, they have on average spent an increasing amount of time on research and a decreasing amount on teaching.

In chapter 11 we will look at the mechanisms through which individuals change. If faculty members are going to change the organizational habits that they have been conditioned to, they need to pass through a series of stages. We will examine these *stages of change* and consider what stage most faculty members have reached and why.

In chapter 12 we will turn to how the organizational culture and environment affects the ability of people to move through the stages of change. We will see that the dissemination of innovations in an organization depends on a social support network and that such networks are much more robust in faculty research than in teaching. We will see that while the main reason individual faculty members give for failing to change—lack of time—is often true, it doesn't tell the whole story. In many cases, the social networks that are required to disseminate change fail to function very well when it comes to teaching. We will examine some of the efforts to change this by creating communities around good teaching practice and creating genuine peer review of teaching. Both of these approaches have proven effective when used, but very often the structural barriers that we saw in earlier chapters prevent their widespread application.

The privacy of teaching and the instruction myth serve to deflect change in large measure because they suppress feedback both to individual teachers and to the institution on the consequences of their work. Thus the myth of teacher professionalism is in fact a myth because institutions prevent teachers from taking a scholarly approach to teaching by denying them access to the evidence that a scholar would need to become expert in the field. In chapter 13 we will look at the mechanisms that might make teaching a genuinely scholarly endeavor. We will see that nearly ubiquitous reliance on student evaluations as the major mechanism of both feedback and evaluation has trivialized teaching and inhibited improvement. We will consider what genuine peer review of teaching might be like and explore how institutions could promote scholarly teaching.

Higher education institutions face a number of learning disabilities when it comes to change. But we can identify certain key processes that could facilitate change. Perhaps the most important involves information flow in the organization. In chapters 14 and 15 we will explore two mechanisms that could create feedback loops for the teaching and learning process: the teaching inventory and the outcomes transcript with portfolio.

Of course, feedback won't change behavior in the way we want unless people are aiming for the right goals. To a large extent, the goal of faculty is to protect their endowment, to keep the valuable rewards that academic life offers. In chapter 16 we will explore how to change the faculty endowment so that faculty professional goals are better aligned with the educational goals they have for their students.

The Instruction Paradigm, of course, is not simply an invention of colleges. The external regulation of institutions and the competition for students have generated a peculiar kind of a market for educational products based on imitation and reproduction of high-prestige models. This regulated market discourages innovation and promotes the mythology of the Instruction Paradigm. In chapter 17 we will examine this market and the regulatory role of accreditors and government agencies to see how current regulations do much to lock the instruction myth in place. We will explore how we might adjust regulation and information flow to create a real market based on educational value rather than imitation and reinforcement of existing models.

By this stage we will have identified several points of leverage that could dislodge the instruction myth and create incentives for change that could promote student learning. In chapter 18 we will summarize how these levers could alter the system as a whole and create a new kind of market for quality learning in higher education.

In the end, I hope to show that colleges and universities as educational institutions are very resistant to designed change. But the reason for this resistance is not the personalities or personal preferences of either college administrators or faculties. It is the structural characteristics of the colleges themselves, as organizations, that insulate them against change.

To see the whole picture accurately, we will need to keep in mind some apparently inconsistent facts. University faculty are in fact seriously averse to large-scale change. But that is not because the people who go to work at universities are particularly change averse. (Indeed, many of them would be happy to completely restructure the world *outside* their institutions, but they remain averse to changing their own places.) They are averse to change because working at universities makes them so. Colleges and universities are locked in the Instruction Paradigm not because the people who work there do not value learning. Quite the contrary. The terms of their employment, in many cases, make their personal preferences irrelevant. They do what they need to do to thrive in institutions that have made immunity to change in core processes a condition of employment. The problem is not that most of the people who work in higher education do not want to change. The problem is that they do not know how to.

But they can learn. If higher education is going to embrace the Learning Paradigm, it must learn the lesson of how to change core practices. Like most important learning, this will not be easy to achieve. But it is neither impossible nor impractical. I hope to show that if we can alter certain key points of leverage in the system, institutions can learn to change in ways that they have been unable to before.

There will always be resistance. Change always means letting go of something, and that means that loss will always contest with gain when we contemplate different ways of doing things. Change invites regret, suggests an admission of past failures, and makes us inconsistent with our prior selves. Hence, often enough, we want to change without changing, to hold on to what we have while reaching for something else. Institutions, and quintessentially colleges and universities, are designed to do what they are already doing. To design changes that call upon them to do new things or do things in radically different ways is always challenging.

Yet to live is to change. The great challenge of life, for individuals and institutions alike, is to grow, to embrace new tasks and new ideas, while remaining true to those central values that give us a place to stand and a way to be. If all were truly flux, then we would be quickly lost in the shifting and roiling confusion of an ungraspable reality. We need to find a still place amid the maelstrom. I cannot change the world if there is no "I," no constant agent who can push and pull against the shifting events around me. So the core question must be: Who am I? Who are we? For many of us, the practical answer to that question, the theory-in-use, as we will call it, that lets us function in the world, is that we are a collection of habits, we are people who do such-and-such things in such-and-such ways. When a habit takes the place of a purpose, we become set in our ways without recalling the object of our efforts, we keep sailing in the same direction but without a destination.

If we are to ask who the people who do the work of colleges are, then we must ask: What is a college? Ask the students. What makes you a college student? What do students do? The answer, for most, is that a student is someone who takes classes and takes tests. Observe then the college teachers. What do they spend their time doing? Presiding over classes and assigning grades. But what is it all for? That is, what is there about it that is essential to preserve, that makes the rest worthwhile, that constitutes the still place where we can stand and say, "This is what we do that is of value, this is what counts, this is what we must preserve, changing everything else, if need be, to keep it." What is the purpose by which we can judge the habits?

Change for the sake of change, we often hear, is pointless. So the question becomes, "Change for the sake of . . . what?" That question brings to light that the prospect of self-conscious change always has at least two sides. In asking what we would change, we are also asking what we would preserve, and what we want to create. How can difference make us better? Difference can make us better if it brings us closer to what we want to be.

What do colleges and universities want to be? That is the question that we need to answer if we hope to resolve the conundrum of change. It is a question that has been blurred and obscured in a thousand ways for nearly a thousand years. But along the way, they have answered it, often well, but usually temporarily. And repeatedly, familiar habits have supplanted conscious purpose. We have forgotten who we are, taken up in the daily ritual of what we do. But we can never achieve anything that really deserves to be called progress unless we can stick to a consistent answer, hold on to a constant purpose. Given an answer, we have a fulcrum, and a solid place to stand. If we can say, "this is what we are, this is what we choose," then we can see what we must do. Then we can change for a purpose, to preserve what we really are, to become what we choose to be.

PART I WHERE ARE WE AND HOW DID WE GET HERE?

1 · THE CHRONIC CRISIS

American colleges and universities as places of undergraduate learning have assumed an increasingly important role for the last century. The job of preparing young people for serious and important work has increasingly moved from secondary schools to colleges and universities, and most colleges and universities have neither understood nor met the challenge. And when I say "work" here I don't mean just earning a living. I mean also the job of living well and participating fully in the world. Indeed, the quality of educational preparation that students receive in colleges has probably declined as our reliance on those colleges for providing the intellectual capital to fuel further growth has increased. As we have asked more of higher education in terms of educating undergraduate students, it has provided less, and at a higher price.

The current default setting for colleges and universities is dysfunctional. It cannot prepare most students for the promising future they hope for. Traditional colleges and universities have become transcript-generating factories that lack the organizational capacity to achieve the mission that they claim to achieve and that society wants them to achieve. The governing paradigm for colleges and universities is that they offer classes, enroll students in classes, keep records of evaluations of student work in those classes using a brief and vague scale, count the classes "successfully" completed, and grant degrees when a sufficient number of classes have been completed. In other words, higher education is in the business of providing instruction in the form of discrete classes, counting them, and crediting students for having been instructed.

In this framework, which Robert Barr was the first to call the Instruction Paradigm,[1] the following things are invisible and irrelevant to the institution granting degrees: What did students learn in their classes? What and how much do they remember, and for how long? What are they able to do? How well are they prepared to learn new things and master new skills during and after college? I do not mean to suggest that the faculty, administrators, and staffs of most colleges do not care about these things. Of course they do. And in performance, occupational, or professional programs where students engage in internships or authentic activities, their teachers often do attend to these questions. But colleges and universities as institutions generally fail to measure or respond to what students learn or to change their own organizational behavior in response to it. Colleges and universities, allegedly the depositories of the "higher learning," do not themselves, as institutions, learn very well.

Most of those who teach in and work at colleges and universities believe in the Learning Paradigm: the fundamental doctrine that what matters most is how much and how well students learn. But as institutions, colleges and universities are stuck in the Instruction Paradigm.

For the most part, colleges and universities cannot distinguish between teachers whose students learn little and forget it quickly and teachers whose students learn much and remember it and apply it for years. Charles Blaich and Kathleen Wise, director and associate director of the Wabash College National Study of Liberal Arts Education—one of the most sophisticated and careful studies of how college affects students—put it this way: "Colleges and universities are capable of accomplishing many complex tasks, among them managing admissions, scheduling courses, allocating resources, and creating and maintaining information technology infrastructures. The governance and bureaucratic structures at most colleges and universities are not built to use assessment evidence to make changes."[2]

Richard P. Keeling, head of the educational consulting firm Keeling & Associates, and Richard H. Hersh, former president of Hobart and William Smith colleges and Trinity College, make the point even more directly: "Making the sanguine but dangerous assumption that passing grades equal learning, most colleges and universities do not adequately support, measure, or strive to improve learning itself."[3] This assumption, that passing grades equal learning, is the core belief that sustains the instruction myth.

The architecture and design of higher education is built on the foundation of the instruction myth. The physical campus, the semester or quarter calendar, the curriculum, the schedule of classes, and the daily activities of teachers and students emerge from the central idea that taking classes is what being a student consists of and that scheduling and administering classes is what the college exists for. In other words, colleges and universities are in the business of putting students through a *process* and observing and recording the steps of that process without paying much attention to the *results* that the process achieves.

Nearly everyone who goes to college intends to get a degree—though many never accomplish this. A degree is, by definition, granted for the completion of a defined number of courses, or more precisely a defined number of credit hours, usually 120. A credit hour is one hour per week spent in a classroom being instructed by a teacher. By the standards not only of nearly all institutions but of their formal accrediting agencies and the U.S. Department of Education, accumulating credit hours is what students do in college and is the criterion for successful completion. And in enforcing this foundational definition of college work, these parties all embrace the myth that Keeling and Hersh so accurately identify above: "the sanguine but dangerous assumption that passing grades equal learning," the substitution of process for outcomes. Eduardo M. Ochoa, assistant secretary for postsecondary education in the U.S. Department of Education in the Obama administration, states on behalf of his department, "At its most basic, a credit hour is a proxy measure of a quality of student learning."[4] This is, as we shall see, nonsense looked at from any angle at all. A credit hour is simply a measurement of time (supposedly) spent in a particular room and carries no information about what happens as a result. But the Department of Education, along with nearly every college and university in the country, treats a process as if it were an outcome. That is the core of the instruction myth.

By and large, colleges and universities as educational institutions do not get better. And in an environment in which the level of preparation of incoming students is declining and the number and variety of students is increasing, if they don't get better, they get worse. We have seen a boomlet in recent years in books and commentaries on the *Crisis on Campus* (the title of a 2010 volume by Mark Taylor). If we look back a few years, however, we note something interesting. The criticisms of higher education that have gained much public notice in the first decades of the twenty-first century are not new. Even at a fairly detailed level, the critique goes back at least to the 1980s, and in many respects to the 1920s. Alfred North Whitehead's *The Aims of Education* was first published in 1929. Alexander Meiklejohn's *The Experimental College*, which contains many elements of the contemporary critique of higher education, was published in 1932. Evidence has accumulated, new voices have been added to the chorus of criticism, but the essential critique persists in a very consistent form. So if higher education is experiencing a crisis, we have to acknowledge that it has become a chronic crisis. How can such an oxymoronic problem persist for so long? Only one way. The institution in crisis has averted its gaze from its problems and persisted with the practices that cause those problems. The problem is not just that higher education is failing. Today's distinctive problem is that the system has refused to learn from its failures but has embraced and preserved the causes of its dysfunction, repeatedly deflecting calls for change.

These are, of course, generalizations, and there are exceptions to all of them. I hope the exceptions are increasing in both number and quality. But the exceptions get attention these days in part because they are so exceptional, so different from the norm.

Colleges and universities, like other human institutions, have changed in many respects over the years. But they have reached a state of equilibrium, especially in the past half century or so, and while they have gone with the flow of social and technological changes, they have been especially resistant to *designed change*. Keeling and Hersh describe a state of affairs that has now persisted for decades: "A large percentage of what students have learned vanishes after the grades are in; almost half of students who begin college never finish; and the results of national tests of college student achievement have been dismal for years. Worse, these data are largely ignored by leaders in positions to respond and instigate reform."[5]

I am speaking here of colleges and universities as educational institutions, as the organizations that facilitate and certify significant learning for adolescents and adults. This is not the only role that such institutions serve. They also conduct research and serve their communities in a variety of ways. These are important functions. Indeed, universities have probably been the major engine of progress in human life for more than a century through their research in a broad array of fields. Universities have changed rapidly and aggressively as research institutions. It is fair to say that, in terms of their research function, since the Second World War American universities have been seedbeds of innovation that have responded avidly to the developing markets for new knowledge and discovery. So you will often hear the claim that the United States has the best universities in the world, that our higher education system is the envy of other countries. Most of the top-ranked universities in the world, by the most widely accepted rankings, are American, and American universities have produced over a third of all Nobel Prize winners.[6]

But if we contrast the operations of the laboratories and research centers at any major university with the operations of teaching and student learning, we will see something that should be rivetingly interesting but usually goes without notice. Research in most fields today is answering very different questions, using very different technology and very different methodology than it was in, say, 1960. But teaching, for most students at most universities, is largely the same. Indeed, if we peel away the veneer of usually superficial technological tools—PowerPoint has replaced the chalkboard—it is almost as if we are caught in a time warp. Dominic Brewer and William Tierney, scholars of higher education at the University of Southern California, have noted the contrast: "Whereas research infrastructure—how one conducts research, with whom, its funding, its transfer, and the like—has gone through enormous transformation over the last century, the same cannot be said of teaching and learning. . . . Indeed, if one transported John Dewey from when he first started teaching in the early twentieth century to a classroom of today, he most likely would recognize the basic components and infrastructure; the same could not be said if Emile Durkheim investigated how researchers now conduct research."[7] Or, in the words of Eric Mazur, a physics teacher at Harvard, "The way physics is taught in the 1990s is not much different from the way it was taught—to a much smaller and more specialized audience—in the 1890s, and yet the audience has vastly changed."[8]

Why is this? Is it because research fifty or one hundred years ago was undeveloped and in need of improvement while teaching had already been perfected? Hardly. No, teaching in higher education has been caught in a strange time warp for other reasons, and we will discuss them in the pages to come. One of those reasons is that research has become the defining mission of the university; in the words of Stanford University's Larry Cuban, it has "trumped teaching" in the internal calculations of the university.[9] My focus here is on the university's role of promoting undergraduate learning rather than the research function because the research function has gone relatively well while the undergraduate learning function, as we shall see, has not. The two roles

are neither mutually exclusive nor mutually reinforcing, but both are important. We can see them clearly only if we see them separately.

DOES HIGHER EDUCATION NEED TO CHANGE?

Most students get both smarter and more knowledgeable in college. So
do most young adults whether they are in college or not. But college students probably grow in many ways that non-students don't. They are, after
all, in a setting for several years where knowledgeable people are intentionally exposing them to important information and ideas. But it is still true
for many of the twenty million or so American college students that being
a student consists largely of preparing through short-term reinforcement
for multiple-choice tests that call upon them to sort correct from incorrect
information in structured and isolated debriefing contexts. If they can
pass enough of these tests, they get the degree. The best evidence we have
suggests that many students fail to understand much that they learn, that
most fail to remember what they learn, and that very few are able to transfer
what they have learned to new settings. If this account is even partly correct,
the implications are dire, and colleges and universities need to change.

The evidence for the effects of college has been hard to interpret because
there has been so little of it. And this is one of the most important ways in
which universities as research institutions differ from universities as educational institutions. The results of academic research are made public and vetted openly by critical experts. Research is an ongoing process of testing and
evaluating ideas, of generating and reviewing evidence, so that researchers
get smarter about what they do, and the world gets smarter about what
researchers study. Most colleges and universities, on the other hand, can provide no credible evidence one way or the other about what their students
have learned or can do as a result of their college experience. What evidence
there is remains tightly held in the secret sanctum of the classroom, known
only to the teacher who gathers it. But doubts have been growing for a long
time as to the value and meaning of a college degree.

Alexander Astin, for many years director of the Higher Education
Research Institute (HERI) at UCLA, began in the 1970s to do longitudinal research tracking the development of college students during and after
college. His 1977 book *Four Critical Years* raised serious questions about

conventional assumptions about college education. The 1983 report of the National Commission on Excellence in Education, "A Nation at Risk," brought questions of educational quality to public attention in a powerful way. It treated higher education only tangentially, but focused some attention on another project, that of the Study Group on the Conditions of Excellence in American Higher Education. This group, under Astin's leadership, concluded in its 1984 report—"Involvement in Learning"—that existing measures of performance in higher education were not very informative: "None of them tells us what students actually learn and how much they grow as a result of higher education. None of them tells us anything about educational outcomes. As a result, we have no way of knowing how academic institutions actually perform."[10] That, they explicitly stated, won't do: "Institutions should be accountable not only for stating their expectations and standards but for assessing the degree to which those ends have been met. . . . They should . . . acquire and use better information about student learning, the effects of courses, and the impact of programs."[11] That was over thirty years ago.

Close on the heels of the Study Group, in 1985 the Association of American Colleges (AAC—now the Association of American Colleges and Universities, the AAC&U) published its report "Integrity in the College Curriculum," which concluded that "evidence of decline and devaluation are everywhere."[12] The principal author of the report was Frederick Rudolph, a leading scholar of the history of higher education from Williams College. "What is now going on," it found, "is almost anything, and it goes on in the name of a bachelor's degree."[13] These reports were widely praised and much discussed. The AAC pursued the conclusions further. Robert Zemsky and Susan Shaman, of the Institute for Research on Higher Education at the University of Pennsylvania, conducted an analysis of thirty institutions, tracing how seniors who graduated in 1986 had made their way to their degrees. They concluded, "Those who would argue that the current critique of the undergraduate curriculum exaggerates the problem will derive little solace from our findings. . . . We find the undergraduate curriculum in the liberal arts lacking sufficient breadth of study, particularly in the natural sciences and mathematics, and lacking substantial depth as measured by either structured or temporally focused coursework."[14]

By the early 1990s the accumulated research and analysis of the higher education picture had achieved something like a consensus among those who were paying attention. In 1991 Ernest Pascarella, then at the University of Illinois at Chicago, and Patrick Terenzini of the Pennsylvania State University published their massive and careful review of nearly all the extant research on higher education for the previous twenty years: *How College Affects Students*. In an environment in which parents and students were beginning to go deeply into debt to pay the rapidly increasing prices of elite institutions, Pascarella and Terenzini found that "there is little consistent evidence to indicate that college selectivity, prestige, or educational resources have any important net impact on students in such areas as learning, cognitive and intellectual development, other psychosocial changes, the development of principled moral reasoning, or shifts in other attitudes and values. Nearly all of the variance in learning and cognitive outcomes is attributable to individual aptitude differences among students attending different colleges. Only a small and perhaps trivial part is uniquely due to the quality of the college attended."[15] In other words, the elite colleges with extraordinary research accomplishments were pretty good at *selecting* students who were good at doing school. But there was no persuasive evidence that students learned more at elite colleges than at run-of-the-mill ones.

Furthermore, there is no very persuasive evidence that attending selective colleges does much to improve students' general life prospects. Economists Stacy Berg Dale and Alan B. Kreuger in 2002 conducted about as careful a study as has yet been done on the effects of college selection. They concluded that "students who attended more selective colleges do not earn more than other students who were accepted and rejected by comparable schools but attended less selective colleges."[16] Indeed, they found something that might at first glance seem rather remarkable: "The average SAT score of schools that a student applied to but was rejected from has a stronger effect on the student's subsequent earnings than the average SAT score of the school the student actually attended."[17] It appears that the ambition and inclinations of individual students are much more important than their choice of college.

These revelations have done nothing to deter sales of the *U.S. News & World Report* College Issue. Nor did Alexander Astin's updated report of his continuing longitudinal research in his 1993 book *What Matters in College? Four Critical Years Revisited*. By this time, Astin's Cooperative Institutional Research Program (CIRP) had conducted longitudinal tracking of over half a million students at thirteen hundred institutions and had been operating over a period of twenty years. Astin found increasing confirmation for the view that colleges and universities were generally doing the opposite of what research indicated worked best to promote student learning and development. They were, he concluded, "guided more by *economic* than by *educational* considerations."[18] It was a problem of values: "Research universities can continue shortchanging undergraduate education as long as they value the acquisition of resources and the enhancement of reputation more than they do the educational and personal development of the undergraduate."[19]

In 2005, Pascarella and Terenzini updated *How College Affects Students* with a second volume, covering research in the decade since their first volume was published. Again, they found no basis in evidence for the conventional criteria for quality: "After adjusting for differences in the characteristics of the students enrolled, the *degree of net change* that students experience at the various categories of institutions is essentially the same."[20]

In the last decade or so the critique has become more focused and acute. And evidence has accumulated that the results of college education have declined in recent years. The National Assessment of Adult Literacy is a nationwide assessment administered by the Department of Education. If we compare the results from the 1992 and 2002 surveys we find that the scores for college graduates fell thirteen points in prose literacy, seventeen points in document literacy, and four points in quantitative literacy.[21]

It is increasingly noticeable that nearly all the credible evidence on what students learn in college is collected by third parties. The institutions themselves have almost willfully distanced themselves from any effort to find out whether they are accomplishing what they say they want to do. As Astin noted in 2016, echoing the observation of the Study Group thirty years earlier, "When it comes to the basic question of whether, and how much, students are actually *learning*, there's a notable lack of information in most colleges and universities."[22] It has taken a long time for the message to get through to the larger public, but it may finally be doing so. In 2013, Robert Zemsky, the same who surveyed curricula in 1985, long professor of higher education at the University of Pennsylvania and a perceptive critic of the system, concluded, "The American public is just now beginning to discover that no one, either within or outside the academy, has any real evidence on what undergraduates are learning."[23]

Many interested parties have attempted to create a more specific and credible picture of exactly what happens to students in college. Perhaps the most important and influential of these is the National Survey of Student

Engagement (NSSE—pronounced like the nickname of the Loch Ness Monster). That survey and its two-year-college companion, the Community College Survey of Student Engagement (CCSSE—pronounced to rhyme with *Nessie*), have gathered evidence from thousands of colleges and millions of students on just what students are doing in their classes, looking especially at those activities that research shows make a difference to student engagement and effort. The NSSE—the brainchild of Russell Edgerton, president emeritus of the American Association for Higher Education (AAHE) and later the director of education funding for the Pew Charitable Trusts—is a survey that asks students about their experience as students. Drawing on previous research, the NSSE forms a profile of the students' experience at the institution, seeking to find out to what extent students are involved in activities that predict academic engagement and achievement, in the classroom and elsewhere. The NSSE has had a powerful effect in part because it provides colleges, sometimes for the first time, credible evidence of what the students are actually doing.

For just one example of the many measures of student engagement that the NSSE includes, consider the level of academic effort students make. For all institutions surveyed, in the first year of the survey, 2000, 34 percent of freshmen and 36 percent of seniors reported spending ten hours or fewer per week in academic work: "studying, reading, writing, doing homework or lab work, analyzing data, rehearsing, and other academic activities."[24] On the 2014 survey the comparable percentages were 40 percent for freshmen and 39 percent for seniors. The NSSE and CCSSE reveal how much students write, how much they read, how often they work with other students and with faculty inside and outside of class, and a variety of information about the kinds of activities that are consequential for learning and academic success.

The NSSE is based at the Indiana University Center for Postsecondary Research. George Kuh, the founding director of the NSSE, and Alexander McCormick, who succeeded Kuh as director in 2007, have supervised the expansion of the survey and the development of parallel surveys of faculty and beginning college students. The organization has conducted a vast research project by plumbing the annual results for evidence of what works best in promoting student learning. The CCSSE, under the leadership of Kay McClenney at the University of Texas at Austin, pursues a parallel project among community colleges. The NSSE and CCSSE have vastly increased the amount of consequential information that institutions have about what is really going on with their students. The results of the NSSE and CCSSE have generally confirmed what we thought we knew about the problems and limitations of most colleges and universities. But institutions have not generally been quick to take action on the basis of this new information.

Several groups and researchers have moved beyond the survey format in an effort to collect direct evidence of what students learn in college. Two such projects are especially worthy of attention. The first is the Wabash National Study (WNS), mentioned above, initially a longitudinal study of 17 four-year institutions in eleven states (now expanded to more), which has tracked a number of indicators of progress among students after they enter college. The Wabash study uses the Collegiate Assessment of Academic Proficiency Critical Thinking Test, a multiple-choice test that seeks to evaluate students' ability to analyze and evaluate arguments after reading prose passages. Based on this and other tests and student surveys, the study seeks to assess students' progress in developing critical thinking skills and other skills and attitudes important to learning.[25]

The second project of special interest, probably the most thorough and carefully controlled research of this kind, is the study conducted by Richard Arum of New York University and Josipa Roksa of the University of Virginia, sponsored by the Social Science Research Council, and reported in their 2011 book *Academically Adrift* and a follow-up volume in 2014, *Aspiring Adults Adrift*. Arum and Roksa administered the Collegiate Learning Assessment (CLA) to over twenty-three hundred students at twenty-four colleges and universities when the students were in their first semester in college in 2005 and then again at the end of their sophomore year in 2007 and their senior year in 2009. The CLA is a sophisticated assessment that provides students with a set of documents on a problem and asks them to produce a written response. In one instance, the student takes the role of an intern to the mayor of a town. Given an in-basket of material including "information regarding crime rates, drug usage, relationship between number of police and robberies, research studies, and newspaper articles," the student's task is to advise the mayor on proposals for drug education and increasing the number of police.[26] The materials and the problems are carefully validated in trials with multiple groups of students, and detailed scoring rubrics are developed before a given problem is used for student assessment. The CLA also includes two other analytical writing tasks. The goal in using the CLA was to test not for specific content knowledge but for the ability of students to use and apply knowledge, what is generally referred to these days as critical thinking. In addition to the CLA, Arum and Roksa administered surveys and analyzed student demographics and academic records.

In their initial review, they concluded, "We observe no statistically significant gains in critical thinking, complex reasoning, and writing skills for at least 45 percent of the students in our study. An astounding proportion of students are progressing through higher education today without measurable gains in general skill as assessed by the CLA."[27] After following up the same students past graduation, they reported, "Over four years of college, if the CLA was scored on a one-hundred-point scale, 36 percent of students would not have demonstrated even a one-point gain."[28] Comparing the progress students made in their first two years with their upper-division work when they were specializing in their academic majors, Arum and Roksa found "that improvement on the CLA was not significantly larger in the last two years of college than in the first two."[29] By comparing a variety of institutions, they were able to contrast institutional types and found what others had found before them: "The issues we have identified, namely weak academic engagement and limited learning, are widespread. They are not concentrated at a few institutions, or even at a specific type of institutions. While students in more selective institutions gain more on the CLA, their gains are still modest, and while they spend more time studying alone, their average is still only slightly over ten hours per week."[30] Hence, the authors conclude, "Large numbers of U.S. college students can be accurately described as academically adrift. They might graduate, but they are failing to develop the higher-order cognitive skills that it is widely assumed college students should master. These findings are sobering and should be a cause for concern."[31]

Of course, some questions have been raised about the study, and about the CLA as a meaningful measure of what students are learning. Charles Blaich, director of the WNS, and Ernest Pascarella, now director of the Center for Research on Undergraduate Education at the University of Iowa, along with Georgianna Martin and Jana Hanson, research assistants with the center, conducted an analysis of Arum and Roksa's research to discover whether it closely replicated the results of other studies, especially the WNS. They found that

> the findings from the WNS, based on an independent sample of institutions and students and using a multiple-choice measure of critical thinking substan-

tially different in format than the Collegiate Learning Assessment, closely match those reported by Arum and Roksa.

This suggests that an important part of what Arum and Roksa found is not simply the result of an anomalous sample or the use of [an] . . . unconventional method of measuring critical thinking and reasoning skills. . . . The WNS results do suggest that Arum and Roksa should be taken seriously. Their findings are not going to go away simply because they make academics uncomfortable.[32]

What Arum and Roksa and Blaich and his colleagues have done is something that, with very few exceptions, colleges and universities themselves do not do. They have attempted to measure in a meaningful way what difference college makes in students, what the students really learn in college. There has been serious criticism of Arum and Roksa's work. No less an authority than Alexander Astin has raised questions about the statistical methodology of their study. And I do not suggest that *Academically Adrift* is the last word on the subject.

Still, there has not been a full-fledged argument on the issue of quality raised by this work. The reason is straightforward. There is simply no credible evidence on the other side. Nobody is making the case with persuasive evidence that college is raising the intellectual caliber of students across the board—for the simple reason that the evidence doesn't exist. Robert Zemsky, who has voiced criticisms of Arum and Roksa's work, nonetheless concludes that "higher education cannot win this argument simply because there is no evidence to the contrary."[33]

Of course, many students learn a great deal in college. But much of that learning is casual, transitory, and ultimately trivial. There does not seem to be any dispute on the point that the world we live in is more complex and challenging to negotiate than the world of fifty or one hundred years ago. Yet all of the extant evidence seems to indicate that the quality of college learning, on average, is lower rather than higher than it used to be.

At the most rudimentary level, we can say that how much and how well students learn will be a product of how much effort students put into the task. Two economists recently undertook an analysis of the evidence on the question of how much time students spend studying in college. Philip Babcock of the University of California, Santa Barbara, and Mindy Marks of the University of California, Riverside, examined a range of surveys and longitudinal studies going back to 1961, including the NSSE research we discussed above: "We find that full-time college students in 1961 devoted 40 hours per week to academics, whereas fulltime students in 2004 invested about 27 hours per week. . . . Study time fell for students from all demographic subgroups; within race, gender, ability, and family background; overall and within major; and for students who worked in college and for those who did not. The declines occurred at four-year colleges of every type, size, degree structure, and level of selectivity."[34] If twenty-seven hours per week is the average, then a large portion of students spend less than that—according to the NSSE results we discussed above, often considerably less.

And when they do study, apparently, many college students are just studying for tests, and that with the minimum possible effort. Kylie Baier and four colleagues from Ball State University and Bowling Green State University in Ohio conducted a study of the response to reading assignments of 395 students at two Midwestern universities. The results were striking: "A staggering 62% of students spend an hour or less [per week] reading their assigned materials and only 6.1% spend more than two hours reading." Over 40 percent reported that they read assignments only when preparing for exams. Over 18 percent simply didn't complete the reading assignments at all. "Approximately 89% of students believed they could receive a C or better without completing any of the assigned readings." Over 30 percent believed they could get an A while doing none of the assigned reading.[35]

If students are spending less time studying and investing less effort and attention, does that mean that they are having less success by institutional measures? Are universities noticing and responding to the fact that students are increasingly disengaged and making less effort? Quite to the contrary. The measure of student success at nearly all colleges and universities is course grades. Stuart Rojstaczer of Duke University and Christopher Healy of Furman University have gathered contemporary grade records from 160 colleges and universities and historical grades going back to the 1930s from over eighty institutions. What they have found is that grades increased greatly in the 1960s, then adjusted slightly downward in the 1970s, and have been rising at a gradual but steady rate ever since. They find that "over a period of roughly 50 years, with a slight reversal from the mid-1970s to the mid-1980s, America's institutions of higher learning gradually created a fiction that excellence was common and that failure was virtually nonexistent."[36] Reviewing evidence of the sort we have just seen, they conclude, "The cause of the renewal of grade inflation, which began in the 1980s and has yet to end, is subject to debate, but it is difficult to ascribe this rise in grades to increases in student achievement."[37] They conclude, in fact, that "it is likely that the decline in student study hours, student engagement, and literacy are partly the result of diminished academic expectations."[38]

The argument over grade inflation has persisted for some years but has been muddied by a confusion over purposes. If we see college as a filter that aims to remove the inadequate students from the system, then grade inflation is a problem because it means that too many unprepared students are not being taken off the assembly line before graduation. But such a view degrades or ignores the educational potential of college. However, grade inflation is problematic from the perspective of the Learning Paradigm as well. Fluctuating standards, over a long period of time, indicate that there really is no standard, that there is no common code that different grades at different institutions can be compared to. Grades, as we shall see in more detail later, are a largely subjective standard of quality reflecting the personal judgment of individual teachers, not the shared judgment of whole faculties or groups of evaluators. This is not to say that the professors who assign grades are being arbitrary; they may be quite thorough and consistent. But it is to say that they are not using a common standard but are making up their own. It is not that grades are meaningless; they mean something to the teacher who assigns them. But it is a private language, not easy to translate for anyone else. The rich meaning that may be carried through the assignments, comments, and conversations that go on in an excellent class is left behind by the single evaluative blot, the lone letter that means "good" or "average," without any specific reference to what students have done or can do and without any link to a larger set of standards.

One suggestion we never hear in the conversation about grade inflation is, "Why don't we calibrate the grades to their true value?" The reason nobody says that is that nobody knows their true value, and everybody knows that nobody knows it. It would be pretentious nonsense to talk of the "real" or "true" meaning of grades without any shared frame of reference. So even though the individual faculty member may know what he or she is doing in teaching an individual class, the institution doesn't know what it is doing and can't describe what has been done to or for the student based on the only information it preserves.

Grade inflation, in an environment in which nobody can make a plausible claim to know what grades really mean, suggests that institutions themselves have no grip on the relationship between student effort and student reward. Indeed, one of the chief reasons Arum and Roksa found for the dismal performance of college students was the lack of rigor in the curriculum.

The critique of higher education, going back at least to the 1970s, is aptly summarized by cognitive psychologists Diane Halpern of Claremont McKenna College and Milton Hakel of Bowling Green State University: "It would be difficult to design an educational model that is more at odds with current research on human cognition than the one that is used at most colleges and universities."[39] Hersh and Keeling draw what has become a fairly obvious conclusion: "Under these conditions it becomes possible—even likely—to be in good academic standing, stay in school, and earn a baccalaureate degree with little evidence of knowledge or skill mastery. With such learning, a degree holds a hollow promise."[40]

EQUAL OPPORTUNITY?

It should go without saying that in a nation dedicated to the proposition that all men and women are created equal, a central goal of education should be to make opportunity widely available to all. In a liberal democracy, higher education should serve as the ladder by which those born with fewer advantages can rise to greater accomplishments. Yet the reputational and financial and academic structure of higher education seems almost willfully designed to do the opposite. The most highly regarded colleges and universities, both in the public folklore and in the formal rankings of the most widely read publications, are the most selective. These are institutions that as a matter of policy admit only students who have already established their bona fides as outstanding school-goers. Thus it is the highest mark of excellence for these educational institutions that they admit the students who require the least education. As Astin puts it, "Institutions and the public define the *excellence* of a college or university in terms of *who* enrolls rather than how well they are *educated* after they enroll. In the health care field, this would be the equivalent of judging a clinic or hospital on the basis of the condition of the patients it admits rather than the effectiveness of the care and treatment patients receive once they are admitted."[41]

I will discuss later the paradoxical fact that the criterion of selectivity, which almost directly determines academic reputation, always and everywhere excludes any information about students actually attending the institution. Selectivity is measured by the ratio of students who have applied and been accepted to students who have applied and been rejected. None of the students in the calculation have attended the institution, ever. Thus the selectivity sweepstakes becomes a kind of self-fulfilling prophecy: the more students who apply, the more selective the college will become and the higher its reputation will rise, leading more students to apply. I think we have already seen that we have no reason to believe that students learn any more at selective institutions than they otherwise would, but that is irrelevant to reputation by prevailing standards.

If we look not just at who is admitted to college but at who succeeds there, the problem is even more dire. As Paul Tough, a journalist specializing in education issues, has written, "Whether a student graduates or not seems to depend today almost entirely on one factor—how much money his or her parents make. To put it in blunt terms, Rich kids graduate; poor and working-class kids don't. Or to put is more statistically: About a quarter of college freshmen born into the bottom half of the income distribution will manage to collect a bachelor's degree by age 24, while almost 90 percent of freshmen born into families in the top income quartile will go on to finish their degree."[42]

We can hardly doubt that the substantive benefits of college will be greatest for those who have the most to learn. The student who attended an inadequate high school needs college more than the student who attended an excellent one. The student who was raised in poverty needs college more than the student who was raised among the benefits and stimulations of well-to-do families. The student whose parents did not themselves attend college needs college more than the student whose parents are college graduates. They all need college, of course, in our contemporary economy. But those who need it the most are those whose learning has been delayed, who have lacked the advantages that middle-class upbringing can provide. For them, almost their entire hope of upward mobility rests in the prospect of college success. They need college more than anybody else.

This is not controversial. Indeed, colleges and universities themselves and educational leaders of all stripes recognize it. It is the rationale behind vast efforts to recruit, support, and graduate at-risk students of various categories. It is the rationale for efforts to increase the population of racial and ethnic minorities and the economically disadvantaged through affirmative action and minority recruitment. It is essentially the rationale for the massive drive for diversity in the college population. Today most major universities have several administrators whose job is to promote and advance diversity, defined as a mix of racial and ethnic groups in the student population.

And yet, all of the diversity effort has been essentially bolted on to a system that has no way of measuring success or correcting its errors because it doesn't know what students are learning or why. The instruction myth constrains the ability of colleges and universities to respond to the needs of students who need education the most.

Of course, the difficulties of low-income students are not the fault of the higher education system. Still, the success and completion rates of African American and Hispanic students compared with those of white students have barely budged in the last decades. For example, considering young adults, ages twenty-five to twenty-nine, as of 2012 more than 44 percent of Hispanic females and 35 percent of males had some college, but only 17 percent of females and 11 percent of males had completed a bachelor's degree. Contrast that with the white completion rate of 43 percent for females and 35 percent for males.[43] African Americans, Hispanics, and students from low-income families are much more likely to attend community colleges than four-year institutions, and community colleges have significantly lower completion rates than others. Overall, fewer than four out of ten community college students complete any kind of a degree or certificate within six years.[44]

The costs of these failures are borne not just by the individuals who fail to realize their potential, though those costs are so heavy that they alone should move us to action. Astin points out that "high school graduates who do not attend college . . . are *five* times more likely to be imprisoned than are people who complete college."[45] The unemployment rate for more than a decade, no matter what the economic conditions, has been much higher for those without a college degree.[46]

The costs to both the individual and society are difficult to calculate but unquestionably large. The waste of human potential is paralleled by the waste of public resources. And this is the easily calculated cost, the cost of education forgone by those who do not attend or do not complete colleges. The cost of the failure to learn much in college is much harder to calculate but is almost certainly as great.

It is interesting to note that the *institutions* that generate extraordinarily low rates of success, including but not limited to most community colleges, do not themselves seem to suffer much from the failure. There is certainly no direct connection between poor academic results and poor financial ones. That is because the institution's "success" is measured by the standards of the instruction myth. Thomas Bailey, Shanna Smith Jaggars, and Davis Jenkins—scholars who study community colleges at Teachers College, Columbia University—note the notoriously poor performance of these institutions and that "colleges designed to maximize *course enrollment* are not well designed to maximize *completion of high-quality programs of study*."[47] The same critique, of course, could be applied to nearly all four-year colleges.

Colleges fail to move at-risk students toward degrees for essentially the same reason they fail to maximize learning for all students—because, forgive the repetition, they don't know what they're doing. Because, as institutions, they do not attend to the outcomes of the processes they mandate, they count classes completed but don't know whether those classes succeed or fail. Those students who are facile at jumping through academic hoops and giving teachers what they want can complete the courses much more efficiently than those who are not. But in no case will the institution learn from its own mistakes or effectively guide the students to learn from theirs. And it is nearly axiomatic that where the instruction myth holds sway, those students who need to learn the most will generally learn the least.

The dimensions of this problem are hard to overstate, and the consequences for the future are dire. This is true in terms of all students, but especially in terms of those students most in need of education. And what matters is not, I repeat, college completion, but student learning. Eric A. Hanushek of Stanford University and Ludger Woessmann of the University of Munich in a 2010 paper for the National Bureau of Economic Research analyzed educational and economic outcomes in the countries in the Organization for Economic Cooperation and Development from 1960 to 2000. Separating out years of schooling from cognitive development, as indicated by comparative international tests, they have found "cognitive skills are highly significantly associated with economic growth. At the same time, the association between years of schooling and economic growth becomes statistically insignificant and drops to close to zero."[48]

How much difference could increases in learning make? Hanushek and Woessmann extrapolate from existing data that an increase of one-fourth of a standard deviation in average performance on the PISA (Programme for International Student Assessment) test would increase GDP in the United

States, now about $18 trillion, by roughly $43 trillion over the next eighty years.[49] In another scenario, bringing all students up to a minimum skill level (a score of 400 on the PISA) would increase GDP by roughly $86 trillion, an increase of 567 percent in GDP.[50] These impacts would take time, but would have massive consequences. Such studies demonstrate that improved learning, and perhaps especially improved learning for those not succeeding today, have the real potential to accelerate economic growth and well-being in the long term.

This point does not, of course, apply just to those students who are at risk in today's universities, but it does apply to them. The underserved students in college today are often seen as a drag on the system, as intruders where they don't belong, grit in the gears of the educational machine. But the fact is that these students are the greatest single resource the country has for improving economic growth and raising living standards in the long run. Knowing this, many have invested much energy in the effort to help these students complete college. Yet, completion is a mirage, a simulacrum of accomplishment if students fail to learn. Students will succeed not based on the degrees they complete but based on what they know and what they can do. In other words, increasing student ability, learning, is money in the bank and raises the income and productivity of the entire society, in addition to the welfare of the individual learners. Years of schooling, however, are nearly irrelevant to growth.

Astin concludes that "the education of the underprepared student is the most important issue in American higher education."[51] The goal of access to higher education for underprepared students is a noble one. But as long as access is to institutions bounded by the instruction myth, access will not mean education.

ARE THEY CHANGING BY DESIGN?

Change is a word that can be freighted with all manner of symbolism and emotional baggage. But the question I am asking here is straightforward. Do colleges and universities, as educational institutions, need to significantly alter their practices? Do they need to do things differently than they are doing them today? Do they need to change? And the only plausible answer is that they do. Are they doing so? In the face of well-nigh overwhelming evidence of failure and dysfunction, is higher education accepting the challenge? Certainly some institutions are. And we may hope—and I am inclined to believe—that their number is growing. But the overall picture is not a happy one.

The touchstone of progress is feedback. Feedback, of course, is information that tells you how you're doing, and how to do better. If colleges don't know how they are doing, how can they do better? Like students, if colleges and universities are going to learn then they need information about where they have succeeded and where they have fallen short. They need information about how well students are learning. Hence the great push for the past few decades among accrediting agencies, education scholars, and professional organizations for systematic and meaningful assessment of student learning. Of course, all teachers assess how well their students are learning; if they did not, how could they assign grades? The problem is that the substance and content of that assessment, even the specific conclusions that emerge from it, are locked in the classroom. All that the institution preserves is the grade, which is not helpful for improving the way the process works because it says nothing about the strengths or deficiencies of the student—or the teacher. And, as noted above, it is highly subjective. Not only do two different teachers assign grades with different degrees of rigor, they may be grading completely different kinds of student activity—even in the same subject. The grade conceals, rather than reveals, these differences.

In the 1980s, the period of the national reports we discussed above, the lack of information about what students were really learning drew the attention of the governors and state governments and sparked discussions within the regional associations that accredit colleges and universities. A widespread movement to promote learning assessment arose, and the AAHE under Russell Edgerton's leadership initiated an annual Assessment Forum. At the third of those forums, held in 1987, Peter Ewell of the National Center for Higher Education Management Systems (NCHEMS) spoke about a core issue in education reform: what is the purpose of assessment? Ewell was (and, now as president emeritus of NCHEMS, still is) deeply involved in assisting both institutions and governments to find ways to more meaningfully assess student learning. One possible motive for assessment, he pointed out, was a desire to improve student learning. Another was a desire to meet external requirements—of state governments or accreditors. Overwhelmingly, he found, institutions were pursuing assessment not for improvement but to meet external accountability requirements.

Twenty-two years later, in 2009, Ewell revisited the issue in a paper for the National Institute of Learning Outcomes Assessment, tracking the arguments in that previous research. He found that much had changed. All the regional accrediting associations had adopted explicit requirements that institutions define the learning outcomes they hoped to achieve and assess student learning in those outcomes. Pressure from states had increased for evidence of the value of higher education in terms of student outcomes. At the federal level, the Spellings Commission (convened by Bush administration secretary of education Margaret Spellings) had recently made a set of recommendations highly critical of many existing practices and calling for more accountability. In response to all of this, Ewell found, universities and colleges engaged in a great deal of activity around assessment. But most of it fell into what he called the Accountability Paradigm rather than the Improvement Paradigm: "Far too many institutions, dominated by the need to respond to external actors like states or accreditors, approach the task of assessment as an act of compliance, with the objective being simply to measure something and the exercise ending as soon as the data are reported."[52] In other words, what Keeling and Hersh said of students in higher education is largely true of the colleges and universities themselves: "A large percentage of what [they] have learned vanishes after the grades are in."

It is not just assessment. We have learned, with a high level of confidence, how to do teaching better and how to design for better learning. Experimental psychology, cognitive science, and neuroscience have made great advances, helping us to understand how people learn. Much has been written about this already, so I will not belabor the point. But we should recognize the fact that the risk calculation in seeking to improve teaching and learning has changed markedly in recent decades. We still have much to learn, but we have learned enough to know how to confidently and demonstrably improve the performance of teaching and learning in almost every institution. The foundational research has shaped the scholarship of teaching and learning, which has largely been translated into knowledge that can be implemented in classrooms.

Consider as just one example the meta-analysis done in 2014 by Scott Freeman, a biologist at the University of Washington, and six of his colleagues. They synthesized 225 studies comparing the effectiveness of teaching courses in science, technology, engineering, and math (STEM) disciplines using traditional lecture methods and using active learning techniques that have been developed in recent years. They found that "active learning increases examination performance by just under half a [standard deviation] and that lecturing increases failure rates by 55%."[53] Furthermore, these improvements "hold across all of the STEM disciplines and occur in all class sizes, course types, and course levels,"[54] and "active learning confers disproportionate benefits for STEM students from disadvantaged backgrounds and for female students in male-dominated fields."[55] So powerful was the more effective pedagogy, the authors concluded, that "if the experiments analyzed here had been conducted as randomized controlled trials of medical interventions, they may have been stopped for benefit—meaning that enrolling patients in the control condition might be discontinued because the treatment being tested was clearly more beneficial."[56] If lives or health were at risk, institutions would not be teaching the way they are.

But, of course, mediocre educational practice puts the welfare of both students and society at risk. So, what has been the response to the nearly overwhelming evidence that we can do better? In 2018, four years after Freeman's study, Marilyne Stains, associate professor of chemistry at the University of Nebraska–Lincoln, and two dozen of her colleagues reported on a thorough and labor-intensive research project seeking to confirm directly how teachers were really teaching in the STEM disciplines. They personally observed 709 courses taught by 549 instructors at twenty-four research universities and one college. They found that lecture was the most common pedagogy. Fifty-five percent of the courses used a "didactic" style, which meant that more than 80 percent of class time consisted of lecturing; 27 percent employed "interactive lecture"; and 18 percent were "student-centered."[57] The researchers conclude, "Didactic practices are prevalent throughout the undergraduate STEM curriculum despite ample evidence for the limited impact of these practices and substantial interest on the part of institutions and national organizations in education reform."[58]

"Substantial interest" in reform has failed, over several decades now, to translate into changed practices. Robert Zemsky of the University of Pennsylvania has been a close observer of reform efforts for over three decades. He draws this conclusion about the capacity of higher education for designed change:

> Presenting evidence of a problem—no matter how compelling—is not sufficient to change academic practices. Faculty freedom and autonomy trump evidence

every time. Those who argue that greater transparency, that is, more evidence as to the academy's problems and failings, will either compel faculty to change or force public entities and accrediting agencies to change always underestimate the inertia in the system. The lamenters will complain that it is cowardly for those outside the academy to give in, having first settled for issuing strongly worded statements. . . . The efficiency pundits will similarly protest, all the while proving relatively powerless to change either practices or customs within the academy.[59]

Colleges and universities need to change, to transform, to redesign themselves. This has been the case for decades and is now strikingly obvious to anyone who attends to the evidence. But institutions don't seem able to respond. What we like to think of as the engines of progress for our civilization are becoming a dead weight, dragging us down. It is time to shake things up.

2 · HOW DID IT GET THIS WAY?

The first institution of higher learning in the American colonies was, of course, a college: Harvard, chartered by the Massachusetts Bay Colony in 1636 and accepting its first students in 1638. By 1645, William and Mary and Yale were added to the list. By 1770, nine colonial colleges had appeared, but it was not until after the Revolutionary War that something formally called a university arose on American soil. So in the New World, the college—devoted primarily to the education of undergraduates—preceded the university. This was a reversal of the order in which such institutions first came into existence, for the university was the original institution, and the college grew out of it.

The university emerged in Europe right around the beginning of the thirteenth century. The first universities developed out of the medieval cathedral and monastery schools that were intended mainly to prepare the clergy. The mainstay of the first universities was the lecture, which means literally to read aloud. In the days before print, masters would convey lessons to their students by reading or summarizing the rare and expensive books that were then available.

The college was originally a housing arrangement, an effort to provide someplace for students to live that would reduce tensions with the surrounding town. Emmanuel College at Cambridge University opened its doors in 1584.[1] Among its students were many who would later travel to New England and participate in the founding of the Plymouth Colony, including a young man named John Harvard. His father, a butcher, died of the plague in 1625, leaving John a small inheritance that allowed him to attend Emmanuel College. He joined many other graduates of the English colleges in migrating to New England.

In the words of Frederick Rudolph, the historian of higher education from Williams College, "a particularly self-demanding band of alienated Englishmen got themselves a college almost before they had built themselves a privy."[2] The General Court of Massachusetts Bay commissioned the creation of "a schoale or colledge" for the community, and dedicated resources for its establishment at a place yet to be determined. The following year, John Harvard, having acquired a wife and some property, immigrated to Charlestown, across the harbor from Boston. After a brief period as the assistant minister in the local church, Harvard died suddenly of consumption, leaving half of his estate, some seventeen hundred pounds, and his entire library of over four hundred volumes, to the new college, which was duly named in his memory.

TEACHING

In colonial times, the American universities stuck close to the medieval pattern. Frederick Rudolph describes the daily regimen at Harvard: "Morning classes were devoted to recitations: Here students demonstrated whether or not they had learned their lessons. Afternoons were given over to disputations (debates): Here students demonstrated not only whether they could think but also whether they could think correctly."[3] Until 1767 all tutors at Harvard were responsible for teaching all subjects.

Latin remained the language of instruction and preserved the central role of the recitation in student life. But changes in the intellectual life of Europe filtered into the colonies with books donated from the continent. In 1782, Yale students engaged in Latin debates strictly limited to Aristotelian syllogistic argument once a month, but engaged in forensic debates in English, modeled after the argument of law courts and legislatures, every Tuesday and three Mondays each month.[4] With the advent of new knowledge and increasing use of English, the lecture began to take on a different character. Benjamin Stillman, who became professor of chemistry, geology, and mineralogy at Yale in 1802, introduced experimental demonstrations to his lectures and became an influential model for both his science and his showmanship. One of Yale's overseers expressed the concern, "Is there not danger that with these physical attractions you will overtop the Latin and the Greek?"[5]

The critique of lecture, that it tended to make the student a passive listener rather than an agent of learning, has persisted to the present day, but in a changing context. By 1869, when Charles William Eliot assumed the presidency of Harvard, he could comment that "lectures alone are too often a useless expenditure of force. The lecturer pumps laboriously into sieves. The water may be wholesome but it runs through. A mind must work to grow."[6]

THE TRIUMPH OF RESEARCH

The primary role of the professor in colonial and antebellum colleges was to teach undergraduates. This began to change after the Civil War. This innovation came about through the enormous influence that the new German university system had on American scholars.

At the beginning of the nineteenth century, European universities were largely backward-looking institutions. The Enlightenment did not emerge from the university and, in many ways, bypassed it. In England, for example, the Royal Society played a much more important role than the universities in the advancement of knowledge. Daniel Fallon, in his history *The German University*, summarizes the state of things around 1800 in Germany: "It was widely believed within universities that knowledge was fixed within a closed system, and the only task of the university was to transmit what was known to students, usually by reading aloud from old texts."[7]

Yet while the universities languished, a rich intellectual life was thriving, with philosophers lecturing to enthusiastic Berlin audiences that included many of the elite and members of the court of King Frederick William III. Prussia at this time was under the thumb of Napoleon, and repressed nationalism no doubt emerged in indirect ways. The juggling for authority, with appointments vetted through the French overseers, led to the appointment of Wilhelm von Humboldt, a diplomat and pioneering scholar of linguistics, as director for education in the interior ministry. He held this position for a little more than a year, but in that time he established the blueprint for a new university, Friedrich Wilhelm University (to become simply the University of Berlin in 1849). Humboldt showed little concern for the details of the new university, but was utterly clear on its foundational principles, and they were Enlightenment principles of discovery: "Everything depends upon holding to the principle of considering knowledge as something not yet found, never completely to be discovered, and searching relentlessly for it as such."[8]

Thus, for Humboldt, the central and dominant rationale for the new university would be not cataloguing and declaiming established knowledge, but seeking and finding new knowledge: "If ultimately in institutions of higher learning the principle of seeking knowledge as such is dominant, then it is not necessary to worry individually about anything else."[9] The fundamental business of the university, in Humboldt's thinking, was to find the best available scholars and give them the freedom to pursue knowledge as they chose.

This core principle was fleshed out in the new university through certain practical rules. The professor became not just a teacher but a scholar seeking new knowledge. Thus a core sense of academic freedom emerges: *Lehrfreiheit*, the freedom to teach. Corresponding to the professor's freedom to teach what he thinks best is the student's freedom to learn: *Lernfreiheit*.

These principles were enacted through the statutes for the university drafted after Humboldt's departure from the ministry, largely by theologian and philosopher Friedrich Schleiermacher. The university was to be organized as a group of *institutes*, each controlled by a full professor, with only one full professor for each institute. The faculty was thus a group of specialists, each with nearly complete academic autonomy within his field.

The University of Berlin proved to be a model for other German universities, and a powerful model as well for Americans. In the course of the nineteenth century, some nine thousand Americans studied at German universities.[10] George Ticknor and George Bancroft went to the University of Göttingen and returned to Harvard filled with enthusiasm for the rigor and dedication that exemplified German scholarship. Harvard philosopher Josiah Royce wrote, "One went to Germany still a doubter as to the possibility of the theoretic life, one returned an idealist, devoted for the time to pure learning for learning's sake, determined to contribute ... to the massive story of human knowledge, burning for a chance to help build the American University."[11]

It was in the 1870s when the German model of the professor as independent researcher gained a significant foothold. With the establishment of Johns Hopkins University in Baltimore, the research model came to be embodied in an American institution, setting a pattern very different from that to be found at Harvard or Yale or Cornell at that time. Johns Hopkins was established as primarily a graduate institution; the undergraduate college was added as an afterthought, for economic reasons. When the new university opened in 1876 it had twelve undergraduates and fifty-four graduate students.[12] Daniel Coit Gilman, who left the presidency of the University of California to become the founding president of Johns Hopkins, pronounced the mission of the new university: "the acquisition, conservation, refinement and distribution of knowledge."[13] And in this transition to a focus on knowledge, the role of the faculty began to change.

The rest of higher education followed the example of Hopkins with alacrity. Charles W. Eliot, president of Harvard, said, "I want to testify that the Graduate School of Harvard University, started feebly in 1870 and 1871, did not thrive, until the example of Johns Hopkins forced our faculty to put their strength into the development of our instruction for graduates." The same, he asserted, "was true of every other university in the land which aspired to create an advanced school of arts and sciences."[14]

In 1892, William Rainey Harper, the founding president of the University of Chicago, declared, "It is proposed in this institution to make the work of investigation primary, the work of giving instruction secondary."[15] In 1891 the newly established Stanford University in Palo Alto, California, brought David Star Jordan from Indiana University to become its first president. In his first address to the new university, he declared, "Some day our universities will recognize that their most important professors may be men who teach no classes, devoting their time and strength wholly to advanced research. . . . They set high standards of thought. They help to create the university spirit, without which any college is but a grammar school of little higher pretensions."[16]

Specialization for research had the auxiliary effect of changing the organization of the institution and the relationship of faculty to administration. American universities never sought to emulate the unitary and nearly absolute role of the full professor in the Berlin model. But they did exalt the role of the professor, relative to its previous status. Frederick Rudolph reports, "The institution in Baltimore . . . saw the faculty, its needs, its work, as so central to its purpose that Gilman insisted that the faculty be given only students who were sufficiently well prepared to provide the faculty with challenging and rewarding stimulation. Nothing could have been more remote from the spirit of the old-time college, where the teachers were theoretically busily engaged in stimulating the students. As a consequence, there developed at Johns Hopkins the apparatus and the spirit, as well as the salaries, necessary to the creation of a respected profession of university teachers."[17]

In the American version, the research specialization was carried over and embedded not in a single individual but in a group: the academic department. The established division of faculty into departments was designed to improve the efficiency of teaching undergraduates, but it was also the first step toward putting the faculty in effective control of the curriculum.

When departments were seen as research groupings rather than teaching groupings, it changed their role and effect. Gilman reflected in 1875 on the changes in store at Johns Hopkins, anticipating "that each head of a great department, with his associates in that department . . . shall be as far as possible free from the interference of other heads of departments, & shall determine what scholars he will receive & how he will teach them."[18] David Starr Jordan, first as president of Indiana University and more completely after his move to Stanford, introduced the major subject system, which allowed the student to specialize as well.

Far distant from the medieval tradition in which every master of arts would teach every subject, the professors in the new university could sometimes not even understand one another's fields. The university became, in the words of Charles W. Eliot, "a voluntary cooperative association of highly individualistic persons."[19]

THE ELECTIVE SYSTEM AND THE COURSE

The freedom of the teacher to research and teach as he chose was paralleled by a corresponding spirit of freedom for the student. But the most powerful innovation was Harvard's. Charles W. Eliot assumed the presidency of Harvard in 1869, and he would hold the position for forty years. From the outset, he proposed a New World version of *Lernfreiheit* in the elective system. When Eliot arrived as president the curriculum was rigidly inflexible— the courses to be taken and even the books to be read were set firmly, with almost no room for variation.[20] Eliot challenged this system. He asserted in his inaugural address that "the individual traits of different minds have not been sufficiently attended to . . . [and] the young man of nineteen or twenty ought to know what he likes best and is most fit for."[21]

The elective system gave students freedom to choose what courses to take and faculty freedom to choose what courses to teach. But to fully implement it required the creation of the course, as we know it today. Harvard dean Harry Lewis describes the process: "In his second year, Eliot created the concept of a 'course' with a name and number, open to students of several class years. A couple of years later he added the innovation of informing students which professor would be teaching each course before students had to decide which courses to take. Little by little, the required curriculum disappeared. By 1884 there were only a few required courses, and in another decade most of those had been eliminated."[22]

So the new university in which all subjects were equal and nothing was required had supplanted the colonial college in which everything was required and students had virtually no choices. The course system and the elective option fit nicely with a faculty organized into research-based departments. If students could choose what courses to take, teachers could choose what courses to teach. It also blurred the lines between graduate and undergraduate programs. Larry Cuban of Stanford points out, "Professorial choice in the courses to offer melded easily with their freedom to teach as they wished once the door closed or the lab began. Thus, electives were wedded to the prevailing university norm of faculty autonomy."[23] At the same time, as Lewis puts it, "By the 1890s, undergraduates had great flexibility in what to study, but less than ever of what was taught was meant for them."[24]

The growing status of the professor came to be linked to autonomous control in the classroom. Cuban concludes, "Such unhampered individual discretion—the professor as researcher and solo teacher—has created a fierce loyalty to classroom independence and an abiding reluctance to force solutions aimed at improving teaching, such as team teaching, cross-departmental collaboration in planning courses, and using instructional technologies."[25]

In 1906 Andrew Carnegie created the Carnegie Foundation for the Advancement of Teaching. And while the declared mission of that worthy organization was to advance *teaching*, one of its first significant steps led to a system that certainly advanced teachers, but contributed mightily to the atomization and bureaucratization of teaching. Carnegie donated ten million dollars to be used to create a pension system for college teachers. The foundation conducted extensive surveys, on the basis of which it proposed a definition of who would count as a college teacher. The standard adopted was taken from secondary schools: the equivalent of "any one of four courses carried for five days a week during the secondary school year."[26] Thus was the "Carnegie unit" born. The accounting system was made a condition of a college's participation in the pension program, and colleges adopted it wholesale very quickly. In 1910, Morris L. Cooke produced a paper for the Carnegie Foundation that aimed "to measure the efficiency and productivity of educational institutions in a manner similar to that of industrial factories."[27] At the core of Cooke's "calculus" was the idea of the *student hour*, which he defined as "one hour of lectures, of lab work, or recitation room work, for a single pupil."[28] Soon the accounting system was adopted to define the number of student hours that would be assigned to individual classes, based on the length of time the class met. The standard was clear from the foundation's first report: "The fundamental criterion was the amount of time spent on a subject, not the results attained."[29] This accounting system, based on time spent in a classroom, fit nicely with the elective system and made nearly universal Eliot's innovation of the discrete, numbered course. It allowed institutions to define the degree in terms of hours spent in classes, rather than any measurement of ability or accomplishment, so that classes became completely fungible. Three units of sociology equals three units of philosophy equals three units of tennis equals three units of microbiology for the purposes of degree attainment.

When the time came, following the Second World War, that the federal government sought to invest heavily in undergraduate education, the student credit hour was an established framework for measuring the work of education, and it was integrated into accreditation processes and the criteria for federal funding. Frederick Rudolph, referring to the shift to the research university at the end of the nineteenth century, concluded, "Henceforth order, certainty, in an institution of higher education in the United States, would be less a function of the curriculum than of the bureaucracy that held it together."[30]

Eliot resisted the major subject at Harvard because it impaired the student's freedom of choice in the elective system. But eventually the two combined—a prescribed set of courses in the major but largely free choice for students in the rest of the program—to become the standard framework of the college curriculum to this day, and to be seen through the bureaucratic lens of the university as a number of credits completed.

THE COSTS OF CHANGE

By the end of the nineteenth century, the New University, the German-style, research-driven university, was well established. The benefits of this system are substantial and well known. But the costs were substantial as well. Laurence Veysey, in his classic study *The Emergence of the American University*, writes, "The most pronounced effect of the increasing emphasis upon specialized research was a tendency among scientifically minded professors to ignore the undergraduate college and to place a low value upon their function as teachers."[31]

One way this shift manifested itself was through growth in the size of classes. While lecture has a long history in the academy, it has proved in modern times to be an efficient medium for increasing the ratio of tuition income to operating expenses. When Charles W. Eliot began his tenure as president of Harvard in 1869, the entire student body amounted to 570. Toward the end of his time as president, in the first decade of the twentieth century, the largest individual course at the university had 520 students.[32]

When the leading institutions put research at the center of academic life, they created new centers of power in the decision-making apparatus of universities. It did not happen all at once, but gradually discipline-based academic departments largely took the place of the presidents in hiring new faculty and making decisions on who should be promoted and retained. After all, if professors were hired for their research expertise in a specialized domain, who could judge their qualifications but other experts in the same domain? By 1900 most universities considered a Ph.D., a degree granted for doing original research, a prerequisite for being hired for a faculty position. Veysey reports that "Yale declared in 1901 that promotion at New Haven depended upon 'productive work' which gave the professor 'a national reputation.' . . . As far as official demands upon the faculty were concerned, by 1910 research had almost fully gained the position of dominance which it was to keep thereafter."[33] As faculty members became credentialed experts in specialized fields, the power of the faculty grew. As Rudolph says, "The faculty stranglehold on the curriculum was a function of intellectual specialization and academic professionalization: With the Ph.D. went a kind of competence and authority and power that an earlier academic community did not have."[34] So established credentials from university graduate schools and publication to other specialists became the tickets to entry to the faculty club.

And once faculty were in the club, it became increasingly difficult to expel them. At its creation in 1915, the American Association of University Professors (AAUP) declared that those who had been on the faculty for ten years should receive lifetime tenure. But the policy was already the de facto rule at most universities, and over the course of the early twentieth century became set in law and regulation at most of the rest. Seven years became the usual period, and faculty who couldn't move up the tenure ladder were, with increasing regularity, pushed out of the institution completely. So published research became a priority from the very early stages of the academic career.

The vigorous leadership of the powerful presidents of the late nineteenth century created faculties of experts, many members of which were hired directly by those presidents in a breathless competition for the best scholars. This led to a system in which future university presidents would be much more limited and circumscribed in their power and faculties would accumulate a virtual veto power over institutional action. But the power of the new faculty was different from the power of the old presidents. Presidents spoke for and acted on behalf of the whole institution, often in service—for better or for worse—of a central governing vision. But the faculty of the new research university was not a single entity. The faculty exists, as a practical, day-to-day matter, as a collection of departments, each of which is essentially in competition with the others for resources and influence. So they can come together only on a limited number of issues. The new faculty was powerful, but it was a fragmented—and fragmenting—power. Veysey describes the trajectory of the post–Civil War institution: "The university went several different ways at once. It crystallized into a collection of divergent minds, usually ignoring each other, commonly talking past one another, and periodically enjoying the illusion of dialogue on 'safe' issues."[35]

GROWTH AND RIGIDITY

The patterns of change set at the end of the nineteenth century solidified in the twentieth. Universities grew as a broader cross section of the population sought higher education. By the time the country went back to work following the Second World War, higher education was poised for unprecedented expansion, what came to be known in some circles as the golden age of higher education. Louis Menand, professor of English at Harvard, describes the explosive growth of the period: "In the Golden Age, between 1945 and 1975, the number of American undergraduates increased by almost 500 percent and the number of graduate students increased by nearly 900 percent. Those are unprecedented and almost certainly unrepeatable figures. The rate of growth was nearly fantastic. In the sixties alone, undergraduate enrollments more than doubled, from 3.5 million to just under 8 million; the number of doctorates awarded every year tripled; and more faculty were hired than had been hired in the entire 325 years of American higher education prior to 1960. At the height of the expansion, between 1965 and 1972, new community college campuses were opening in the United States at the rate of one every week."[36]

This enormous growth was propelled, in the first instance, by the infusion of soldiers coming back from the war and supported by the GI Bill to attend college. But it was augmented by a vast influx of funding from the federal government, spurred by the Cold War and Sputnik, to support academic research. As Menand puts it, "Because public money was being pumped into the system at the high end—into the large research universities—the effect of the Golden Age was to make the research professor the type of the professor generally."[37] Hence, "For the first time in the history of American higher education, research, rather than teaching or service, defined the model for the professor—not only in the doctoral institutions, but all the way down the institutional ladder."[38]

This is the time when most community colleges were created, and they were created specifically as "teaching colleges" that imposed no research responsibilities on their faculty. But the vast number of faculty they hired were trained at institutions that prioritized research over teaching. Thus community colleges, like liberal arts colleges, came increasingly to structure their departments and organize their curricula on the model of research-focused graduate schools. From top to bottom, this period of growth reinforced the structure of the research university as the definitive framework of higher learning. As Menand points out, "Federal research grants increased by a factor of four between 1960 and 1990, but faculty teaching hours decreased by half, from nine hours a week to four and a half. . . . This is how it was that the system of higher education become more uniform even as it expanded between 1945 and 1975. The Cold War homogenized the academic profession."[39]

THE PRICE OF PERSISTENCE

What persisted from the very earliest universities was the lecture. What was, in the days before movable type, a necessity continues to characterize the role of university teachers eight centuries later, surviving the critiques of Eliot and a host of others. Recital and disputation faded away with the classical curriculum. Students came to be evaluated first by written examinations, then by tests of recognition—in which rather than recalling and generating what they had learned from their own resources, they were presented with lists of suspect knowledge, like the lineup that the witness to a crime might view in a police station, and had to select the item guilty of truth. First the essay then the multiple-choice test weakened the link between faculty and student, especially when the growth of graduate schools provided an abundant supply of graduate students who could read the papers or mark the exams. By the 1930s multiple-choice exams could be graded by machines, further atomizing assessment and removing students even further from their teachers. Increasingly, the professor became just a lecturer, to ever larger classes. And as the system of research universities advanced its raison d'être and grew more specialized and atomized, the faculty lecturer became more and more removed in perspective, worldview, and concerns from undergraduate students.

Today there is a great variety of colleges and universities. They differ in size, staff, purpose, culture, and students. As we discuss the difficulties of higher education, it is important to keep this in mind. But with all their diversity, the vast majority of these institutions have in common some of the characteristics we have been discussing. And there is also a great diversity of teachers.

There have been teachers at all times and places who have made young men and women think, who have induced them to the labor of self-conscious learning. But such teachers have not usually risen to become exemplars or leaders of the academic world. Clark Kerr, who was president of the University of California in 1963 when he wrote *The Uses of the University*, noted therein, "There seems to be a 'point of no return' after which research, consulting, graduate instruction become so absorbing that faculty efforts can no longer be concentrated on undergraduate instruction as they once were. This process has been going on for a long time; federal research funds have intensified it. As a consequence, undergraduate education in the large university is more likely to be acceptable than outstanding; educational policy from the undergraduate point of view is largely neglected. How to escape the cruel paradox that a superior faculty results in an inferior concern for undergraduate teaching is one of our more pressing problems."[40] The problem is even more pressing today, over fifty years after those words were written.

The movement of educational practice from its early days to the present has not brought us to educational enlightenment. The critique of higher education that I recounted in the last chapter has often raised objections to common practice first made a hundred years—or several hundred years—before. It is not the case that everybody is happy with things or that the current arrangement of colleges and universities works well for undergraduate education. It doesn't. And I would argue from this brief survey of academic history, *it never has*. There is no golden age to return to, though certainly college has been a wonderful experience for some students and some aspects of college education have been better in other places and at other times.

How far have we come? In some ways, very far indeed. In other respects, progress is harder to see. David Damrosch of Columbia points out that "one of the world's chief centers of high-tech research, the American university is also in many ways a holdover from the Middle Ages, complete with an entrenched guild mentality and the indentured servitude of graduate student apprentices and postdoctoral journeymen."[41]

And for undergraduates, the ritual recitations of the medieval university, adopted with adjustments by the colonial college, have given way to the new ritual of lecture and machine-graded tests. The creation of the research university and its conquest of higher education have advanced the cause of research richly and abundantly. We can see no evidence on the record to suggest that the university has advanced the cause of education at all.

PART II WHY IS CHANGE
SO HARD?

3 · THE STATUS QUO BIAS

As we saw in the last chapter, there are historical reasons why universities and their faculties have developed as they have. In the period of transformation over a hundred years ago and during the "golden age" of the postwar period, the prospect of change offered to expand and extend the work of the faculty and to increase the importance and the power of universities. The changes in prospect today appear to many in higher education to threaten what have become expected power and privileges, and seem likely to limit rather than expand their scope of control. I believe that those who take this view may be mistaken, but if we are to understand the nature of the challenge we need to understand why such views are so widely held. To do so, we need to explore both the causes of and the reasons behind the enormous inertia that holds higher education in a dysfunctional holding pattern in a rapidly changing world. From the perspective of many faculty and administrators in higher education, they are fighting for the very integrity of their work and their institutions against fads being urged by snake oil salesmen—like me.

Why do they believe this? Some of the reasons are rooted in the structure of their institutions and the culture of higher education that has grown up in the last century. But some are rooted in common habits of thought that academics share with most other people. Indeed, the resistance to designed change is not unique to higher education but is a common feature of most people and most organizations.

In this chapter I will argue that most people, most of the time, embody certain ways of seeing the world and thinking about it that lead them to resist designed change. Of course, I am making no assumption that change is always, or even usually, a good idea. Most proposals to redesign the world are probably bad ones, and many people may oppose them for good and credible reasons. The only way to tell whether a specific design for change is worth adopting is to weigh its merits. And very often ideas for change lack merit and deserve to be rejected. But what I am suggesting is that most proposals for designed change do not get evaluated first on their merits or on valid or credible evidence. That is an illusion.

I am arguing that this generic resistance to change is *irrational*, that it is not a result of reasoned thought, but is a systematic bias or set of biases. To call a way of thinking irrational is not to say that it is evil or useless or even necessarily wrong. It is just to say that it emerges not from a balanced and self-conscious consideration of the evidence but from something else.

A *bias* is an irrational inclination or tendency. The word is a metaphor, quite an old one, from the game of lawn bowling. If the wooden ball is heavier on one side than the other, either due to its shape or because it has been weighted, say, with lead on one side, then it will roll not in a straight line but on a curve oblique to the path on which the player sets it. Such a ball is said to have a bias. So a bias is a characteristic of someone or something that causes it not to follow the normal rules, not to take the designated path, but to diverge because of its shape or internal inclination.[1]

The particular bias we will be discussing in this chapter is in fact a complex of several such tendencies. But the overall tendency has been given a name. In 1988 two economists, William Samuelson of Boston University and Richard Zeckhauser of Harvard, published an influential article in the *Journal of Risk and Uncertainty* titled "Status Quo Bias in Decision Making." What they found, in brief, was that most people had an unconscious tendency to prefer a decision that confirmed existing practice or policy over one that changed it. In both controlled experiments and real-world cases, they found that people exhibit a powerful bias in favor of the status quo.

To refer to the preference for the status quo as a bias is not to suggest that it necessarily leads to bad conclusions or always has bad effects. That must be determined case by case. Indeed, if we are going to have a bias in one direction or another, it's much more desirable to be biased in favor of the status quo than against it. The bias in favor of the status quo means that we generally prefer the tried over the untried. A systematic bias *against* the status quo would put us in a state of frequent first-time trials and invite a bevy of dangers and threats into our daily lives. But the choice is not between one irrational bias and its polar opposite. It is between choices guided by bias and choices guided by informed deliberation. What I want to suggest is that informed deliberation is not the standard pattern for most of us; the status quo bias is.

To understand the way the status quo bias works, it will help to lay a foundation by exploring how people make decisions.

UTILITY AND CHOICE

Economists and decision theorists have long been fascinated by gambling— as have a good number of non-economists, of course. The thing that makes a gamble interesting to economists is that a bet is a case study of choice when we lack knowledge of the outcome. In other words, it is an isolated case of the sort of decisions we have to make every day. Thus thought experiments about who would bet how much under what circumstances have long been the petri dish of new thinking about choice. Swiss scientist and mathematician Daniel Bernoulli was seeking to explain betting behavior when, in 1738, he propounded one of the most productive complications in the history of decision theory: *utility*. He noted that most people seem to try to avoid risks, but that this aversion to risk seems to decline as people grow wealthier. From the perspective of the individual, Bernoulli pointed out, a dollar isn't just a dollar. The subjective worth—utility—of a given amount of money is not absolute but relative to individual wealth. "A gain of one thousand ducats," Bernoulli wrote, "is more significant to a pauper than to a rich man though both gain the same amount."[2] Since Bernoulli, discussions about choice have most often used the idea of utility.

In 1947 legendary mathematician John von Neumann and economist Oskar Morgenstern laid down the rules for *expected utility theory*, a prescription for making rational choices when the outcomes are uncertain. For example, among the axioms they offered for rational decision makers was *transitivity*: if the decision maker prefers Outcome A to Outcome B, and Outcome B to Outcome C, the decision maker must prefer Outcome A to Outcome C. Expected utility theory was enormously influential, and made obvious good sense. Another of its principles was *invariance*: the rational decision maker cannot be swayed by the way alternatives are presented. For instance, in choosing between a gamble involving multiple bets and a simple gamble with the same odds, there can be no preference. The way a gamble is explained or sequenced can have no effect on the rational decision to take the bet or not because it has no effect on the expected utility of the bet. The answer to the question should always be the same, no matter how the question is worded.[3] One way of looking at the rules that von Neumann and Morgenstern propounded is that they were seeking a theory that would free decision making from bias.

Von Neumann and Morgenstern were offering a prescription, not a description. They were telling decision makers how to be rational, not claiming that most decision makers were. And evidence cropped up frequently that people were far from rational and consistent in their choices.

THE FRAMING EFFECT

One arena distant from economics where evidence of odd patterns of choices turned up was public opinion on questions of policy, and the growth of public opinion polling brought the oddness to light. For example, in June 1969, Gallup and Harris polls on troop withdrawal from Vietnam showed dramatically different results. In one national survey a large plurality said the troop withdrawal was too slow, and in another an even larger plurality said that it was just right.[4] So was the public severely confused (always a live possibility), or was there something different about the surveys?

Of course, something was different. The Harris survey specifically listed the option of "about right," while the Gallup version only gave two options, faster or slower. Many respondents rejected the two options and created a third, but not as many as chose it when it was presented as an option. So, contrary to invariance, it did seem to make a difference to many people how the question was posed. Similar apparently contradictory outcomes turned up in polling about issues such as abortion, public schools, and nuclear arms policy.[5]

Such results encourage a healthy skepticism about public opinion polling, and also suggest that the way you ask the question does influence the answer.

Psychologists began to explore this issue and soon accumulated a substantial store of evidence for systematic inconsistency not just in people's choices but in their perceptions. Richard Harris, at the University of Illinois, explored whether the adjectives used to form a question would affect the answer. They did. So, for example, when subjects were asked how high the office building was, they estimated an average of twenty-six stories, but when asked how low it was, they estimated thirteen. When they were asked how tall a basketball player was, they guessed 78.8 inches, but when asked how short he was, they said 69 inches. These results were consistent across sixteen pairs of contrasting questions. People gave significantly different answers based on the way the question was worded.[6]

Asking questions differently could also affect what people remembered— or thought they remembered. Elizabeth Loftus, a psychologist at the University of Washington studying the reliability of eyewitness testimony in legal cases, conducted research on how leading questions might influence the responses of witnesses. She found that even apparently subtle variations in the way a question is presented can make significant differences in what people "remember." So, for example, she presented a questionnaire to subjects as market research on products for treating headaches. She asked one set of subjects, "Do you get headaches frequently, and if so, how often?" The average response was 2.2 per week. But altering just one word changed what people remembered. She asked another group of similar subjects, "Do you get headaches occasionally, and if so, how often?" These respondents reported an average of only 0.7 headaches per week.[7]

Mounting evidence seemed to confirm what psychologists called a *framing effect*. People's opinions, their memories, and even their subjective sense of their own perceptions were powerfully influenced by the way the question framed the answer or the way the initial information framed subsequent thinking. If framing influences people's very perceptions, then it must also affect their choices.

PROSPECT THEORY AND LOSS AVERSION

Amos Tversky and Daniel Kahneman were both psychologists working at the Hebrew University in Jerusalem when they began their joint exploration of decision theory in the 1960s. They discovered that the way choices are framed has a much more powerful and consistent effect on behavior than had been previously thought. Tversky died of cancer in 1996, and Kahneman was awarded the Nobel Prize in Economic Science in 2002 for their joint work. (The prize is not awarded posthumously.) They sought a "descriptive analysis . . . concerned with people's beliefs and preferences as they are, not as they should be."[8] They called it *prospect theory*, and it was at odds with expected utility theory in some significant ways. For one thing, Kahneman and Tversky corrected an error in Bernoulli's idea of utility. Bernoulli had conceived utility too narrowly. As Kahneman puts it, Bernoulli's "idea was straightforward: people's choices are based not on dollar values but on the psychological values of outcomes, their utilities."[9] So far, so good. The flaw, what Bernoulli did not recognize, was that the subjective value of a choice is a function not just of one's current wealth but of *changes* in wealth over time and especially changes in wealth that seem relevant to the choice. Kahneman offers the following illustration to make the point:

Today Jack and Jill each have wealth of 5 million.
Yesterday, Jack had 1 million and Jill had 9 million.
Are they equally happy? (Do they have the same utility?)[10]

No, they are not equally happy! "Indeed, we know that Jack would be a great deal happier than Jill even if he had only 2 million today while she had 5. So Bernoulli's theory must be wrong."[11]

In prospect theory, the value of Jack's and Jill's relative wealth is determined by the change in their wealth as calculated from a *reference point*: the starting point from which they figure gain or loss—in the example, 1 million for Jack and 9 million for Jill. The reference point, we might say, frames the individual's perception of subsequent events. Say Jack has 1 million to start and Jill has 4 million. They are both offered a choice between (1) a gamble in which they will have a 50 percent chance of owning either 1 million or 4 million and (2) a sure 2 million. Because of their different reference points, the sure thing would more than double Jack's wealth, while it would cut Jill's in half. She would be more likely to take the gamble than he would. They are both thinking in terms not of the total amounts, but of how much they would gain or lose as measured from their reference points.

If risky choices are basically a balancing of gains versus losses, then this raises the importance of framing because nearly any choice can be framed in terms of either a gain or a loss. According to the invariance principle, it should make no difference. Kahneman and Tversky set out to test this claim in a series of carefully designed experiments. They were, of course, thinking about the way people make policy choices of all kinds, not just monetary gambles. So they considered a range of policy decisions in which the outcome was uncertain. One of their studies, for instance, introduced a choice with this background information: "Imagine that the U.S. is preparing for the outbreak of an unusual Asian disease, which is expected to kill 600 people. Two alternative programs have been proposed. Assume that the exact scientific estimates of the consequences of the programs are as follows." They randomly separated the subjects into two groups and gave each group a different pair of alternatives that were logically identical but framed differently. In the first instance the alternatives were as follows:

If Program A is adopted, 200 people will be saved.
If Program B is adopted, there is a one-third probability that 600 people will
     be saved and a two-thirds probability that no people will be saved.

In the second version the identical outcome was described, but the alternatives were framed, not in terms of the number of people saved, but in terms of the number of people who would die:

If Program C is adopted, 400 people will die.
If Program D is adopted, there is a one-third probability that nobody will die
     and a two-thirds probability that 600 people will die.[12]

In both versions, the same number of people live and die. Logically there is no difference between the two, and invariance would dictate that we respond the same way to both. (Indeed, the value of the two alternatives in each version is statistically the same.) In both versions, the first alternative is an assured, small gain while the second is a risk taken for a chance of a larger gain. In this study, and many others conducted since, the way the choices are framed has a powerful effect on how people respond. In the first version, where the outcome is described in terms of people saved, 72 percent of respondents chose Program A and 28 percent chose B. The vast majority chose the sure thing over the risk for a greater gain. In the second version, where the outcome is described in terms of people who die, 22 percent chose

Program C and 78 percent Program D—the opposite result. When the choice was presented in terms of a gain (people "saved") respondents were risk averse—they took the sure thing over the gamble. When it was presented in terms of loss (people "die") they became risk seeking. (I once presented the problem to a group of faculty from different institutions. The results of this informal survey were very similar to those in the original study.) Furthermore, as Kahneman and Tversky concluded, "The failure of invariance is both pervasive and robust. It is as common among sophisticated respondents as among naïve ones, and it is not eliminated even when the same respondents answer both questions within a few minutes. Respondents confronted with their conflicting answers are typically puzzled. Even after rereading the problems they still wish to be risk averse in the 'lives saved' version; they wish to be risk seeking in the 'lives lost' version; and they also wish to obey invariance and give consistent answers in the two versions. In their stubborn appeal, framing effects resemble perceptual illusions more than computational errors."[13]

"Invariance," they concluded, "is normatively essential, intuitively compelling, and psychologically unfeasible."[14] Most people view risky situations through a decidedly imperfect lens, with a powerful bias that causes them to take much greater risks to avoid a loss than to achieve a gain.

THE ENDOWMENT EFFECT

The idea that people are not in fact perfectly rational in their transactions but driven by biases such as loss aversion has led to a new approach to the science of economics: behavioral economics. One of its founders, and an early collaborator with Kahneman and Tversky, is University of Chicago economist Richard Thaler, who won the Nobel Prize in Economic Science for his work in 2017. He summarizes the evidence on loss aversion: "Roughly speaking, losses hurt about twice as much as gains make you feel good."[15] He reasoned that loss aversion implies something about the relative value of gains and losses. If we will not take as big a risk to gain what we don't have as to keep what we do have, that implies that we see things that we already have as more valuable than what we don't have but might gain. Thaler called this the *endowment effect*. My things gain value just by virtue of being mine. One of his first tests of the effect, and one frequently repeated, was conducted in his economics classes at Cornell University back in the 1980s. He gave every other student in the class a coffee mug with the Cornell logo on it. He then gave students a chance to exchange the mugs, for tokens representing money in one instance and for pens in another: "Those who got the mugs were reluctant to sell them. . . . But those who did not have a mug were not eager to buy one."[16] These conclusions went against the conventional wisdom of economics at the time, so the experiment was repeated frequently: "We ran numerous versions of these experiments to answer the complaints of various critics and journal referees, but the results always came out the same. Buyers were willing to pay about half of what sellers would demand. . . . Again we see that losses are roughly twice as painful as gains are pleasurable, a finding that has been replicated numerous times over the years."[17]

Dan Ariely, professor of behavioral economics at Duke University, and his colleague Ziv Carmon conducted a creative study of this phenomenon that found an even larger effect. At Duke, basketball is such a popular sport that the stadium won't accommodate all the students who want to attend a big game. Students who want tickets must camp out in tents in front of the stadium, sometimes for days or weeks, in order to be at the head of the line when tickets go on sale before the games. Officials check periodically to make sure that the tents are occupied, and cheaters lose their place in line. For games in great demand, even being first in line doesn't guarantee tickets: students receive a lottery number and the ticket winners are chosen by lot. So those who get into the lottery have made a considerable investment of time and effort even to get that far. It appears that they place a high value on the tickets. But they don't all get them. In the spring of 1994, Ariely and Carmon got the list of students who were in the lottery. They called them all and told the winners that they had a chance to make some money by selling their tickets and the losers that they had a chance to buy one. They asked them how much they would pay or how much they would accept for the transaction. Ariely describes the outcome: "What was really surprising . . . was that in all our phone calls, not a single person was willing to sell a ticket at a price that someone else was willing to pay. . . . We had a group of students all hungry for a basketball ticket before the lottery drawing; and then, bang—in an instant after the drawing, they were divided into two groups—ticket owners and non-ticket owners. It was an emotional chasm that was formed, between those who now imagined the glory of the game, and those who imagined what else they could buy with the price of the ticket. And it was an empirical chasm as well—the average selling price (about $2,400) was separated by a factor of about 14 from the average buyer's offer (about $175)."[18]

We can see the endowment effect at work in financial and real estate markets, in garage sales and swap meets, and in sales and marketing strategies. It explains, for example, why companies that offer a "money-back guarantee" on a product or a "30-day free trial" seldom pay out much for returned products. Once the customer has the product in hand, it becomes more valuable. And as Ariely points out, an endowment can be *virtual*: "we can begin to feel ownership even before we own something."[19] Much advertising is aimed at creating virtual ownership, which will then lead directly to purchase. The shoppers who have set their hearts on an item, especially one that carries a heavy emotional and financial load like a car or a house, often begin to speak of it as "mine" or "ours" before any money has changed hands.

Furthermore, and crucially important when we come to discuss people's behavior in organizations, the sense of endowment does not stop with physical property. We can "own" an idea or a privilege or a mark of status as well as an object. Thus, the *confirmation bias* acts like the endowment effect. I read the columns in the newspaper that confirm my existing ideas, which I know to be more valuable than those that compete with them. And status can be an endowment: the loss of relative standing before my peers is as real a loss as the loss of income.

ANCHORING

The reference point for any decision, recall, is the point from which we measure change. Such a reference point in terms of price or value can constitute an *anchor*, the point where we start in our thinking, adjusting upward or downward in response to circumstances. And such an anchor point can be created on purpose or by chance.

The evidence for the power of anchoring is substantial. Kahneman and his colleagues Ilana Ritov and David Schkade contend that "anchoring effects are among the most robust observations in the psychological literature."[20] In cases of anchoring, they point out, "*the response is strongly biased toward any value, even if it is arbitrary, that the respondent is induced to consider as a candidate answer.*"[21] The phenomenon has been tested many times, using purely arbitrary anchors. Elizabeth Loftus, in her studies in the 1970s on framing, used anchors as part of the suggesting frame. She asked subjects how many products to treat headaches they had tried, suggesting different ranges of possibilities. One set of subjects she asked, "In terms of the total number of products, how many other products have you tried? One? Two? Three?" The average number of products they claimed to have used was 3.3. But when she asked the same question, but suggested the range "One? Five? Ten?," they claimed to have used an average of 5.2 products.[22]

One interesting experiment was conducted by Drazen Prelec, a professor at MIT's Sloan School of Management, George Loewenstein of Carnegie Mellon University, and Dan Ariely. Prelec asked the fifty-five MBA students in his MIT class in marketing research to participate in an auction. He displayed a series of items: a rare bottle of wine, a cordless keyboard and mouse, a design book, and a box of chocolates, among others. He distributed a list of the items and asked the students to first write the last two digits of their social security numbers at the top of the sheet. This was the anchor. Then he asked them to convert that number into dollars and write it next to each item, indicating whether they would pay that price for the item or not. He then asked them to write a bid for each item, the maximum amount they would be willing to pay. Ariely reports the results: "Did the digits from the social security numbers serve as anchors? Remarkably, they did: the students with the highest-ending social security digits (from 80 to 99) bid highest, while those with the lowest-ending numbers (1 to 20) bid lowest. The top 20 percent, for instance, bid an average of $56 for the cordless keyboard; the bottom 20 percent bid an average of $16. In the end, we could see that students with social security numbers ending in the upper 20 percent placed bids that were 216 to 346 percent higher than those of the students with social security numbers ending in the lowest 20 percent."[23]

It goes without saying that these MIT graduate students were not naïve rubes—and that they knew perfectly well that their social security numbers had no relevance whatever to the value of a keyboard or a box of chocolates. But they could not resist the pull of the anchor, which they were almost certainly unaware of. In other studies, researchers have used arbitrary anchors to influence subjects' estimates of the average temperature, the tallest trees, the cost of conservation programs, real estate prices, and a variety of other things.[24] Once an anchor is set in our minds, we tend to make estimates not on a blank slate, but by adjusting from the anchor point, even when we know the anchor is arbitrary and irrelevant. Our own ideas of what is a "fair" price are probably formed in large part by the anchors that were set when we shopped for our first car or television or house. So the normal operations of inflation will lead persons of a certain age to feel that nearly everything is expensive these days. Furthermore, it is hard to escape the anchor. As Ariely points out, "Our first decisions resonate over a long sequence of decisions. First impressions are important, whether they involve remembering that our first DVD player cost much more than such players cost today (and realizing that, in comparison, the current prices are a steal) or remembering that gas was once a dollar a gallon, which makes every trip to the gas station a painful experience. In all these cases the random, and not so random, anchors that we encountered along the way and were swayed by remain with us long after the initial decision itself."[25]

So anchoring is not something that happens only in experimental studies. A common example that we encounter every day is the "manufacturer's suggested retail price" for a product. As Thaler points out, such a price is "largely fictional" and "actually just serves as a misleading suggested *reference price*."[26] It allows retailers to make an adjustment from what may be a purely arbitrary price and claim sometimes extravagant "savings," even though few consumers—or none—may ever purchase the product at the listed price. Suggested prices lock customers into a pattern of adjustment that will make them feel good about saving money with respect to an essentially fictional anchor.

THE STATUS QUO BIAS

If arbitrary anchors affect people's calculations of gains and losses, how much more so must the real reference point derived from their lived experience? That is, the status quo. As Kahneman and Tversky put it, "The status quo defines the reference level for all attributes. The advantages of alternative options will then be evaluated as gains and their disadvantages as losses. Because losses loom larger than gains, the decision maker will be biased in favor of retaining the status quo."[27] The endowment effect means that what we have will seem more valuable than what we have not yet gained, leading us to hold on to what we have, to protect the status quo.

This was the idea that Samuelson and Zeckhauser tested for their 1988 article. They presented a variety of subjects with sets of choices, in each case presenting the choice with *neutral framing* in one instance and with *status quo framing* in the other. For example, in one experiment they presented subjects with a situation in which they had recently inherited money and had to decide how to invest it: in Company A, Company B, treasury bills, or municipal bonds. They described briefly the performance of the various investments and their predicted returns. In the neutral framing subjects were told merely that they had inherited the money and had to invest it. In the status quo framing they were told that their deceased great-uncle had most of the investment in Company A, and they had to decide whether to leave it there or move it to another investment. In other experiments, the researchers gave the subjects a preliminary survey in which they made a choice that established a status quo option and then were presented with a subsequent case calling for a decision. Samuelson and Zeckhauser concluded that "the controlled experiments demonstrate that for a variety of decision situations individuals exhibit a significant and predictable status quo bias."[28] This was even the case when the "status quo" was an essentially meaningless state in a fictional scenario: "In drawing inferences from past behavior, individuals fail to discriminate to some degree between imposed actions, random selections, and choices voluntarily (and thoughtfully) undertaken."[29] Even when the fictional status quo was clearly arbitrary, people still leaned toward preserving the existing state of things over changing them. The more alternatives they faced, the stronger the status quo bias.

In addition to controlled experiments, Samuelson and Zeckhauser offered a series of examples from the real world that confirm the bias. The authors were able to conduct two field studies that are especially interesting for our purposes because they involved employees of colleges and universities. The first was an analysis of the changes in enrollment in various health insurance plans at Harvard University. During the 1980s Harvard increased the number of health plans available to employees from four in 1980 to double that by 1986. A previous study had shown a very low rate of employees switching plans: about 3 percent. (A similar study at the Polaroid Corporation found the same thing.) To determine whether a status quo bias was present Samuelson and Zeckhauser separated new employees from existing employees. If new employees chose different plans than continuing employees, it would suggest that the two groups were using different criteria. To test this hypothesis, the researchers grouped employees as *continuing* or *new* and then within each of those categories grouped employees by age. The overall result was unambiguous: "To sum up, a comparison of plan choices between new and old enrollees provides strong evidence of status quo bias. Old enrollees persist in electing the incumbent plan . . . much more frequently than do new enrollees, and enroll in the new HMO plans . . . much less frequently."[30]

The other field study involved the TIAA/CREF retirement fund, which at the time had about 850,000 participants, most of them college and university professors. Participants in the fund had to decide each year how much they would contribute and how it would be distributed between the Teachers Insurance and Annuity Association (TIAA)—a portfolio including bonds, mortgages, real estate, and loans—and the College Retirement Equities Fund (CREF), invested in stocks. Participants could, free of charge, change the allocation of their funds in any year. Yet "a TIAA study . . . finds that only 28% of those surveyed had ever changed their distribution of premium between the funds (8% had changed more than once, 20% exactly once). Given a 12-year average length of participation, fewer than 2.5 percent of all participants alter their distribution in a given year."[31] Whether this stability reflected the status quo bias may depend on the reasons why participants chose a given allocation for their investments. The TIAA survey asked several questions that sought to explore the rationale for investors' choices. Nearly all of the participants, the survey showed, knew that they could change their allocation in any year. But when asked for the reasons behind their current allocation, "only one in three participants surveyed felt his or her initial allocation was an informed choice. One in four said it was a guess, with the others characterizing it as something in between."[32] The minority who changed their allocation were able to state a reason for the change, usually trends in the stock market. "But very few participants had a particular reason for *not* changing their allocation. As Samuel Johnson observed, it is easy to 'decide' to do nothing."[33]

Why is the status quo bias so pervasive and powerful? Samuelson and Zeckhauser consider several factors. One is certainly loss aversion augmented by anchoring. When the professor setting up a retirement plan makes his or her initial allocation, even if that allocation is based on a "guess," it serves as an anchor and becomes the point of reference from which changes need to be made. The anchoring effect, as we have seen, limits movement away from the anchor. And since losses loom larger than gains, the potential losses that might result from changes will likewise loom larger than the potential gains, making it easy to decide to do nothing. As Kahneman puts it, "Loss aversion is a powerful conservative force that favors minimal changes from the status quo in the lives of both institutions and individuals."[34]

The status quo bias may also reflect a particular mode of psychological accounting, sometimes called the *sunk costs effect*. Sunk costs are resources already lost that cannot be recovered. For the rational person, sunk costs are irrelevant to decisions about the future, since no current action can affect the loss. But most of us are not rational persons. Thaler offers this example: "Vince paid $1,000 to an indoor tennis club that entitled him to play once a week for the indoor season. After two months he developed tennis elbow, which made playing painful. He continued to play in pain for three more months because he did not want to waste the membership fee."[35] We also see the sunk costs effect in the tendency of gamblers to increase their wagers after losses. Thaler summarizes one implication this way: "Paying for the right to use a good or service will increase the rate at which the good will be utilized."[36] Since most of us have invested something in creating the current state of affairs in our lives, we all have sunk costs in the status quo. And the greater our investment, in our minds, the more likely we are to hold on to it. We can see this phenomenon in terms of investments of time and effort as well as money.

Akin to the sunk costs effect is the psychological *drive for consistency*. As psychologist Leon Festinger first argued, we all try to reduce *cognitive dissonance* in our lives.[37] That is, when we find ourselves holding incompatible beliefs or ideas, we will tend to change something so as to reduce the stress created by that incompatibility. To a great degree, the status quo each of us lives in is a product of our own choices. The lives we live today are the result of our beliefs about the world and of the quality of decisions we have made. Samuelson and Zeckhauser point out that the desire to avoid cognitive dissonance reinforces the status quo bias: "With his or her self-image as a serious and able decision maker comes a need to justify current and past decisions, whether or not they proved successful. Past choices are rationalized, and the rationalization process extends to current and future choices. Thus, an individual tends to discard or mentally suppress information that indicates a past decision was in error (since such information would conflict with his or her self-image as a good decision maker)."[38]

4 · HOW THE STATUS QUO BIAS DEFENDS ITSELF IN ORGANIZATIONS

The status quo bias goes a long way toward explaining why designed change is so difficult to execute. One of the most remarkable things about the status quo bias, given its ubiquity, is that most of us are unaware of it most of the time. Indeed, much of our behavior in organizational settings is a product of habit or tacit rules that we are unaware of. And many of these hidden patterns of behavior accentuate the status quo bias. Chris Argyris of the Harvard Business School suggests that most organizations are beset with limitations that keep them from changing even when they want to. "It is as if," he says, "they are compulsively tied to a set of processes that prevent them from changing what they believe they should change."[1] Argyris and his colleague the late Donald Schön from MIT explained this in part by pointing out that the way people behave in organizations involves two kinds of thinking. We hold a theory of action, but most people have two kinds or levels of theories of action operating simultaneously.

ESPOUSED THEORY AND THEORY-IN-USE

Ask a person why she is doing what she is doing and she will probably provide an explanation. This is an example of what Argyris and Schön call *espoused theory*. But watch the way that individual behaves, and you may find that her actions don't match her espousals. She is acting out her *theory-in-use*. "Espoused theories are those that an individual claims to follow," Argyris and his colleagues Robert Putnam and Diana McLain Smith point out: "Theories-in-use are those that can be inferred from action."[2] For example, a president or provost may espouse change but may act in a way that penalizes it. R. Eugene Rice and Mary Sorcinelli interviewed 350 new and early-career faculty members, with special emphasis on questions of the tenure and promotion process. Many of them reported major differences between what they were told or what the documents said and what turned out to be the case. For example, "an assistant professor at a large research university reported that an appointment might be represented as a mix of 45% research, 45% teaching, and 10% service when in actuality the expectation was that 90% of one's efforts should be directed to research."[3]

What is important about espoused theory and theory-in-use is that each is a coherent theory; people do not just act randomly or follow what seems like a good idea at the time. Their behavior follows patterns. The Learning Paradigm expresses the espoused theory of most educators, but the Instruction Paradigm is the theory-in-use of most colleges and universities.[4] Likewise, loss aversion and the status quo bias are not beliefs that most people embrace—they are not the espoused theories of most of us—but they do affect our theories-in-use, our patterns of behavior.

This does not mean that our espoused theories are insincere or deceptive. Often, we believe that we are following our principles and don't recognize the compromises we make in practice. We follow our theories-in-use without being aware of them. As Argyris puts it, "Although people do not behave congruently with their espoused theories [much of the time], they do behave congruently with their theories-in-use, *and* they are unaware of this fact."[5]

ORGANIZATIONAL DEFENSIVE ROUTINES

The conflict between what we believe and what we do in an organizational setting creates contradictions. The contradictions will lead to cognitive dissonance if brought into the open. One of the ways we deal with them is by attempting to camouflage them through *organizational defensive routines*. "These are actions and policies," report Argyris and Schön, "enacted within an organizational setting, that are intended to protect individuals from experiencing embarrassment or threat, while at the same time preventing individuals, or the organization as a whole, from identifying the causes of the embarrassment or threat in order to correct the relevant problems."[6] Defensive routines work against organizational learning and tend to freeze existing practices. They also promote false and misleading accounts of organizational problems. Because they obscure or distract from the grounds for change, they tend most of the time to reinforce the status quo bias.

Management writer Harvey Hornstein has characterized the kinds of routine comments that block new ideas as "idea killers."[7] He lists among these responses to change proposals the following: "It's not policy," "I don't have the authority," "It's never been tried," "It's not *my* job (or *your* job, or *their* job)," "It's not in the budget," and "We've always done it that way."[8] These are all examples of defensive routines, and they extend the reach of the status quo bias to processes and procedures: We must follow the same routines we have in the past. If we are to change, we must do so without doing anything differently. Hornstein refers to this action bias as "the rule of repeated action": "In doubt, do what you did yesterday. If it isn't working, do it twice as hard, twice as fast and twice as carefully."[9] The effort to improve the quality of teaching at universities is often stymied by the rule of repeated action. As we shall see in the next chapter, defensive routines tend to deflect inquiry away from the real causes of ineffective teaching, which are often rooted in the organization, not the individual teacher. So where a problem does arise, the solution seems to be to "teach better." But without any accepted criteria of what good teaching consists of, that often boils down to the advice to do the same thing you did last semester, but do it more.

Argyris and Schön point out that defensive routines usually involve crafting messages that contain inconsistencies and then presenting them as if they were consistent. An example they offer is of an executive saying to subordinates, "We encourage everyone to be innovative and risk oriented. This is what we mean by empowerment. Of course, we also expect you to keep out of trouble."[10] In other words, take risks, but don't do anything risky. Because defensive routines are intended to deflect threat or blame, one effect they have is to "make the ambiguity and inconsistency in the message undiscussable" and then to "make the undiscussability of the undiscussable also undiscussable."[11] Defensive routines aim to deflect embarrassment or threat from the speaker, yet to publicly raise the inconsistency or its undiscussability would be to invite embarrassment or threat of another kind. If we cover up rather than resolve the source of dissonance, then the cover-up itself threatens to become a source of dissonance. Hence, we must cover up the cover-up, and defensive routines tend to proliferate. The result is "organizational loops that are known to all and manageable by none."[12] The effect of widespread defensive routines on the communication in an organization is corrosive:

> One way to live with having little choice about defensive routines is to develop a cynical attitude about them. Cynicism leads to pessimism and doubt. For example,
>
>> Nothing will change around here.
>> They don't really mean it.
>> I doubt if anyone will listen.
>> Hang on. Don't get fooled. Next year there'll be a new fad.
>
> Cynical attitudes make it more likely that individuals will ignore or sneer at evidence of positive intentions. The cynic automatically mistrusts other people and sees the world as full of evidence that nothing will change.[13]

When we camouflage the sources of our dissatisfaction and then camouflage the camouflage, we make the real problems undiscussable and preserve them as sources of harm. We also undermine the possibility of rationally weighing the costs and benefits of designed change; we lock in the status quo bias.

What happens in many decision-making processes is that people think and act out of a narrow frame of reference (their department, their courses, their research interest) but they camouflage this fact and pretend to think and act out of a larger frame of reference (the university or college, the students, the community). Many people do this, but all of the people who do pretend not to. Most people know that others are doing it—and in many cases assume that everybody else is doing it—but they refrain from pointing this out because then they would be vulnerable to the same revelation. So the source of inconsistency and incoherence becomes undiscussable.

This dynamic gives rise to myriad defensive routines. When people's positions are attacked they tend to change the subject, raise the stakes, shift assumptions without saying so, or attack the motives of their opponents. When disputes come to be seen as personal, it makes them emotionally toxic so that people tend to avoid the topic in question. Thus the shift to ad hominem framing of issues is often a defensive routine with the effect of making the underlying problem undiscussable. Kinds of defensive routines abound, often introduced by expressions such as the following, each paired with a brief description of the style of defensive routine it represents:

But the real problem is . . .	I want to change the assumption behind your comment, thus making your idea beyond examination, but I don't want to be seen to be doing so.
But that's not the point . . .	I want to change the subject, but don't want to be seen to be doing so, thus I will preempt your intention by substituting my own.
But we've always done it this way (or we've never done it that way).	I want to avoid examining new evidence or new ideas, but I don't want to be seen to be doing so, hence I will make newness itself grounds for considering an idea undiscussable.
We can't afford that; the budget will never support that.	I want to suppress or avoid examining the reasons for and benefits of your idea, so I will shift the conversation to costs, which will make benefits undiscussable. (This routine is almost never accompanied by any actual financial analysis, but carries with it the assumption that everything already in the budget is inevitable so therefore everything not already in the budget is unaffordable, though this is never made explicit.)
But faculty/administration /staff/the community/I/the good guys had no input on this proposal. Or: This proposal came from the administration/the	I want to avoid examining the merits of these ideas, so I will shift the focus to their origins. If the real origins of the proposal are indeterminate or unrecorded, the controversy over origins can continue indefinitely without resolution, thus

president's office/the dean /the bad guys.	blocking out any discussion of merits. Other appeals to process can have the same effect.
We've been over ideas like this a hundred times, and it's never gotten us anywhere. Let's move on to practical matters.	I want to avoid examining the merits of these ideas, so I will put them in the category of failed ideas on grounds, not of their novelty (as in a previous defensive routine) but of their familiarity.
You're saying that I am—or our faculty/administration /department is—incompetent /inept/dishonest.	I want to avoid examining the substance of your argument, so I will personalize it, making it an attack against the competence or intentions of colleagues. The result is to make everyone defensive, making the substantive issue toxic and hence undiscussable.

Of course, comments such as these do not always initiate defensive routines; they might lead to reasonable points in a given context. But they are often used as means of changing the subject and derailing the examination of ideas. And they might be both true and defensive routines. We may really have discussed this idea many times in the past, but each time the conversation might have been deflected or derailed by defensive routines that prevented a real examination of the issue. The new proposal almost by definition will not fit in the current budget. Readjustment of policy often requires a readjustment of the budget. But to accept this as grounds for taking a proposal off the table amounts to committing in advance to resisting nearly all significant change. There may be real personal antipathy between various people, and it may or may not be related to the issue in question. So it is not that defensive routines are necessarily false. And indeed, if the conversation is successfully waylaid by a dispute over the truth of the claim that it was really so-and-so's idea, then the defensive routine has been successful: it has suppressed or seriously tainted or confused any examination of the threatening idea.

What organizational defensive routines do is make evidence on certain topics inaccessible, out of reach. When a topic is undiscussable and its undiscussability is undiscussable, we can't learn about it. We can't get better at it. We can't advance our understanding. We do things the way we do, not because the evidence shows that it is the best way, but because to ask for evidence would be out of the question. And in the absence of evidence, we are thrown back onto myths and superstitious reasoning, which we will examine down the line.

Often people find that the sense of threat fed by loss aversion that triggers defensive routines creates a high level of anxiety accompanied by a low level of clarity. Where emotions are high and the reasons are muddy, the most direct route to seeming coherence may be to blame the other guy or gal. This leads to a tendency to raise the rhetorical stakes and rely on ad hominem arguments, even where the issues involved don't seem particularly earthshaking. This sort of high-octane, high-dudgeon debate drives many, or even most, faculty members away from public conversations, leaving the floor to the hotheads and aficionados of hyperbole. I have often had the sense that people would not speak the way they do if they thought anyone were really listening—certainly anyone from outside the fishbowl of overwrought faculty-speak. Robert Zemsky has commented on the general phenomenon and notes that "those faculty who have better things to do mostly withdraw, leaving their more combative colleagues to duke it out either with each other or, as is more often the case, with the administration or the trustees."[14]

The tendency to raise the emotional stakes has the side effect of increasing the number of taboo topics. It creates a breeding ground for defensive routines—a big supply of topics that are potentially embarrassing or threatening and that need to be taken off the table and distracted from. And when defensive routines or raising the emotional stakes continually deflect conversations from a given topic, it creates a pattern of self-censorship. Faculty members who want to maintain a relatively peaceful work environment learn to simply avoid trigger topics.

In one instance an institutional assessment committee was grappling for a way to meet accreditation requirements when one member of the committee suggested that they look for examples of how other institutions were handling assessment. Another committee member—a woman who had long opposed assessment—spoke at some length, her voice breaking with emotion, to oppose the idea of seeking examples or models from other institutions. I spoke with several people who had attended the meeting and asked them what arguments had been made. Nobody could say. Indeed, nobody seemed to have really understood what the woman said in her long stream-of-consciousness tirade. All they knew was that the topic had triggered a ferocious emotional outburst. So the topic became forbidden in future meetings and the committee spent an inordinate amount of time quibbling over undecidable questions in the absence of any clear framework for thought. Until, that is, the college was warned in its next accreditation review that it had failed to do anything about assessment. And, of course, the question of why they could not discuss this subject also became undiscussable, and remained so even after the painful accreditation process. The president of the institution avowed that he was shocked, shocked to find that his institution had been inert on assessment for several years. Who knew? Everybody knew, but they couldn't talk about it. Similar examples abound, cases where defensive behavior by faculty members or administrators simply takes topics off the table, trains everyone not to talk about the issue.

Defensive routines tend by their very nature to reinforce the status quo bias as it applies to designed change. The only way to design a new process or product is to talk about it. Defensive routines work to prevent new ideas from being talked about, hence they tend to lock existing procedures in place. Because the status quo bias is a bias, it is almost inherently embarrassing, and especially so in an organization that is purportedly aimed at advancing reason and clear thinking. So, while the status quo bias is embedded in the theory-in-use of most organizations, it becomes undiscussable, and its undiscussability becomes undiscussable. Defensive routines systematically arise to deflect attention and discussion from the irrational foundations of many choices and decisions. The more skillful the organizational politicians are at manipulating the system to get the results they want, the more entrenched becomes their avoidance of the underlying problems. This means that rational scrutiny of the biases underlying most resistance to change becomes very hard to achieve.

When people become highly skilled at the use of defensive routines, they can carry out what Chris Argyris calls *fancy footwork*: "Fancy footwork includes actions that permit individuals to be blind to inconsistencies in their actions or to deny that these inconsistencies even exist, or, if they cannot do either, to place the blame on other people. Fancy footwork means to use all the defensive reasoning and actions at their command in order to continue the distancing and blindness without holding themselves responsible for doing so."[15]

Because the organizational theory-in-use involves inconsistencies, people often *distance* themselves from it, and from the consequences. By distancing, people can hold themselves above the process, condemning the outcomes while disclaiming any responsibility. So when the issue of the budget comes up, we often hear from faculty that that is an administrative problem. Indeed, I have heard the same faculty member use the budget as a defensive routine when issues of educational reform came up and distance himself from it when he thought faculty interests were at stake. When implementing a learning outcomes assessment system was proposed, he said, "We could never afford that, there's no way the budget could support it." But when a similar argument was made about a proposal for a faculty salary increase, the same individual responded, "That's not our problem. It's the administration's job to find the money if it's the right thing to do." Of course, these comments were made at different times to different groups, and no one seemed to notice the inconsistency. Selective distancing is a way to deflect responsibility and at the same time keep one's powder dry, so to speak, in order to impede action by others.

DESIGNED IGNORANCE

As members of the organization become more skillful at doing their technical work, there can be a paradoxical result that they become less aware of the sources of their behavior. A similar paradox affects teachers who are highly skilled in their disciplines: the more skilled they are, the more automatic their processing of information in the discipline, and hence the more distant they are from the thinking processes of the novices they are trying to teach. The math teacher who rattles off the solution to what seems to him a simple problem is dumbfounded at how ill-prepared and inept his students are and loses track of the fact that the cognitive load of solving the problem for students is greater by orders of magnitude than it is for him. They have not been practicing these skills for the last seventeen years. As Argyris puts it, "The very action required to become skillful produces unawareness. Once human beings become skilled, they forget much of what they went through to become skillful. Skillful actions are those that 'work,' that appear effortless, that are automatic and usually tacit, and that are taken for granted. A consequence of generating skills is designed ignorance."[16]

Psychologists Keith Stanovich and Richard West were the first to introduce the idea of two "mind systems." Daniel Kahneman expands on this idea in his 2011 book *Thinking, Fast and Slow*. The systems are not intended to correspond exactly to portions of the brain or even strictly defined psychological functions. But they do provide a rough but reliable framework for thinking about how we engage different kinds of tasks differently. Kahneman defines the two systems this way:

System 1 operates automatically and quickly, with little or no effort and no sense of voluntary control.

System 2 allocates attention to the effortful mental activities that demand it, including complex computations. The operations of System 2 are often associated with the subjective experience of agency, choice, and concentration.[17]

Many tasks that begin as System 2 operations come, with familiarity and practice, to be conducted in System 1. This is how, as Argyris points out, skill development promotes a lack of awareness. Driving is an example, as well as becoming proficient at tennis, baseball, or woodworking. One of the differences between experts and novices is that skills that novices perform in System 2 experts can perform in System 1. And I use the term *skills* in an expansive sense. Perception and intuition are often skillful behaviors.

Many organizations suppress discussion of the real causes of dysfunction among people with high skill levels; these people have high status, earned through their performance, and therefore receive deference, but not just deference in their specialties. This produces a body of people who operate "successfully" in the organization while disabling the organization from being able to address its underlying problems. Thus the organization is insulated against learning by designed ignorance. And people who are very good at doing what they are specialized to do are strictly insulated against being able to see the effect of their practice on the organization.

As we will see in more detail later, specialists who deserve respect and deference for their mastery of a given specialization often become victims of designed ignorance in other activities. The specialist who acts largely in System 1 in his or her specialization may tend to fall back on System 1 behaviors in other activities. Designed ignorance is never designed on purpose. It is almost always the product of skilled people's failure to see the limits of their skills. The key to thinking clearly about any task (*metacognition* is what cognitive scientists call it) is the ability to move from System 1 into System 2 when appropriate, to see when we need to step back and reassess things. But highly skilled people, who operate successfully in System 1 much of the time, may fail to monitor the shifting nature of the environment, may act in the unawareness natural to System 1, in designed ignorance. And because designed ignorance tends to be embarrassing when discovered, the skillful will often use defensive routines to camouflage that ignorance. When high-preforming people and organizations fail disastrously, designed ignorance is often at work. The *Challenger* disaster, Pearl Harbor, and the recession brought on by an excess of high-risk mortgages can all be traced to very smart and talented people staying in System 1 when the circumstances called for them to move into System 2.

5 · THE DESIGN OF COLLEGES AND THE MYTHS OF QUALITY

Not long ago, I was speaking with the provost of a large state university, who was describing initiatives his campus had under way to promote student learning. He stopped in midsentence, raised both hands in a gesture of frustration, and said, "Here's my problem: How can I get my faculty to go along? It seems that every new idea starts a war! We have some folks who aren't willing to do anything differently." I have heard variations on that complaint many times, and not only from administrators. Faculty members who have taken the lead in change initiatives often express frustration at the roadblocks created by other faculty members or faculty groups. In 2009 George Kuh and Stanley Ikenberry undertook a survey of provosts for the National Institute for Learning Outcomes Assessment to explore the progress that was being made on the assessment of student learning. They found that "gaining faculty involvement and support remains a major challenge." Of provosts at all institutions, 66 percent said more faculty engagement was needed, and "about four-fifths of provosts at doctoral research universities reported greater faculty engagement as their number one challenge."[1] Some hear from the chorus of the faculty the famous refrain of Groucho Marx in *Horse Feathers* (playing the role, interestingly, of a college president): "I don't care what you have to say / It makes no difference anyway! / Whatever it is, I'm against it!"

As Clark Kerr put it in a more sophisticated way, "The faculties are substantially in control, and they are most conservative about their own affairs, never more so than when their own affairs are not going too well."[2]

As we have already seen, the shift to a major emphasis on research in the last part of the nineteenth century also greatly increased the power and control of the faculty over the university. It moved to the faculty themselves much of the authority to hire new faculty and to arrange the curriculum, acting through their departments and committees, and constrained the authority of presidents and provosts. The great growth of higher education following the Second World War served to extend the departmental structure designed for research and graduate education to every level of nearly every college. It is this structure, solidified during the period of the greatest growth of faculty in history, that frames the status quo for today's faculty, that defines their endowment, and that creates the lens through which faculty view ideas for change and improvement.

A LONG TRADITION

Faculty opposition to change initiatives is not new and is not distinctive to North America. In 1908, F. M. Cornford, a classics professor at Oxford, penned a delightful satire of the academic decision-making process at his own university: *Microcosmographia Academica: Being a Guide for the Young Academic Politician.* The Greek title might be translated "A Study of a Tiny Academic World." Among the principles repeatedly called upon as rationales for obstruction is the Principle of the Dangerous Precedent: "Every public action which is not customary, either is wrong, or, if it is right, is a dangerous precedent. It follows that nothing should ever be done for the first time."[3]

Today the long-standing tradition of aversion to change needs to be viewed against a backdrop of a new body of research on the way people learn and the way schools and colleges work. We reviewed some of that research in chapter 1. Yet many faculty members seem unaware that there is a problem or resist giving it serious attention. As Derek Bok, president emeritus of Harvard, has put it, "No faculty ever forced its leaders out for failing to act vigorously enough to improve the prevailing methods of education. On the contrary, faculties are more likely to resist any determined effort to examine their work and question familiar ways of teaching and learning."[4] Faculties, in other words, tend to be living embodiments of the status quo bias.

Charles Muscatine describes his own efforts in the 1970s to sustain Strawberry Creek College at Berkeley, a wonderfully innovative program for undergraduates. Muscatine was a leading scholar in English and comparative literature with a powerful reputation. But his attempts at undergraduate reform were effectively blocked. Strawberry Creek, not the first creative departure smothered in its youth by that great university, was terminated by a faculty committee because of concerns about "educational quality." But in the long process of review, he notes, *"No faculty group, to my knowledge, had ever attempted to determine the actual 'quality' of the courses in the regular academic program, against which the quality of unconventional courses might be judged."*[5] This double standard, in which quality becomes a question only when contemplating change and no common standards of comparative evidence ever emerge, is widespread in discussions of curriculum and pedagogy. Indeed, many teachers in higher education exhibit a deep-seated resistance to devoting attention to the evidence about teaching and how it might be done better. "Underlying the neglect of pedagogy," Bok writes, "is a studied disregard of the research on student development in college. By now, empirical papers on teaching undergraduates lie thick on the ground. . . . Yet rarely does one discover a reference to this literature in the published reports of faculty committees reviewing their own colleges' curricula. Individual instructors do no better in their own teaching."[6]

The focus of the research Bok refers to is how students learn, and learning is the touchstone for reformers' thinking about pedagogy. The key question for teachers, in this view, should be how they can help students to learn better. While this will strike most people outside the academy as painfully obvious, it remains a trigger for defensive retrenchment for many faculty members. Mary Burgan, formerly general secretary of the American Association of University Professors, suggests that "the most general effect of the reformist program for higher education pedagogy has been an emphasis on the word 'learning' in all talk about pedagogy. An insistence on this term is so obligatory as to have become politically correct in educational circles, where 'teaching' is seldom mentioned without being yoked to 'learning.'"[7] And how does this persistent yoking strike the faculty, at least in Ms. Burgan's view? "Far from creating a balance in pedagogy . . . , such a semantic move radiates a sense that individual faculty are inveterate hams or gasbags, and—more disastrously—that the masses of aspiring students sentenced to their tutelage are actually eager learners who have hitherto been thwarted in their longing to take part in mutual discovery."[8]

Does the very use of the word *learning* in the context of education raise defensive hackles in teachers? Does the word itself "radiate a sense" of threat to faculty? As a certified (some would say "certifiable") reformer, and one who uses the term *learning* consistently if not obsessively when discussing the work of colleges, I can testify that I do not hold either of the views that Burgan associates with my kind. Yet, it is not an unusual experience for me to find myself associated with views I do not hold through such strange yoking of oddly matched ideas. Indeed, this sort of red herring is a defensive routine often seen in university discussions of reform. We can see the classic move of personalizing the argument for the purpose of changing the subject. The mention of students as learners triggers a fear of loss in the faculty member who deflects the threat by pointing out a conspiracy to abuse faculty, lower standards, attack academic freedom, or something similar. I will point out in a later chapter that there is good reason to believe that Burgan's views do not represent those of most college teachers. However, this kind of resistance to change is not unusual in the pronouncements of faculty leaders, speaking on behalf the "official" faculty position.

The fact of the matter, and one source of faculty insecurity and defensiveness, is that most faculty members, while they are probably experts in their disciplines, are by no means experts about teaching. As Muscatine notes, "Your typical professor is hardly aware of new thinking in education, does not read educational periodicals, and rarely goes beyond the academic department in discussing problems of teaching and learning."[9] I would add that within the academic department discussions of teaching and learning are often, but not always, deformed by a resistance to evidence that in any other setting would be labeled "anti-intellectualism." While it is not at all the case that most faculty members are "hams or gasbags," it appears that the fear of being so caricatured—or the fear of something else—has raised a defensive shield around some faculty minds that seems to insulate them from argument. "Though the ideas have been out there for decades," says Muscatine, "... on a national scale our progress has been very slow. We will not by any means get substantial educational reform until we confront the faculties themselves."[10]

THE FACULTY ENDOWMENT

Changes in pedagogy and curriculum are offered as a way of making gains in student learning. But, as we have seen, when it comes to a weighing of gains versus losses, losses will simply be heavier; loss aversion and the endowment effect will keep a thumb on the scale, leading losses to outweigh gains. This principle applies to faculty and administrators alike. Both will seek to protect existing programs and activities against possible threats and will be sensitive to such threats. But those who have the greatest interest in protecting against loss are those who have, relatively, the most to lose. And losing ground in the quest for more control and more autonomy over research activities most directly affects faculty, who are actually doing the research.

I once attended a regional conference that featured a number of sessions in which faculty members described new work they were doing to promote student learning. In one session a senior faculty member in a science discipline described a large-scale study he was involved in to explore how students regulate their own learning and how the design of courses could lead them to do so more effectively. It was an interesting presentation, based on good evidence, and during the question period a young professor expressed his enthusiasm for the approach and asked about an idea for implementing some of the principles in his own teaching. Before directly answering the question, the senior faculty member asked the questioner what his academic rank was. He was an assistant professor—one on the tenure track but not yet tenured. The senior faculty member began his answer by saying, "There are some things you can do, but don't let this get in the way of your own research. Your first priority has to be what your departmental tenure committee wants. After you get tenure, you'll have more freedom to experiment with your teaching. But you have to put your own interests first now."

The senior faculty member was clearly concerned that he not undermine the career of his junior colleague by sparking too much enthusiasm for effective teaching. His intentions were good. But they also revealed vividly a design flaw of the university. Following the rituals that will preserve the faculty endowment comes before good teaching.

The message of this anecdote is confirmed time and time again. For example, Julie Foertsch, Susan B. Millar, Lynn Squire, and Ramona Gunter, researchers at the University of Wisconsin–Madison, did a series of interviews with faculty members from several universities who had been offered opportunities to pursue reformed approaches to their teaching: "Many of the university research professors we talked to were concerned that time spent on reform activities would take too much time from their research."[11] The authors quote one department chair who put it quite explicitly: "If you don't have tenure, you are told not to mess with any of this stuff. Publish and get grants, make a reputation in your field."[12]

The way the endowment effect works in any given case depends on the subjective beliefs of people about what they think they "own." If a change entails no cost to me, then I am much more likely to accept it than if it leads to a loss. So what does a faculty member's endowment consist of? What does the faculty member potentially have to lose in this transaction of organizational change?

In 2000, William Massy and Andrea Wilger of Stanford University conducted a series of interviews with 378 faculty members from nineteen varied colleges and universities for the National Center for Postsecondary Improvement (NCPI). The purpose of the study was to find out what incentives or rewards faculty members considered important. Their results can stand as a reasonable estimate of the faculty's sense of their own endowment—and they confirm the judgment of the senior faculty member described above. The researchers found that "nearly every faculty member interviewed (94 percent) finds tenure and promotion to be an important goal. Almost three-quarters of faculty are also motivated by salary and merit increases."[13] Salary increases, of course, are usually linked to promotion, which is linked to tenure. The next most frequently mentioned reward was release time or sabbaticals—time released from teaching duties to do more research.

The most obvious endowment is money—the salary and other monetary rewards a faculty member receives for doing his or her job. When salary or other income is not implicated in curricular or pedagogical change the virtual or immaterial endowments that are connected with monetary rewards may be more important. And these often involve a sense of prestige or self-worth connected to expertise. Higher salaries, stipends, grants, and monetary awards recognize ability and accomplishment. What do faculty members think they are getting rewarded for? What are the material rewards emblematic of?

The shift to research that began in the nineteenth century and continued through the twentieth shows no signs of abating and is reflected in dollars and cents. James Fairweather, then at the Pennsylvania State University, conducted a detailed study of nationwide faculty salary and work patterns for his 1996 book *Faculty Work and Public Trust*. He found that "regardless of institutional type or mission and irrespective of program area, faculty who spend more time on research and who publish the most are paid more than their teaching-oriented colleagues."[14] Fairweather reviewed a number of studies of faculty attitudes about what determined their rewards. Uniformly, they "found that faculty perceived their rewards to be dependent on research, not teaching, including faculty from institutions with a strong emphasis historically on teaching."[15] Furthermore, this process was explicit in the rewards for newer faculty members, and it was true in all kinds of four-year institutions: "The . . . data show that professed differences in institutional missions are not matched by difference in faculty pay. Instead, pay in all types of 4-year schools contributes to early faculty socialization by paying assistant professors who spend their time on research and publishing considerably more than their counterparts who devote their time to teaching and service."[16]

One of the most treasured endowments of college and university faculty, the most highly valued according to the NCPI study, is tenure. Not only is tenure a valuable reward in its own right, as an assurance of continuing employment, higher salary, and increased autonomy; it also has enormous symbolic weight. So like a product that we've set our hearts on but can't yet afford, tenure enters the virtual endowment of nearly all faculty members for whom it is conceivably within reach—and many for whom it isn't. Most faculty members see tenure as linked strongly to research and linked weakly, if at all, to teaching. Mark Taylor, chair of the Department of Religion at Columbia and an emeritus professor at Williams College, says, "Though most universities pay lip service to teaching and rely on student course evaluations, in my experience, teaching ability plays no significant role in hiring and promotion decisions. Publications and the evaluations of other specialists in the field are virtually all that count."[17] Jack Schuster of the Claremont Graduate School and Martin Finkelstein of Seton Hall University reviewed faculty survey results and other research for the past several decades in their 2006 book *The American Faculty*. They found, "The proportion of faculty agreeing that it is difficult to attain tenure without research or publications rose steadily from about two in five (39.9%) in 1969 to nearly two-thirds (65%) by 1997."[18]

It is not just faculty who are aware of this; students notice as well. Elaine Seymour and Nancy Hewitt, sociologists at the Bureau of Sociological

Research at the University of Colorado Boulder, spent three years in the 1990s interviewing and conducting focus groups with students who majored in math, science, or engineering—some of whom stayed with those majors and some of whom started with them and then switched or dropped out. The purpose of their research, reported in their 1997 book *Talking about Leaving: Why Undergraduates Leave the Sciences*, was to find out why the attrition in technical and scientific fields was so high. One of the reasons, they found, was the very low quality of teaching. One female student who stuck with her engineering major reported how the system worked: "The basis for tenure is not whether or not you're a good teacher, it's how much money you bring in. It's well-known that they can't teach, but they bring in research money. They usually teach the toughest classes too. Or maybe they're the toughest because they're teaching them."[19]

Thus, time and resources for research become, in the faculty mind, the causes of highly valued endowments: money, privilege, prestige, and tenure. So research time itself becomes an endowment. Schuster and Finkelstein found that by the 1990s, "faculty members almost universally expressed a desire to shift some portion of their time from teaching to research."[20] "Teaching load," for most faculty members, is not a dead metaphor. Time spent on teaching is itself seen as a loss rather than a gain, a burden to be carried in order to pay for the real value, the true endowment, of research time.

LOOSE COUPLING AND THE BINDING MYTHS

Most colleges and universities extend a great deal of autonomy to units of the institution and to individuals acting within them. Cornell University organizational theorist Karl Weick pointed out that colleges and universities tend to be *loosely coupled* organizations.[21] Loose coupling implies that the work done in one division of the organization is not dependent on or connected with the work done in another. In, say, a manufacturing company, the various departments—production, marketing, accounting, transportation— are tightly coupled. The production units aim to produce close to the number of products the marketing unit can sell and the transportation unit can get to the customers. If the various parts of the organization fail to provide continuous feedback to one another and act in concert, the result will be waste and lost revenue. In a university, on the other hand, what one department does is not, in most cases, linked in any significant way to what another department does.

To get an idea of what loose coupling looks like, consider the experience of the average undergraduate. She may be taking classes from three, four, or even five different departments. She has no expectation that her math teacher will teach in the same way as her sociology teacher or her life sciences teacher. She will expect to take tests, but she will have no idea how many or what kind until she starts the class. How much, if anything, she will need to read, and write, how many assignments of what kind she will have to do are purely at the option of the individual teacher. In one class, her entire grade may be based on two multiple-choice tests, a midterm and a final. In another, she may have to write an essay every week. In another she may be involved in projects with other students. But she won't know until she gets there. And, indeed, she is perfectly well aware that her life sciences teacher will have no idea what she is doing in her math class, and will probably have no interest in finding out. Each class in each separate department stands on all fours, with its own pedagogy, assignments, and criteria for grading. It would not even occur to her to complain about the fact that her experience in one class is completely unrelated to what she does in another.

How does such a loosely coupled organization hold together? Through symbolic or ritualistic linkages. In discussing them, we need to keep in mind the double meaning of the term *myth* that we noted earlier. A myth is a fable or a fiction, a false or misleading account, not to be trusted. But myths are also "true" to those whose lives they organize, true in the sense of giving meaning to actions that might otherwise be inexplicable. Myths give meaning to rituals—routine and standardized actions that gain significance because they are seen as repeating or following some exemplary models.

RITUAL CLASSIFICATIONS

There is an obvious sense in which the university thrives on ritual: commencement, robes and hoods, traditions that go back to earlier generations. But rituals, in a larger sense, pervade and define colleges and universities. Return to our hypothetical student: some things are the same in all classes for her. Every class meets at a designated time, usually in the same place, a specific classroom, and for a specific period of weeks, not subject to varia-tion and the same for all classes. The teacher sets the rules for the course, usu-ally by distributing a course syllabus. And the student's performance in the course will be judged; she will be given interim grades on a five-point scale (A-B-C-D-F) and will be assigned a final grade for her overall performance in the course at the end of the term. These things are standard across all courses and departments; our student knows going into every class that she will be assessed and graded, and that the teacher of the class will be respon-sible for both stating and applying the criteria of success. There is not a shadow of a doubt about this, while there is nearly complete uncertainty about what the actual work will be from one instructor to another.

John Meyer and Brian Rowan, Stanford University organizational theo-rists, characterized the stable and constant aspects of educational institutions as *ritual classifications*. These are the categories that colleges and universities (and elementary and secondary schools as well) keep track of, enforce, and gather information about. Meyer and Rowan point out that "instructional activities—the *work* of the organization—are coordinated quite casually in most American educational institutions. But the ritual classifications and cat-egories that organize and give meaning to education are tightly controlled."[22]

The ritual classifications provide the framework for the theory-in-use of educational institutions. They name and identify what become the nodes and reference points for the routines that define people's jobs. They entail a largely separate world from the espoused theories of educators, what they really believe about what matters in their work. So the rituals of education that gen-erate the tacit theory-in-use that everyone follows are carefully monitored and observed. The productive work, the efforts to carry out the espoused theory that defines the goals the system exists to promote are unobserved and unmonitored.

What is interesting about this pattern of loose and tight control is that what is loosely controlled is much more important to the purported mission of the institution than what is tightly controlled. The things that colleges and universities pay the most attention to often deserve the least attention. The daily rituals of college life are severed from the real value of the work that both faculty and students do. The implicit connection between ritual and reality, between theory-in-use and espoused theory, is achieved by the gov-erning myths of higher education.

A vast body of research points to the fact that the pedagogical choices teachers make, the ways they teach, make a great deal of difference in terms of how much students learn, how long they remember what they learn, and how well they can transfer their learning to new settings. I mentioned earlier Richard Arum and Josipa Roksa's work in *Academically Adrift* and the ongoing projects of the NSSE and CCSSE, all of which have demonstrated that pedagogies that lead to increased student engagement and effort lead to vastly better learning. Another compilation of research that illustrates this point quite vividly has been produced by John Hattie, an education scholar at the University of Auckland in New Zealand. His 2009 book *Visible Learning* is a compilation of over eight hundred meta-analyses of studies of classroom learning. A meta-analysis is a study that collects a number of experimental studies that address the same question and statistically synthesizes those studies to extract a common body of evidence. Hattie has done remarkable work in synthesizing these eight hundred meta-analyses, which themselves synthesized the results of over fifty thousand empirical studies of student learning. My purpose here is not to identify what works and what doesn't for teaching. (I have already written a book on that question,[23] and Hattie's book is one of many other excellent ones on the subject.) I am making the simpler claim that what teachers do "in the classroom" really does make a difference. Hattie summarizes many of his major findings as follows: "The remarkable feature of the evidence is that the biggest effects on student learning occur when teachers become learners of their own teaching, and when students become their own teachers."[24] Teachers' choices, the kinds of things that are buried in the syllabus and that are completely outside the control of anyone but the individual instructor, count.

In contrast, the ritual classifications that institutions obsessively observe, record, and preserve count for very little in the real world of learning. And, indeed, the whole range of activities that constitute what we might call *the myth of educational quality* are basically irrelevant to educational value. In chapter 1 I referred to the work of Ernest Pascarella and Patrick Terenzini and cited their two-volume compilation and summary of research on higher education, *How College Affects Students*. As we saw, they found that the societal myth of educational excellence was without foundation: the "great" institutions had no better outcomes than the "average." What did make a difference, they found, was what the students did, the kinds of things that the ritual classifications that link the parts of the university together completely miss: "What the evidence indicates consistently, as it has for the past 30 years . . . , is that what happens to students after they enroll at a college or university has more impact on learning and change than the structural characteristics of the institution these students attend. What matters is the nature of the experiences students have after matriculation: the courses they take, the instructional methods their teachers use, the interactions they have with peers and faculty members outside the classroom, the variety of people and ideas they encounter, and the extent of their active involvement in the academic and social systems of their institutions."[25]

This should not surprise us. After all, the ritual classifications that define progress and success through college—grades, credit units, courses—are the same at almost every accredited institution. A bachelor's degree represents 120 units completed with an average of C or better at almost all the colleges and universities in the country. With small variations, transcripts of a student at an Ivy League university and one at a rural community college will look pretty much the same: a list of classes with final grades. The experiences—the assignments, the work, the level of effort, the strength of engagement—are invisible on the transcript, yet these are the experiences that may shape the trajectory of a student's life and that may be vastly different not just from one college to the next but from one class to the next in the same institution. The credits are fungible, interchangeable—three units in math or history at virtually any accredited institution will be accepted at most other institutions as of the same educational value as three units from anywhere else. But the experience, the learning, is definitely not fungible. The student who knows and understands what she studied cannot be exchanged on the job or in any place where the knowledge or skill matters with a student who learned little and forgot most. In the long run, the learning matters a great deal, and the transcript matters not at all.

The structure of colleges and universities, by and large, conceals the important and reveals the trivial. The ritual classifications—majors, grades, credit hours—that the institution preserves and displays are the basis of societal beliefs about higher education that have little or no basis in reality. But in the loosely coupled structure of the modern university, the important work that goes on is invisible. As Meyer and Rowan put it, "It is very clear whether a given school has an economics major or not, but there may be no one in the organization who keeps track of exactly what economics majors study or learn."[26]

One result of this is that the quality of teaching goes largely unnoticed at the institutional level. Seymour and Hewitt conducted their interviews with students randomly selected from science, mathematics, and engineering classes at seven very different colleges and universities. They found that among both the students who switched majors (switchers) and those who did not (non-switchers), "reports of poor teaching . . . were by far the most common complaint. . . . Poor teaching was mentioned by almost every switcher (90.2%), and by far more non-switchers (73.7%) than any other issue."[27] Reading through the hundreds of interview excerpts from anonymous college students is a sobering experience.

Students see that many of the classes they are required to take have the purpose of "weeding out" students. Several students confirmed that the medieval model of lecture thrives in many of today's science and engineering classes: "I had one professor who would literally pick up the book and read it to the class. I mean, he would just read. We had 60 percent of the class drop the course. . . . I was happy with the course content, and the facilities were wonderful, but the teaching was just a *vast* disappointment to me."[28] Another, a science major, reported, "A lot of professors are really bad teachers. There doesn't seem like there's any pattern. They'll give you a syllabus, but they kind of go off on tangents and there's really no lesson plan."[29] While most found the teaching wanting, they were clear on the fact that the quality of teaching was in many ways the key to their education. An engineering student put it well: "The professor is *by far and away*, I think, the main determining factor in how well you do in a class, and how much you learn. I could give several examples of courses I've taken with one professor, which my room-mate had taken with another. And you'd think they were teaching two different subjects. It's definitely the teacher thing."[30] Yet "the teacher thing" gets scant serious attention in either the hiring or the promotion of faculty in higher education. And institutions nationwide conduct the business of education as if teachers were entirely interchangeable, as if it were obligatory to treat them as if all were doing the same quality of work.

It is not, of course, just the teacher; it is also the design of the class and the pedagogy. I was privileged to sit in on a class at a community college in Washington State that was a team-taught learning community combining basic English and basic math. Students would do nearly all of their work in groups of six or so, working through math problems and then writing about how they solved them and creating examples to illustrate the math principles. Nearly all of the students in this class were fairly hard-core failures, in their own eyes and in the view of the system. All had done badly in math and most in English in high school and many had managed to avoid both subjects for years. I asked these students to report both anonymously in writing and in an open discussion how they felt about the math they were doing in this class.

They were unanimously glowing in their praise. It was the first time in their lives they had enjoyed math. They finally understood concepts they had never been able to comprehend before. They loved the collaboration and had discovered they could learn from one another. A few years later, when I read John Hattie's book and came across the line quoted above—"the biggest effects on student learning occur when teachers become learners of their own teaching, and when students become their own teachers"—I thought of this class.

I said nothing to prompt them but just asked questions. One young woman raised her hand in the back of the room. "You know," she said in a quiet voice, "it's funny, but just by coincidence, my sister is taking this math class too. She's older than me, but she's taking a regular class, where the teacher just lectures, not a learning community like this. And when we go home at night, she asks me to help her with her homework. We're using the same book, taking the same tests, but she doesn't understand any of it from class. I have to explain it to her. And I can." That learning community was probably not going to be offered in the next semester because it depended on the efforts of the two teachers who had partnered together, and one of them was called to other things. And on the student's transcripts, the fact that the class had a completely different pedagogy would just disappear. The young woman who was teaching her sister and the sister who needed tutoring after class would, if they came away with the same grades, be identical, interchangeable on the transcript. As evidence of the ritual classifications that determine progress through the curriculum, Math 80 (or whatever it was) would appear just as any Math 80 class. On the transcript, in the records of the institution, in the planning of the institution, the mind-deadening lecturer who drives students away washes out, becomes invisible, as does the brilliant team of teachers who materially changed the lives of many students for the better. All that survives is A, B, C, a letter that stands for nothing definable, all the meaning, all the value, for better or for worse, washed away. The institution preserves the ritual and ignores the reality.

THE INSTRUCTION MYTH AND SUPERSTITIOUS REASONING

How can such a strange reversal of common sense survive in institutions populated by scholars and thinkers? The fact of the matter is that the scholars and thinkers think in a very different way when it comes to their own institutions than they do when doing their research, or even their teaching. As Meyer and Rowan point out, "Attempts to tightly link the prescriptions of the central theory of education to the activities of instruction would create conflict and inconsistency and discredit and devalue the meaning of ritual classifications in society. Educators (and their social environments) therefore decouple their ritual structure from instructional activities and outcomes, and they resort to a 'logic of confidence': higher levels of the system organize on the *assumption* that what is going on at lower levels makes sense and conforms to rules but avoid inspecting it to discover or assume responsibility for inconsistencies and ineffectiveness."[31]

What Meyer and Rowan refer to as the logic of confidence is part of the instruction myth. The instruction myth, as we have seen, is the keystone of the Instruction Paradigm: its root assumption is that instruction and learning are interchangeable, that if a student has been instructed, has taken the class, then he or she has successfully accomplished what needs to be done. By extension, the instruction myth extends to nearly all the operations of the institution: if the procedures that ritual classifications require have been carried out, then the job has been done. The instruction myth sustains the myth of educational quality, which in turn obscures the conflict between the organizational espoused theory and the theory-in-use.

The institution extends the myth to the individual faculty member in the classroom. If what we know about learning is to have an effect, it needs to be linked to the experience of students, and everyone—in an act of ritual assent—assumes that the individual faculty member will make that connection. Thus we have the corollary *myth of teacher professionalism*. Given the assumption that all teachers are "professionals," and hence worthy of confidence, the system can then deflect responsibility to these individuals. Weick points out that "linkages that occur within universities tend to be person-specific and occur among units of very small size. At the most molecular level, linkages among research, service, and teaching are presumed to occur *within* the single individual, a presumption found in few other organizations."[32]

The definition of myth I quoted earlier used the term *sacred*, and that may have put some academics in a lather. Of course, I do not intend to imply any belief in the supernatural among the bulk of the faculty, many of whom are a determinedly secular bunch. However, it does seem clear that the instruction myth—the assumption, for instance, that each faculty member will teach wisely and well—is a faith, an ardent belief in things unseen, rather than any kind of a conclusion from observation or evidence.

Still, every teacher—and every administrator—encounters evidence every day that tends to undermine the instruction myth and cast doubt on the myth of quality and the myth of teacher professionalism. Even those who scrupulously avoid reading any of the vast output of educational critique encounter the evidence from their own students that things are not working well. How do they think through these problems? In many cases they rely on what Weick calls *superstitious reasoning*. In the face of feedback, usually long delayed, that reveals the problems in present practice, "the only kind of learning that is likely to occur is superstitious learning. Superstition is evident when people perform elaborate rituals to produce good outcomes because some unknown piece of the ritual has produced the outcome in the past, though no one knows for sure which portion it is."[33] Like the athlete who wears the same socks for every game or the gambler who won't sit down at the table without his rabbit's foot or lucky coin, the faculty member repeats last semester's syllabus and last semester's lectures because to not do so might be to omit the ritual that keeps the demons at bay. This is the academic version of Harvey Hornstein's rule of repeated action. Such superstition is often a product of loss aversion, repeating the ritual act because the possible loss of failing to repeat it looms so much larger than the possible gain from a risky innovation. F. M. Cornford was describing superstitious reasoning precisely and elegantly when he spoke of the Principle of the Dangerous Precedent. And such reasoning does indeed lead us to the conclusion that nothing should ever be done for the first time.

The institution is loosely coupled when it comes to the actual work of teaching but tightly coupled when it comes to the rituals and mythic beliefs that organize the work, so the very structure of the organization accentuates the status quo bias. To gather people together to oppose a change requires only that they act on the assumptions—the instruction myth—that govern and organize their work and their daily lives. To gather people together to support a change requires that they question those underlying assumptions. Frank W. Lutz, a professor of education at New York University, went so far as to suggest of universities that "they are tightly coupled in some aspects and uncoupled in other aspects. *Tight coupling* occurs when an issue supports the status quo. *Uncoupling* occurs when an issue challenges the status quo."[34]

6 · FRAMING THE FACULTY ROLE

Graduate School, Departments, and the Price of Change

For most faculty members who come to work at a college or university, their thinking about the nature of faculty work is framed by their prior experience at a university, and their thinking about the institution where they will work by the initial contacts there. Most of the time, the initial contacts and the interview are carried out by the academic department. And when the faculty member is hired, the department, formally or informally, provides the introduction to the institution and the initial version of the ground rules. And it is clear from the outset that, just as the department was the chief agent of deciding who to hire, it will be the chief agent in deciding about future promotions and eventual tenure. It is not much of an exaggeration to say that most untenured faculty members work for their departments rather than for the college or university that is their titular employer.

Beginning with the preparation for a faculty position in graduate school, the university experience of future and beginning faculty members frames time spent on teaching as a loss and time spent on research as a gain. The training and preparation for a teaching career sets up faculty to see time invested in teaching as a risky endeavor that can threaten one's prospects for hiring and advancement but that probably cannot improve those prospects. Likewise, the price of changing existing arrangements appears to be high, and so efforts to change the existing practices of an institution are framed from the very outset as a losing proposition.

THE FORMATION OF TEACHERS

The educational qualification for a faculty position is a graduate degree; for four-year colleges today—and given the glut of doctorates in some fields, often at two-year colleges as well—that almost always means a doctorate. The initial frame for thinking about what a faculty member does is the individual's experience of graduate school. This poses a challenge for improving the quality of undergraduate education because the barriers to change in the undergraduate college derive in large measure from the structure of graduate schools. Since the triumph of research in the late 1800s academic departments have been formed and structured primarily as research engines, collaboratives of specialists organized in the first instance to conduct research and in the second to prepare apprentices to do more of that research.

The autonomous and inward-looking character of academic departments is most pronounced at the graduate level. And the graduate program is at the head of the undergraduate department; the most senior faculty are most likely to teach graduate courses and supervise doctoral students, and also have the most influence in the decision-making process of the department at the undergraduate level. Graduate school frames the faculty role: it is where future teachers are socialized to the academic culture and absorb the tacit rules of the game. The Modern Language Association, the largest professional association in the humanities, summarizes the point in the report of their 2014 task force on doctoral study: "Doctorate-granting universities confer prestige on research rather than teaching. A coin of the realm is the reduced teaching load—even the term *load* conveys a perception of burdensomeness—while honor and professional recognition, not to mention greater compensation, are linked largely to research achievements. The replication of the narrative of success incorporates this value hierarchy and projects it as a devaluation of teaching."[1]

In the first decade of this century, the Carnegie Foundation for the Advancement of Teaching conducted an extensive study of doctoral programs, the Carnegie Initiative on the Doctorate, under the direction of George E. Walker of Florida International University. They made detailed studies of eighty-four Ph.D.-granting departments in six different academic disciplines. Walker, Chris Golde, Laura Jones, Andrea Conklin Bueschel, and Pat Hutchings reported on the project in their 2008 book *The Formation of Scholars: Rethinking Doctoral Education for the Twenty-First Century*. To oversimplify only slightly, they found that the traditional apprenticeship model of the doctorate, in which senior scholars guide students through the preparation of a dissertation, failed to prepare most doctoral students for whatever they ended up doing afterward. "It is hard . . . ," they conclude, "not to be disheartened by the waste of human talent and energy in activities whose purpose is poorly understood."[2]

Kenneth Prewitt of Columbia University notes a fact that is central to both the successes and the failures of graduate education: "The genius of doctoral training in American higher education is that *no one is in charge*."[3] Graduate education is much less strictly regulated, in most fields, than undergraduate. And even at a given institution, graduate programs are only loosely controlled by the institution and more tightly bound to the disciplinary guild. If the undergraduate college is a loosely coupled system, the graduate program often seems completely uncoupled from the larger institution. There is no equivalent in doctoral programs to general education, a shared enterprise in which departments must cooperate to some degree. The doctoral program is a pure major and the gateway to membership in the academic guild. Thus departments have almost complete control. Walker and his coauthors point out that "doctoral education remains a locally controlled process: admissions, curriculum, and quality standards are all controlled by the department's graduate faculty. As any graduate dean will testify, disciplines and departments rule the day when it comes to shaping the experience of doctoral candidates. In short, departments have tremendous power and are deeply resistant to external pressures for change."[4]

The result is what we might expect: "This highly decentralized structure makes American graduate education at once messy and unruly, and at the same time highly resistant to systemic change. In this sense, it is an element of stasis, a condition that makes widespread reform much more difficult than it might otherwise be."[5] Hence it is, as Columbia's David Damrosch puts it, "that many of our graduate programs do not run so very differently than they did when our own teachers were graduate students."[6]

The independence of graduate programs has three effects on undergraduate learning. First, it sets a pattern of departmental autonomy that models and reinforces the role of departments as separate and independent centers of authority in the undergraduate programs as well. Second, it invests a major faculty endowment—the right to teach graduate courses and serve on doctoral committees—in senior faculty, thus making them more removed from and less knowledgeable about undergraduate teaching. Third, and perhaps most important, it places the controlling role of mentoring and guiding the next generation of faculty in the hands of those senior faculty who tend to be the most focused on research and the least focused on undergraduate teaching. Of course, there are many senior faculty members who are very interested in undergraduate teaching. But that is not the job of the graduate faculty; their job is to prepare researchers.

Most doctoral students, at some point in their graduate careers, do get some teaching experience. One of the other benefits of a doctoral program to the department is that it provides a supply of inexpensive academic labor in the form of graduate student teaching assistants. But the kind of experience these students get and the way their teaching work is framed by their superiors do not always serve their undergraduate students well. As Walker and his colleagues point out, "Where teaching experience is available, it may not be required. And where it is required, there is no guarantee (or structure to ensure) that experience actually leads to greater understanding of the complicated dynamics of teaching and learning. In teaching, as in other complex practices, more experience does not automatically lead to more expertise."[7] In the fall of 2016, a young professor of history published a short essay called "Teaching Tips for Graduate Students" in the *Chronicle of Higher Education*. Interestingly, hardly any of the tips had anything to do with the actual process of teaching; they all involved how to limit the time devoted to teaching and cut corners on the process. And all derived from the first, central, and controlling tip: "Your research comes first. That's what my advisor always says. Teaching during graduate school helped me to learn what that really means."[8] What it means is that teaching must be limited and constrained to the prior and more important demands of doing the work that is really rewarded. The consequence for newly minted doctors, Prewitt says, is that "although prepared to do original research, they seldom are adequately prepared for their teaching duties or their more general professional obligations."[9]

The apprenticeship relationship between a doctoral student and his or her advisor is often close, but perhaps as often fraught. In the doctoral program the privacy of teaching is often taken to an even greater extreme than in undergraduate education, and the master-apprentice relationship can become nearly a sacred space, one in which even other senior faculty hesitate to interfere. When the relationship isn't working well for the student, it often leaves the student isolated and alone. As Walker and his colleagues point out, "The traditions of solo sponsorship are often coupled with traditions of faculty autonomy that leave students feeling they have no recourse when they are mistreated or, more commonly, when a relationship sours. The culture of privacy extends so far that faculty members and departmental leaders are reluctant to intervene in dysfunctional situations."[10] Catherine Hoffman Beyer, Edward Taylor, and Gerald Gillmore, who conducted the UW GIFTS study of teaching growth at the University of Washington, draw this conclusion about graduate schools: "Programs may differ dramatically across the country, but nearly all are marked by a hierarchy with faculty advisors at the top holding complete power over the futures of the graduate students under them."[11]

The question has been repeatedly asked whether doctoral education prepares students well for faculty positions, and the answer of those who have looked at the evidence objectively has been that it does not. For one thing, it fails to prepare faculty for what most of them went into faculty work to do and for what they will spend most of their time doing: teaching. In 2001, Chris Golde of the Wisconsin Center for Educational Research at the University of Wisconsin and Timothy Dore of the University of Georgia conducted a survey of over four thousand doctoral students at twenty-seven universities across the country. The overwhelming majority of these students aspired to faculty positions at colleges and universities. Golde and Dore asked them why. The most important reason why these students decided to pursue a faculty career was enjoyment of teaching, which 83.2 percent of the respondents listed. Most of the people who go into higher education do so largely because they want to become teachers. Among those working in faculty positions, the researchers found that college faculty spend considerably more time, on average, doing teaching than doing research.[12] Yet graduate programs overwhelmingly emphasize research over teaching, and even to the exclusion of teaching, thus preparing students for what they will do less of and leaving them largely on their own to figure out the larger portion of their work.

University leaders, of course, talk about teaching a lot. That is the espoused theory, for public consumption. But the theory-in-use of most institutions is radically different. The espoused theory, in most cases, has little influence on the academic lives that graduate students live. The UW GIFTS study involved interviews with fifty-five faculty members, almost all of whom were making a real effort to improve their teaching. But 63 percent of them reported that they had received no training in teaching at all as graduate students.[13] Ann Austin of Michigan State interviewed seventy-nine doctoral students at two research universities: "The graduate students often mentioned mixed messages about teaching—the most obvious being public statements by institutional leaders about the importance of teaching contradicted by institutional policies and faculty behaviors emphasizing research."[14] These mixed messages almost certainly contribute to the very high attrition rates in most doctoral programs—about half drop out on average, and more than that in many programs. It is hard to be sure just why, but Austin interviewed one student who was probably not unusual: "I came here because I really wanted to teach. Research was the hoop I had to jump through. . . . I didn't know if it would take more than I was willing to give. I've tried three times to find a 'researchable project,' . . . and, well, I'm just not that interested anymore. . . . I think I'll go into business."[15]

The result of the current design of graduate programs is that most faculty are never trained to teach. Thus, the work of faculty is framed as a research job in which teaching is a fill-in activity that requires no special training. This is, apparently, a problem of international scope. The consequence was reported most colorfully by Anna Tobin when she was a recent graduate of Leeds University in the United Kingdom. She had, she reported, "endured lecturers with IQs to match Einstein's, who have written a series of theses and libraries of books, but who could not teach a dog to sit."[16]

BEGINNING FACULTY WORK

Most students enter doctoral programs because they think it will allow them to do a certain kind of work, and for most that is faculty work in higher education. The success of any doctoral program depends to a great degree on the success of its graduates in finding promising positions. So the colleges and universities that hire students with graduate degrees are largely responsible for the behavior of graduate schools. If being prepared to teach is a criterion for hiring, graduate schools will take preparing their students to teach much more seriously. But today, it is not a significant criterion for hiring at many institutions.

Robert Boice of the State University of New York, Stony Brook, conducted extensive interviews over twenty years ago with new faculty from two large universities. He characterized this remark by a new faculty member as "normative": "No, no one has said much about teaching. Mostly, I've been warned about colleagues to avoid. A lot of it is gossip and complaining. I can only think of two specific things that have been said about teaching here. One is how bad the students are . . . about how unprepared and unmotivated they are. The other one, that maybe two people mentioned, was a warning about the need to set clear rules and punishments on the first day of class. All in all, I'm pretty disappointed with the help I've gotten."[17]

Overall, Boice found that "less than 5 percent of new faculty in their first semesters at either campus could identify any sort of social network for discussing teaching. Moreover, no new faculty were in departments where colleagues met occasionally to discuss teaching."[18]

Left to be enculturated to the institution mainly by their departments, new faculty tend to direct their attention where others do. Boice found that "they are passive about change and improvement. They assume that casual comments from students (and perhaps from colleagues) are sufficient to gauge prowess at teaching. They reluctantly seek outside help from resources including faculty development programs. And when asked to specify plans for improvement, even in the wake of poor ratings and admitted dissatisfaction, they are unable to specify alternatives beyond improving lecture content and making assignments and tests easier."[19]

The new faculty members Boice interviewed are, many of them, now tenured faculty. I am convinced that things are better than this today at many institutions. Still, hiring institutions have little to go on even if they really want to hire good teachers. The basic template, the default setting at too many institutions, is the pattern where graduate students with no serious preparation to teach are hired by departments that pay little attention to their lack of preparation and then do little or nothing to support them in learning how to teach. It should be clear by now that faculty avoid investing time and effort in improving their teaching not because they don't want to but because the risks of investing time in teaching are much greater than the risks of investing time in research. Loss aversion guides them to the safer alternative.

THE ROLE OF DEPARTMENTS

The organizational units that embody the ritual classifications of major and discipline are academic departments. The academic disciplines that define the roles of academic departments are the modern successors of the medieval guilds, the professional associations that define the purposes and the rules that will govern success in the work. As the local representatives of these national and international guilds, departments have a special expertise and authority as the authorized holders of not only the knowledge of the guild but its rules. The standards and criteria for research in history are not the same as those in physics or music, and only a member of the guild can judge another member in the realm of its expertise. The nature of these academic guilds tends to reinforce the status quo bias. As John V. Lombardi, former president of the Louisiana State University System, puts it, "Because their own members hire and retain their successors, an institution's guilds behave as self-replicating organizations."[20]

Departments, seen as organizations for teaching as opposed to research, exist for the purpose of offering classes and assigning grades, for maintaining the ritual classifications that largely define them. As James Fairweather points out, "Academic organization and faculty reward structures are based on discipline-oriented departments. Department chairs often see themselves as preservers of the discipline, ensuring that dominant mores continue. In the modern college and university, valued faculty behaviors focus on research and publication and on minimizing the time devoted to undergraduate instruction. The very structure which ensures maintenance of the disciplines works against faculty involvement in teaching and learning and against developing a more successful undergraduate curriculum."[21]

Fairweather conducted a case study of a coalition of seven institutions that sought to improve curriculum and pedagogy in engineering departments. In his surveys and interviews of faculty he found that "faculty believe that [untenured] assistant professors who devote time to teaching and curricular reform are at risk. Department chairs consistently warned assistant professors to stay out of coalition activities in spite of the commitment by deans."[22]

In the loosely coupled structure of the university, the department becomes the channel for the faculty member's endowment. Departments play a central role in hiring new faculty and deciding who is promoted and who receives tenure. Furthermore, especially at large institutions, the department is the only place where faculty have a sense of control over institutional processes. Schuster and Finkelstein noted that there is "a strong and consistent pattern of about two of every three faculty members perceiving a high level of influence on their department. At the same time, many fewer faculty (15% to 20%) report wielding high levels of influence over campuswide affairs."[23] This reflects the fact that departments, and individual faculty members, are loosely coupled to the institution, but departments are tightly coupled internally, to the standards of the guild and to the ritual classifications that give them their character.

It goes without saying that not all departments are alike and that many take the teaching role quite seriously, as do most of the faculty. But when it comes to contemplating significant change in the way teaching is governed or arranged, many features of departments militate against such change. As we have seen, departments function to protect faculty autonomy from administrative control.

THE MYTH OF ACADEMIC FREEDOM

Closely related to the instruction myth is the *myth of academic freedom*, and the myth of academic freedom has done much to strengthen the role of departments in curriculum and governance. Academic freedom, of course, is a real and important concept. In some times and places it has served as a necessary bulwark against government intrusion in free inquiry and against inappropriate administrative interference in research and teaching. Indeed, preserving this key principle where it is really needed should be reason enough for rejecting its mythic impersonator. In recent years, this valid sense of the term has been all but overwhelmed by the mythic concept of academic freedom as nearly unrestrained faculty autonomy. Arthur Levine, who later served as president of Teachers College at Columbia University, wrote over thirty years ago that "academic freedom has come to be the right of faculty to teach in strict privacy and to do their research in isolation. In fact, student course evaluations have been criticized by faculty for violating their academic freedom. The problem then is that autonomy has become popularly linked with academic freedom, encouraging existing programs and activities simply to continue because scrutiny of any sort is inappropriate."[24]

Much more recently, Derek Bok observed that "faculties have taken the principle of academic freedom and stretched it well beyond its original meaning to gain immunity from interference with how their courses should be taught. In most institutions . . . , teaching methods have become a personal prerogative of the instructor rather than a subject appropriate for collective deliberation. The result is to shield from faculty review one of the most important ingredients in undergraduate education."[25]

Robert Zemsky, of the University of Pennsylvania, provides a vivid example when he relates the response of a "senior colleague" to an initiative to improve the quality of teaching: "When told by one of our program directors that her students were questioning her teaching, [she] responded that such a query on the part of an administrator was a violation of her academic freedom, as were all administrative attempts to either monitor or regulate her classroom performance. In the same breath she reminded the program director that she had no interest in participating in any kind of 'group-grope' that was intended to make the program's instructional offerings less disjointed. What and how she taught was her business and her business alone. By invoking faculty autonomy and academic freedom, she evoked the ultimate defense against any reform effort that asked her to change anything."[26]

Of course, no one would suggest that academic research is a private matter. Quite to the contrary, the whole point of doing research is to be seen to be doing research. Thus the myth of academic freedom and the *privacy of teaching* to which it gives rise leave research as the only public and widely observed work of a faculty member and lock teaching in a dark closet of private practice—"free," and therefore unobserved and inconsequential.

GROUPTHINK AND GROUP POLARIZATION

One of the god words of the academy is *diversity*. But in the public discourse, and sadly within the academy, it is nearly always taken to mean *identity diversity*: differences in race, gender, ethnicity, or background. This is important, of course, and diversity of this sort is valuable for any number of reasons. But when it comes to decision making and problem solving, the kind of diversity that makes a marked difference is *cognitive diversity*. (Identity diversity, in many settings, promotes cognitive diversity, and this is one of the chief reasons it is valuable in an organization. People from different backgrounds and cultures often think differently.) The group in which different members have different perspectives and skills, different mental tools with which to address a problem, will be more likely to solve problems.[27] The value of cognitive diversity is a deep justification for academic freedom, the real thing.

The greatest threat to the genuine freedom of faculty members to speak their minds today is not government or even the administration; it is the department. This is not to say that all departments suppress free expression, but it is to say that their tendency is to do so. In a loosely coupled organization, where the individual faculty member's prospects and opportunities are largely dependent on the choices of his or her immediate colleagues, the tendency is for these small and powerful groupings to enforce a collective conformity around the ritual classifications that it is their mission to protect.

Many departments come to enforce something very much like what psychologist Irving Janis, in his book of the same name, called *Groupthink*. "Groupthink," Janis wrote, "refers to a deterioration of mental efficiency, reality testing, and moral judgment that results from in-group pressures."[28] In other words, groupthink is the active suppression of cognitive diversity. Janis derived his theory of groupthink from an analysis of disastrous decisions made by very smart people, including the Bay of Pigs Invasion, the Cuban Missile Crisis, and the failure to defend Pearl Harbor. What he found was that talented and experienced leaders often failed to examine the options in a rational way when a group consensus seemed to have emerged: "In a sense, members consider loyalty to the group the highest form of morality. That loyalty requires each member to avoid raising controversial issues, questioning weak arguments, or calling a halt to softheaded thinking."[29] And, as we have seen in the case of defensive routines, groupthink makes the weaknesses that it gives rise to undiscussable. Groups often exaggerate the degree of agreement present early in a discussion and then reinforce the illusion. So members often engage in "self-censorship of deviations from the apparent group consensus, reflecting each member's inclination to minimize to himself the importance of his doubts and counterarguments."[30] Often, members adopt a "shared illusion of unanimity concerning judgments conforming to the majority view (partly resulting from self-censorship of deviations, augmented by the false assumption that silence means consent)."[31]

Janis quotes, for one example, Arthur Schlesinger Jr., historian and advisor to President Kennedy during the planning for the Bay of Pigs Invasion. Speaking of the weeks of deliberation among "the best and the brightest" that preceded the disastrous decision to proceed with the invasion, Schlesinger said, "Our meetings took place in a *curious atmosphere of assumed consensus*."[32] In part, this can be another example of framing—how the way of presenting or formulating an issue can influence the way people think about it and what they see as safe or risky behavior. In groups, framing effects are powerful. Janis found that group leaders had a significant effect on the development of groupthink. Insulated groups, where outside voices were not invited in, had more of a tendency to create assumed consensus. And when leaders did not invite alternative points of view, members who had them were more likely to censor themselves. Overall, groupthink tends to push group members to take more extreme positions than they would otherwise, a phenomenon called *group polarization*.

Janis's evidence for groupthink consisted entirely of case studies, albeit very detailed and careful case studies. Subsequent experimental research seems to confirm that it is more than an occasional occurrence. In recent years, for example, a number of scholars have studied the phenomenon of group polarization, and much of their research confirms that people do self-censor and exaggerate the level of consensus in a group. Cass Sunstein, a professor at Harvard Law School, suggests that the phenomenon of group polarization can explain much of the political polarization that we see in the United States. In one study of undeniably smart and well-educated people, he conducted a statistical analysis of federal appeals courts, which consist of three-judge panels. Some of the judges, of course, have been appointed by Republican presidents, some by Democrats. Judges, aside from being highly educated and accomplished in the law, are serving in positions that are almost defined by the aspiration to be free from bias. What Sunstein did was to compare the decisions of courts configured in two different ways: those with three judges appointed by presidents from the same party as opposed to those with two from one party and one from the other. One set of groups had two poles of opinion, the other only one. He found that "in countless areas, Democratic appointees show especially liberal voting patterns on all-Democratic panels. Republican appointees show especially conservative voting patterns on all-Republican panels. If we aggregate all cases showing an ideological difference between the two groups, we find a 15 percent difference between

Republican and Democratic appointees in liberal voting rates. That is a pretty big difference. But the polarized difference is far higher—34 percent!"[33]

There is a tendency, even among highly educated people whose job is to try to be objective, to be swayed by group consensus and by the absence of cognitive diversity.

To what extent do groupthink and group polarization affect academic departments? That varies, and it may depend a lot on the traditions and leadership of the department. But we have strong evidence that these patterns are commonplace. My own experience and that of many others whom I trust on the question has been that departments tend to be insular and self-protecting. When it comes to stepping outside the departmental framework of thinking, many faculty members not only won't do it but won't even talk about it. In years of trying to get faculty engaged in innovative projects, one of the most common rationalizations I have heard for not doing anything new has been the fear that such an activity would transgress "departmental norms," or more straightforwardly, "My department wouldn't like it." There is often no answer to the question "Why?" And in many cases I have found that this isn't because people want to conceal their reasons: they really don't know why the department takes such-and-such a stand. They know, however, that asking for reasons would be dangerous. Groupthink comes about in part because group members who may have different points of view censor themselves, which in turn reinforces the illusion of consensus, which in turn encourages members who believe they are in a minority to censor themselves further. That process is very likely to occur to some extent in most departments. As David Damrosch puts it, "Both initial hiring decisions and tenure votes in particular are influenced only in part by intrinsic merit; equally important is the established faculty's sense of how well the candidate has been socialized into the dominant norms of the department."[34]

The question is whether the "dominant norms of the department" actively suppress cognitive diversity and cause people to censure themselves. In 2006, Stephen J. Ceci and Wendy M. Williams, professors of human development at Cornell, and Katrin Mueller-Johnson, a lecturer at Cambridge University, conducted a survey of 1,004 faculty members at colleges and universities randomly selected from the U.S. News top fifty liberal arts colleges and research universities. They were seeking to find out whether the professors' academic rank affected the likelihood that they would teach classes unpopular with senior colleagues, publish research unpopular with the department, or report ethical violations by members of the department—including plagiarism and sexual misconduct. They were especially interested in testing the idea that professors speak more freely after they have received tenure.

Overall, they found that all faculty below the level of full professor tend to censor themselves and restrict their options in light of what they believe senior faculty prefer. Interestingly, while faculty of all but the highest rank reported that they would censor themselves heavily, they did not believe that their colleagues would. Of course, if individuals who are censoring themselves believe that others are not, then the silence of others (who in fact are censoring themselves as well) will reinforce the illusion of consensus. "Lower-ranked faculty," they concluded, "appeared 'muzzled' by the fear that displeasing senior colleagues could result in denial of tenure and promotion, and the finding that tenured associate professors were perceived as being less likely than full professors to exercise academic freedom suggests a 'hush time' lasting 10 to 20 years or more."[35] The researchers found no differences based on academic discipline or gender. The dependence of faculty on the department, what the authors call "the muzzling effect," has created a system in which "even tenured associate professors refrain from exercising academic freedom for fear of derailing their chance for promotion to full professor."[36] In this system, "The truth is that most of us walk on eggshells until we become full professors."[37] These results show that loss aversion continues to be a major motivator of faculty choices well into their careers and that it almost certainly reinforces the tendency to groupthink.

Consider the implications in terms of departmental willingness to embrace significant change. Those who are least likely to censor themselves in departmental forums are those with the largest endowment in current practice, the largest investment in the status quo. Those most likely to censor themselves are those most likely to have novel or different points of view because they have most recently come from different places. What is the likelihood, in this environment, that faculty will challenge the logic of confidence? Departments instead become fertile fields for the growth and nurturance of organizational defensive routines, and topics that could become troublesome become and remain undiscussable.

In the day-to-day conduct of colleges and universities, academic freedom is often equated with departmental freedom. To preserve a united front against external enemies and at the same time preserve the shared illusion of consensus, departments need guardians of the myths and rituals that sustain them. Janis points to the "emergence of self-appointed mindguards—members who protect the group from adverse information that might shatter their shared complacency about the effectiveness and morality of their decisions."[38] Frank Lutz sees the departmental and other faculty mindguards as protectors of the orthodox mythology, charged with demonizing those who would undermine it: "Shamen emerge who, after having developed a consensus within the society, are allowed to accuse individuals of being witches. The witches are often marginal members of the society, new and/or untenured professors or administrators. They are accused of cursing academic freedom and attempting to destroy the essence of the university." The result of this informal disciplinary system is that "academic administrators uncouple themselves from decisions that may result in such accusations being made about them, and untenured professors attempt to be amiable and unchallenging of the status quo in order to survive."[39]

We reviewed in the first chapter some of the mountain of evidence on the performance of undergraduate colleges. Why do the faculty at most colleges and universities seem unaware of this evidence? In large measure, it is the departmental censoring process that suppresses evidence of the widespread malfunctions of higher education. So it is that in a crowd of learned doctors something like *argumentum ad ignorantiam*, argument from ignorance, rules the day: we have seen no evidence in this room that our methods don't work; therefore, they must be working. As Derek Bok puts it, "Safely insulated from reliable evidence of how their students are progressing, most faculty members have happily succumbed to the Lake Woebegone effect. As surveys have confirmed, close to 90 percent of college professors consider their teaching 'above average.'"[40]

In terms of teaching, the myth of academic freedom works itself out, as Levine said, in the right of "faculty to teach in strict privacy." Many faculty members have not been trained at all in teaching. Thus they are on their own in the classroom, in most cases falling back on the patterns they have observed in their own education, teaching as they have been taught. The privacy of teaching protects poor or mediocre work from observation or correction. Correspondingly, it means that if teachers do work hard to improve and succeed in improving student learning, nobody will know it. Lacking either credible expertise, respected credentials, common standards, or a framework of meaningful review for teaching, many faculty members see pedagogical improvement as a morass in which gains would be invisible if achieved and they can only lose: lose time, lose money, lose energy through vaguely configured efforts that create no enduring value. So privacy becomes an endowment in terms of teaching, a protective cover and defense, and the department preserves the individual space of the teacher to do whatever he or she does unobserved and unmolested.

And the myth of academic freedom becomes a component of a variety of defensive routines that make the teaching process simply undiscussable in many times and places. The more skillfully the department protects its integrity, the more it perpetuates designed ignorance on its members and its institution.

THE MYTHS STAND ALONE

But what of colleges where faculty have no or hardly any research responsibilities, such as community colleges and some small liberal arts colleges? While there is little or no pressure on faculty at these institutions to do research, the organizational structure is usually the same: faculty are hired, promoted, and granted tenure through discipline- or skill-based departments. Faculty at community colleges attend graduate school at four-year universities. And the system of recognition and reward in the community college, like that in the university, is based on individual accomplishment as mediated by the department. In community colleges, the autonomy survives without the research. Thus the privacy and individualism of teaching at most community colleges creates an environment in which autonomy becomes itself a reward, a form of control, an endowment.

At community colleges, while there is a public emphasis on teaching, it usually does not translate into any kind of public or institutional scrutiny of teaching. It is as much the case for community college faculty as for their cousins at universities that teaching is usually done in private and that autonomy translates into a nearly complete absence of scrutiny or real quality control.

The late W. Norton Grubb and his associates from the University of California, Berkeley observed hundreds of classes and interviewed dozens of teachers at twenty-four community colleges throughout the country for their book *Honored but Invisible: An Inside Look at Teaching in Community Colleges.* They found that "a defining aspect of instructors' lives in community colleges is their isolation. Except in a small number of exemplary institutions, most instructors speak of their lives and work as individual, isolated, lonely. A teacher's job is a series of classes, with the door metaphorically if not literally closed. Some faculty view isolation as an inherent part of teaching: 'Teaching is a very individualistic endeavor, and people are often secretive and unwilling to seek out or utilize a different approach.'"[41]

Tenure is relatively easy to achieve at community colleges, and in most cases the review of actual teaching practice is no more serious or credible than at most four-year colleges. There is certainly more emphasis on teaching at community colleges, but there is no better apparatus for reviewing and improving teaching. Serious peer review of teaching is probably most robust in vocational and career-preparation programs where faculty often work closely together and students are assessed on their actual performance. The standards for tenure and promotion are probably more valid and credible for auto mechanics, welding, and graphic design than for English, math, and psychology.

In the absence of any clear standards, in an isolated environment where the work is not seriously examined and its consequences are essentially unknown, the privacy of the classroom becomes the vehicle of control, the personal entitlement of the teacher.

7 · THE MYTH OF UNITY AND THE PARADOX OF EFFORT

Professors at four-year, traditional colleges and universities are trained to be researchers in specialized fields, hired for their research accomplishments, and rewarded by promotion and tenure based on the perceived quality and quantity of their research output. As we have seen, both faculty and administrators at four-year colleges and universities are heavily invested in research. That investment holds them back from changing the basic design of undergraduate learning, and indeed reinforces the status quo bias across a range of activities.

And since the academic disciplines, acting through the academic departments that make up the college, have a structure of assessment and feedback to faculty on the quality of their research, this allows them to substitute the research question for the teaching question. So the logic of confidence and the instruction myth do not completely apply to research. Departments and institutions do not simply assume that faculty members are good researchers; they look at some evidence on the question. But they tend to look at very little evidence on the question of whether faculty members teach effectively; instead, they substitute the research question, as if it were the same question.

QUESTION: Is Professor Evans an effective teacher?
ANSWER: Of course, he's written two books on his subject.

The belief that has held sway for over a hundred years in the academy is that teaching and research are reciprocal, complementary activities. Christopher Jencks and David Riesman, in their classic 1969 critique of higher education *The Academic Revolution*, pointed out many problems for the undergraduate college created by the rise of the research university. But they held fast to the orthodoxy that the research doctorate was the necessary preparation for good teaching: "Those who do not publish usually feel they have not learned anything worth communicating to adults. This means they have not learned much worth communicating to the young either."[1] While this is on its face a non sequitur, and one based on a false premise, it captures the logic of association that has dominated the argument for decades. Their view is widely adopted by higher education administrators and faculty. For example, James Duderstadt, emeritus president of the University of Michigan, asserted in 2000, "Teaching and scholarship are integrally related and mutually reinforcing and their blending is key to the success of the American system of higher education. Student course evaluations suggest that more often than not, our best scholars are also our best teachers."[2] The argument here is a bit circular, of course, because if any teachers were not among "our best scholars," they would never get tenure in the first place. But Duderstadt simply reflects a belief that is nearly obligatory for the president of a research university. James Fairweather points out that "surveys of faculty indicate widespread acceptance of the belief that teaching and research are mutually reinforcing."[3] So it is worth exploring what the real relationship is between teaching and research. It will turn out to be more complicated than we probably expected.

DOES RESEARCH IMPROVE TEACHING?

So what does the evidence tell us? Does doing research make people better teachers? In 1996, John Hattie (who at the time of this article worked at the University of North Carolina at Greensboro) and Herbert W. Marsh of the University of Western Sydney in Australia conducted a meta-analysis of fifty-eight studies that sought to find what the relationship was between teaching and research. The studies they used all examined teacher-scholars at universities or colleges, involved ratings by external parties of both teaching

and research, and used large enough samples to reasonably calculate a correlation using valid statistical techniques. Essentially, what they found about
the correlation of teaching and research performance was that there was no
correlation: "The evidence suggests a zero relationship."[4] The evidence of a
positive relationship, where it occurred, was balanced out by evidence of a
negative relationship elsewhere, and any evidence of a correlation was weak
in both directions: "We must conclude that the common belief that
research and teaching are inextricably entwined is an enduring myth. At
best, research and teaching are very loosely coupled."[5]

Six years later, in 2002, Hattie and Marsh (Hattie now at the University of
Auckland in New Zealand) followed up on their meta-analysis with a detailed
study of a research university in Australia in which they were able to break
down the possible variables that might connect research and teaching in less
obvious ways: "In summary, the multilevel analyses demonstrated that the
near-zero correlation between teaching and research was remarkably robust
across 20 academic departments in the one institution considered in our
research."[6] Reviewing the totality of the evidence, they concluded that

> the results of the present investigation—coupled with the comprehensive . . .
> meta-analysis—clearly indicate that teaching effectiveness and research produc-
> tivity are nearly uncorrelated, thus supporting the hypothesis that they are
> independent constructs. These results have some obvious implications.
> Good researchers are neither more nor less likely to be effective teachers than
> are poor researchers. Good teachers are neither more nor less likely to be
> productive researchers than are [poor] teachers. . . . Research performance does
> not provide a surrogate measure of teaching effectiveness, nor do measures of
> teaching effectiveness provide an indication of research productivity. Similarly,
> if students want to be taught by outstanding teachers, they need to focus on
> measures of teaching effectiveness rather than reputations based on research
> performances.[7]

Research continues on the question. A notable 2017 study was conducted
by two economists at Northwestern University, David N. Figlio and Morton
Schapiro (Schapiro is also the president of Northwestern). It is worth note
because they used a particularly persuasive means of evaluation. To assess
teaching quality they looked at two factors: the likelihood that students in
an instructor's introductory courses voluntarily took later courses in the same

subject and how well they did in those subsequent courses, and the extent to which students subsequently majored in the discipline of the introductory course. To assess research, they looked at whether the faculty member had been recognized by the university or national organizations for excellent research and an index of how influential the faculty member's publications had been in his or her field. Using these criteria, they compared the performance in teaching and research of 170 tenured faculty who taught over fifteen thousand first-quarter students between 2001 and 2008. Their conclusion was nearly identical to Hattie and Marsh's twenty years earlier: "Our bottom line is that, regardless of our measure of teaching and research quality, there is no apparent relationship between teaching quality and research quality."[8] The evidence points still to the conclusion that "the factors that drive teaching excellence and those that determine research excellence appear unrelated."[9]

Why, then, has *the myth of the unity of teaching and research* survived? We do not expect that a great golfer will also be a great tennis player. We do not expect that excellent accountants will also be superior public speakers. Or that skilled managers will be wonderful musicians. Speaking of musicians, we don't even expect that an accomplished pianist will be a good singer. When two activities essentially draw on separate sets of skills, we don't make an assumption of crossover, and when we do, we are usually disappointed. Why, then, do intelligent and well-educated people assume that good researchers will also be good teachers?

Hattie and March suggest that there are two theories that have been used to justify the connection. The first, which they call "the conventional wisdom model," holds essentially that "it is 'obvious.'"[10] Faculty have always been told that the two are connected; they were trained on the assumption that this was true; their mentors and supervisors always assumed it was true; and the organizations where they work are structured on the assumption that it is true. In other words, the belief in the connection between teaching and research is an intellectual habit that most academics have never had occasion to question. The second model is what Hattie and Marsh call "the 'G' model."[11] This is an analogy with the theory that intelligence is fundamentally explained by a general form of mental power that manifests itself in different ways, a g factor. Likewise, advocates of the g model hold that the underlying skills involved with teaching and research are the same. This line of thinking is quickly revealed as a form of special pleading. And, of course, the credible research on the subject fairly well dispatches that theory. It's clear, if we can break out of the conventional wisdom, that John Henry Cardinal Newman, writing 160 years ago, was right: "To discover and to teach are distinct functions; they are also distinct gifts, and are not commonly found united in the same person. He, too, who spends his day in dispensing his existing knowledge to all comers is unlikely to have either leisure or energy to acquire new."[12] There is no reason, just on an observation of what they do, that a good researcher is more likely to be a good teacher, any more than that a good baker will be a good bowler. It might happen, of course. But there's no reason to expect that it usually will.

THE TIME FACTOR

James Fairweather concluded, in agreement with Hattie and Marsh, "The evidence increasingly points to teaching and research as discrete activities having less in common than accepted in conventional academic lore." He added an important qualifier, however: "Effective teaching and effective research share a common feature: both are labor-intensive."[13] This point is important. Because while there is no evidence that better researchers are better teachers, there is a good deal of evidence that teaching and research compete for the limited time available to a faculty member.

In 1996, Fairweather analyzed the data from the 1987–1988 National Survey of Postsecondary Faculty, sponsored by the National Center for Education Statistics, a survey of over eleven thousand faculty from 480 colleges and universities. The data "confirm the competition between time spent on teaching and research for faculty in all types of 4-year institutions. . . . In effect, the more time faculty spend on research, the less they spend on teaching, and vice versa. Since effective teaching requires substantial faculty effort, and because the increased effort must come from time spent on research, the implication for faculty and administrators is clear: improvement in teaching requires faculty to spend less time on research and publishing."[14]

In 2017, ten years after Fairweather's study, Carl Wieman, a Nobel Prize–winning physicist who has long been an advocate for better teaching in the sciences, reflected on his own efforts a two major research universities to raise the profile and effectiveness of teaching through the Science Education Initiative: "The dominant barrier to the adoption of better teaching methods at these and other universities is the formal incentive system, which is actually seen as a disincentive to put time and effort into teaching. The universal concern for tenure-track faculty was how adopting new teaching methods would impact their research productivity. Whenever the issue of changing teaching was brought up, it invariably led to the question 'How much time will this take?' A longer conversation made it clear that this really meant 'How much time will this take away from my research?'"[15]

Students, of course, are perfectly aware of the conflict. Elaine Seymour and Nancy Hewitt, in their extensive interviews with math and science majors and ex-majors, found that "students constantly referenced faculty preoccupation with research as the overt reason for their failure to pay serious attention to teaching undergraduates."[16] They quote a young woman who switched majors away from mathematics: "The full-professors are here for the research. They have the attitude that students are barnacles. Undergraduate students just kind of prevent professors from doing the research they really want to do."[17]

While most faculty, I ardently hope, do not treat students as "barnacles," nearly all faculty at four-year institutions feel the tension between research and teaching. For nearly two decades I have been working with college and university faculty to promote more active, effective teaching and to encourage institutions to set meaningful goals for teaching by formulating learning outcomes and assessing student progress. Overwhelmingly, the greatest source of resistance has been the question "How can we find the time?" I am convinced that this is a sincere concern, not an excuse or an evasion. I am convinced, in part, because I have had the same complaint. Teaching well takes time, and making changes and improvements in courses and pedagogy cannot be done in an instant. Yet, research takes time too! Bryan Barnett, an academic administrator at Rutgers University, concludes, "One cannot produce the quality or quantity of research needed to establish a significant reputation among peers as a part-time pursuit. So the research demands on individual faculty members will never leave enough time or energy for them to meet the need for devoted teaching and curriculum development."[18]

In 2002, Fairweather conducted a study in which he attempted to measure the productivity of faculty in terms of both research and teaching, using the 1992–1993 National Survey of Postsecondary Faculty, which examined a sample of over twenty-five thousand faculty members from 817 institutions. Using the best available measures, Fairweather found that "about 22% of all faculty in 4-year institutions simultaneously attained high productivity in teaching and research. . . . This percentage did not vary substantially by type of institution. When collaborative/active instruction is added to the definition . . . , the overall percentage drops to about 6%."[19] In other words, when we attempt to provide a meaningful quality test for teaching, the capacity to do both at the same time, at a high level, nearly vanishes. Fairweather concluded, "The small percentage of faculty in all types of 4-year institutions who achieved high levels of output in both research and teaching . . . belies the common belief that each faculty member can achieve both simultaneously. Even fewer were able to achieve above the norm in teaching and research productivity while using potentially more effective instructional practices."[20]

The evidence supports the conclusion of Bryan Barnett: "Several generations of official rhetoric notwithstanding, the present requirements for high-quality undergraduate education ultimately are incompatible with the sort of research programs now required to secure tenure, promotion, external support, and scholarly reputation and status."[21]

Ronald Barnett of the Centre for Higher Education Studies in the Institute of Education at the University of London offers what I think is a useful analogy for the relationship between teaching and research: "The relationship of the teacher to research is analogous to the relationship of the musical soloist to the score. There is no demand on the soloist that he or she be a composer, be able to produce new scores. But it is paramount that the soloist be so directly acquainted with the score that he or she is able to offer us a personal interpretation of it; in a sense, a critical commentary on it."[22]

THE PARADOX OF EFFORT

If we explore this relationship more closely we find an interesting discontinuity. Hattie and Marsh, in their detailed study of the faculty at a single institution, identified several factors that may or may not be relevant to faculty productivity in teaching and research. They found, consistent with other research and with common sense, that researchers who spend more time on their research are more productive. However, when they looked at teaching, they found, quite at odds with what common sense would lead us to expect, that faculty who spend more time at teaching are *not* more productive. Not only time but several other factors seem to be unrelated to teaching effectiveness: "A perplexing pattern of results . . . is that teaching effectiveness and even self-ratings [of] teaching ability are mostly not significantly related to other teaching constructs (e.g., satisfaction, personal goals, time expenditures, and activities). In contrast, research productivity and self-ratings of research ability are positively related to most of the corresponding research constructs."[23]

Researchers who enjoy their work, set goals, and spend more time on research and research-related activities are more successful researchers. But teachers who enjoy their work, set goals, and spend more time on teaching and teaching-related activities are *not* more successful teachers. How could this be?

Hattie and Marsh hazard a partial explanation: "Academics receive considerable training in how to be productive researchers and are constantly exposed—through professional reading, conferences, and collaboration—to role models who are productive researchers. Because academics know how to be productive researchers, it follows that greater motivation, time, effort, and appropriate activities should result in increased research productivity. In contrast, most academics receive little or no training in how to be effective teachers and are rarely exposed to role models who demonstrate effective teaching."[24]

Referring to another study, they note that "even teachers who were motivated to improve their teaching and had systematic feedback from their students identifying their strengths and weaknesses did not know how to improve their teaching effectiveness."[25]

This is a strange state of affairs. But we have already seen that both graduate education and the orientation that faculty receive on the job provide little support for improving their teaching. And, if true, the paradox would powerfully reinforce the bias in favor of research, both in the faculty and in the institutions where they work. Most faculty members at four-year institutions would like to spend more time on research and less on teaching. One explanation is that they get results from spending more time on research and don't from spending more time on teaching. It is a paradox—I will call it *the paradox of effort*—but one that could explain a lot.

We should consider another partial explanation for this paradox. It may be that institutions and researchers don't have any very clear measures of just what good teaching is. Research on feedback has shown that people respond to feedback differently according to their situation, goals, and attitudes. People who have clear goals, for example, and believe that those goals are achievable will utilize feedback to improve their performance, but if those conditions are missing they often will not.[26] As we will see in future chapters, the goals of teaching improvement are often unclear. And for a variety of reasons, teachers often have well-founded doubts about their ability to achieve a given goal with a given class. So it may be that teachers are themselves ill situated to use what feedback they receive. And the quality of that feedback is often dubious.

Hattie and Marsh and most other researchers who have attempted to assess teaching quality have chiefly relied on student evaluations of teaching. Though often using careful and sophisticated ways of interpreting these evaluations, they may face the perennial challenge of those attempting of assess qualities that have not been directly measured: as the computer programmers like to say, garbage in, garbage out. I am not suggesting that the data that these studies are based on are useless or completely uninformative. Indeed, I believe that the paradox of effort is really at work on today's campuses. But we should keep in mind that the measures of research productivity are, by orders of magnitude, more specific, reliable, and quantifiable than any existing measure of teaching effectiveness.

8 · FACULTY EXPERTISE AND THE MYTH OF TEACHER PROFESSIONALISM

College professors are, almost quintessentially, experts. If we seek expertise on most subjects, the first place we are likely to look is a college or university campus. Most professors are expert in the subject matter they teach, but the source of their expertise is their training and work as researchers. The myth of teacher professionalism, which we discussed earlier, encourages us to assume that expertise in research translates directly into expertise in teaching. But that is an unsupportable assumption.

What does it mean to be an expert? How do people get there? And is there a difference between saying that an individual is an expert in what she teaches and saying that she is an expert teacher? If there is a difference, it could help to explain the paradox that effort pays rewards in research but often does not in teaching.

We should note at the outset that two of the easy equations that we sometimes make are wrong. We sometimes use the term *expert* when what we really mean is *specialist*. This is a mistake. Many experts specialize, of course. And many specialists are experts. But specialization is not a sufficient condition for considering someone an expert, as I use the term here. The development and maintenance of expertise is something more and different from narrowing the range of one's practice to a smaller and smaller number of cases.

The second erroneous equation we sometimes make is between expertise and experience. It is true that most experts have much experience; it does not follow that experience necessarily leads to expertise. Richard Elmore of the Harvard Graduate School of Education has studied reform efforts in public education for decades. He makes the point in terms of public school teachers, but it certainly applies as well in every other field, including higher education: "So while expertise exists, matters, and can be improved, it is not true that experience equals expertise. That is, deep knowledge in the domains necessary to become a powerful and fluent practitioner does not automatically, or even reliably, come as a result of continuous practice."[1] What, then, is expertise?

EXPERTISE

The key to expertise is learning. An expert is one who has learned more, and perhaps better, than others. One of the clearest differences between experts and novices—and a potentially misleading one—is that novices have to consciously think about doing things that become automatic for experts. As we saw in chapter 4, Chris Argyris points out that skillful actions "appear effortless" and are "automatic and usually tacit."[2] K. Anders Ericsson of Florida State University has studied expertise for years. He notes that skillful activities can become automatic well before the development of what anyone might consider expertise: "After a limited period of training and experience— frequently less than 50 hours for most everyday activities such as typing, playing tennis, and driving a car—an acceptable level of performance is typically attained. As individuals adapt to a domain . . . , their performance skills become automated, and they are able to execute these skills smoothly and with minimal effort."[3]

Thus the development of skill requires practice, and with practice the activity comes to seem automatic (System 1), to require little or no conscious attention. Nearly all adults have reached this level of automaticity in a variety of complex actions, such as reading, writing, typing, and driving a car. Those activities were not easy, much less automatic, when they were first learned. The reason that teenage drivers (or their parents) have to pay such high insurance premiums is that drivers are more likely to have accidents for the first few years of driving. That is true for a variety of reasons, but one of them is that the cognitive load of driving—the proportion of working memory that needs to be devoted to the task—is greater for new drivers than it is for drivers for whom many of the processes have become automatic. Experienced drivers can devote more of their mental capacity to the conditions of the road and the other traffic than can new drivers because they no longer need to devote conscious attention to whether to signal and how soon and how hard to depress the gas or the brake pedal. They have not yet had enough practice to make the rudiments of driving into System 1 activities and so occupy more of System 2 with these fundamentals. Thus they are slower and less accurate in responding to unanticipated challenges.

Many people can perform highly skilled activities in System 1, and if one is to learn to perform at a very high level, this is necessary. But even nonexperts gain familiarity with a variety of processes and learn to carry them out automatically. Experienced drivers don't need to stop to think about decisions under normal driving conditions. But put most experienced drivers on a raceway and challenge them to a test of speed against professionals and the prudent ones—like me—would experience entirely justified terror and run away. Being an experienced driver on the public roads involves nothing like the split-second timing and spontaneous response to serious risks that make professional racers capable of meeting much greater challenges than most of us can.

Learning any skill involves making initially difficult operations automatic. But the mastery of complex skills or knowledge will involve moving back and forth between System 1 and System 2. If we are operating completely in System 1, just going on automatic pilot, we aren't learning at all; we are enacting routines. The key distinction between the expert and the nonexpert is that the experienced nonexpert comes to act in a routine fashion, while the expert continues to learn.

The young pianist learning a new piece carefully studies the score and deliberately reads each note before striking the corresponding key. With practice, reading the notes will become a System 1 activity, yet many players become fairly proficient at sight reading but never reach the level of a professional performer, playing at once with accuracy, sensitivity, and flexibility. What, then, separates experts in a field from competent and experienced nonexperts? It is probably the quantity, quality, and purpose of their practice.

The amount of practice makes a difference. Ericsson estimates that it takes something like fifty hours of practice for us to achieve an "acceptable level" of proficiency in some basic skills. By comparison, the standard estimate of the time it takes to achieve genuine expertise is ten thousand hours.[4] Those who pursue expertise devote more time to practice because they seek to master higher level and more complex skills. But once skills become automatic, they become harder to improve upon. As Ericsson points out, the shift to System 1 puts the skill beyond the range of learning: "When the behaviors are automatized, mere additional experience will not lead to increased levels of performance."[5] How, then, do we make additional practice count? The answer lies in the kind of practice.

People on the road to expertise practice differently from others. Ericsson calls it *deliberate practice*. "Deliberate practice," he points out, "presents performers with tasks that are initially outside their current realm of reliable performance, yet can be mastered within hours of practice by concentrating on critical aspects and by gradually refining performance through repetitions after feedback. Hence, the requirement for *concentration* sets deliberate practice apart from both mindless, routine performance and playful engagement."[6]

Concentration means moving into System 2, becoming aware and deliberate about one's efforts. Deliberate practice is designed specifically to challenge the learner to perform at a higher level. Thus good coaches and teachers—whether the domain is chess, sports, music, science, or law—design challenging tasks for learners to perform, tasks that require concentration and repeated efforts, so that they can expand the repertoire of activities that they can perform automatically and with little effort.

Carl Bereiter and Marlene Scardamalia of the Ontario Institute for Studies in Education at the University of Toronto address this matter in their book *Surpassing Ourselves: An Inquiry into the Nature and Implications of Expertise.* They describe expertise as a process rather than a steady state. (And here is where expertise parts company, in its essentials, from specialization.) While most experts know a great deal more than nonexperts, it is the trajectory and purpose of their knowledge acquisition that really makes them experts: "*The career of the expert is one of progressively advancing on the problems constituting a field of work, whereas the career of the nonexpert is one of gradually constricting the field of work so that it more closely conforms to the routines the nonexpert is prepared to execute.*"[7] Elmore characterizes the view of development that most teachers adopt in their work as precisely nonexpert, in this sense. It is "characterized by narrow focus and routinization rather than active learning and the deepening of knowledge."[8]

As people make skillful activities automatic, they free up time and mental resources. Doing work in System 1 is faster and less effortful than doing the same work in System 2. We might call this the *skill bonus*. Here is the crucial question: What happens to the bonus? Do we spend it or invest it? While Bereiter and Scardamalia don't use the System 1–System 2 construct, they make exactly the same point that Kahneman does about the relationship between them: "Automaticity is the great freer of mental resources, but it is obtained at a cost. The cost is loss of conscious access. It becomes difficult to modify a well practiced procedure."[9]

The nonexpert, having made the process of driving or playing the piano or teaching automatic, expends the attention thus freed up on something else—listening to the radio or playing video games or doing research. The nonexpert constricts the field of operation to those tasks that can be done on the plateau of skill she has reached, so she can accomplish the same tasks in less time. The expert, on the other hand, *reinvests* the skill bonus in more challenging tasks, tasks that need to be engaged through deliberate practice. Of course, even nonexperts may seek out challenges. If you are winning all of your chess games or tennis games, you may seek better opponents. But if you are on the trajectory to expertise, you will *systematically* seek out challenges that stretch your existing skills. Thus, through deliberate practice, the expert engages in, to use Bereiter and Scardamalia's term, *progressive problem solving*, using the skill bonus by seeking out and grappling with ever more challenging problems. "Such moves do not just require trying harder. They confront one with problems that cannot be handled by applying previously learned procedures."[10] We see this process of seeking out and grappling with new and more challenging problems in academic research at its best, no matter what the field.

It is the essence of expertise that the expert never settles in for a smooth ride on the plateau but sets out for the peaks. Thus while the casual practitioner of a skill continues to practice, repeating familiar routines and occasionally expanding them to keep it interesting, the expert consistently seeks out new challenges and engages in deliberate practice. The nonexpert learns to make effortful System 2 activities into System 1 routines and then *stops learning*. The expert reinvests the skill bonus gained from making operations routine in order to *keep learning*.

THE ILLUSION OF EXPERTISE

If we think of expertise as a dynamic, ongoing learning process, it will be clear that not all the activities that we might commonly put under that heading really fit. *The illusion of expertise* is commonplace. And one source of frequent confusion here, as I suggested earlier, is to mistake a specialist for an expert, to assume that because a person can perform a very specific activity very well, he or she is an expert. And the myth of teacher professionalism thrives on precisely this illusion, this confusion of specialization and expertise.

To choose an example that is familiar to me, the beginning composition teacher puts a great deal of emphasis on discovering explicit errors in student writing. But after a few years—or even months—of doing this, the process becomes automatic. The teacher no longer needs to look for fused sentences, the passive voice, or lapses in noun-verb agreement; they leap from the page as if already highlighted. She can't miss them. So the temptation is to make the easy part, what is now a System 1 activity, the whole job. It now takes the teacher less time and hardly any effort to identify the superficial flaws in student writing, and the question arises whether to reinvest that skill bonus into probing under the surface or to simply do the job faster and read a book—or perhaps write one—in the time saved.

If students are aiming chiefly for technical excellence in their writing, it should not surprise us that they rarely have anything interesting to say. To engage the process of invention, the process by which words embody thought and thus furnish the laboratory for testing ideas, is far distant from what most students have learned to do when they set out to write a school essay. But unless they can be engaged at the level of meaning, and meaning that matters to them, they become proficient at spinning out variations on hollow formulas without ever saying anything significant or consequential. Teachers who stay on the surface of student work reinforce students in doing the same, so that both repeat the superficial rituals of schooling without learning anything that will change them—or anyone else. I know—and could name, were I sufficiently rude—several professors who pride themselves on the speed and accuracy with which they can reveal the lapses in student writing. These people stopped teaching years ago, but still don't know it. They have narrowed the scope of their work to what they can do almost effortlessly, in System 1. They have become specialists and abandoned the effort of progressive problem solving; they live on the illusion of expertise. We see the same narrowing of goals that masquerades as expertise in teaching any subject, from astronomy to zoology.

Research, certainly research in the sciences, is designed to push the boundaries of expertise. A good hypothesis should be one that can tell us something we don't already know. It should pull the researcher into reinvesting the skill bonus. In quite different activities artists—writers, painters, musicians—seem almost defined in the public mind by their "creativity," which should mean at least exploring the boundaries of conventional frameworks and representations. But we all know both scientists and artists who have built reputations by repeating themselves. Having conducted a successful experiment, it is tempting to repeat it with sufficient changes to make it credible, but without really pushing the envelope. And we all know of novelists who have built careers, sometimes successful ones, on writing the same novel over again, with new characters and settings.

In some fields, expertise exists, but is often hard to differentiate from its surrogate of opinionated specialization. One such field is political and economic prediction. Philip Tetlock, a psychologist at the University of Pennsylvania, interviewed 284 "experts." For the purpose of the study, "expert" was defined as "a professional who makes his or her livelihood by commenting or offering advice on political and economic trends."[11] A majority of those who participated in the anonymous surveys and interviews held Ph.Ds., and 80 percent had served as consultants on international political or economic issues to either government or private groups. Beginning in 1987, he had them complete a Possible-Futures Questionnaire, which asked them to predict the most likely outcomes out of three alternatives on a variety of current issues, such as the fate of world leaders, the prospects of war, and economic trends. He gathered over eighty thousand predictions, most of them completed by 1995. By 2003 he was able to observe the actual outcomes of the events he had asked about.

The experts, on average, performed worse than average. Human experts basically tied with random predictions—outcomes predicted by "a chimp throwing darts"—and they lost by a considerable measure to sophisticated statistical algorithms. Overall, Tetlock concluded that "in this age of academic hyperspecialization, there is no reason for supposing that contributors to top journals—distinguished political scientists, area study specialists, economists, and so on—are any better than journalists or attentive readers of *The New York Times* in 'reading' emerging situations."[12]

These outcomes were averages, however. One other discovery that Tetlock made was that different experts had significantly different degrees of success. His array of questions attempted to differentiate in several ways among his pool of experts. For example, he used several *content factors*: ideology (left-right), realpolitik (realist-idealist), and optimism (boomster-doomster). None of these categories had any significant value in explaining successful predictions.

Tetlock also asked questions seeking to identify the *cognitive style* of respondents. As a result, he was able to confirm that "*what* experts think matters far less than *how* they think."[13] Here he drew on the distinction that historian and philosopher Sir Isaiah Berlin made in his famous essay "The Hedgehog and the Fox." He took his theme from the Greek poet Archilochus, who wrote that "the fox knows many things but the hedgehog knows one big thing."[14] Berlin argued that hedgehogs "relate everything to a single central vision, one system, more or less coherent or articulate, in terms of which they understand, think and feel—a single, universal, organizing principle" while foxes "pursue many ends, often unrelated and even contradictory, connected, if at all, only in some de facto way."[15] In other words, the hedgehog is a pure specialist, while the fox is more eclectic.

Plato, on Berlin's account, was a hedgehog, Aristotle a fox.[16] Of course, it will be clear that both have accomplished great things, and that one might be suited for some tasks better than the other. Berlin acknowledged that the abstract distinction could go only so far, but held that "like all distinctions which embody any degree of truth, it offers a point of view from which to look and compare, a starting-point for genuine investigation."[17] And that is how Tetlock used it.

In the realm of political prediction, Tetlock found, "quantitative and qualitative methods converge on a common conclusion: foxes have better judgment than hedgehogs."[18] Further, it appears that the more specialized a hedgehog is in background and focus, the worse the quality of his or her predictions. Foxes who specialize intensely "derive modest benefit." On the other hand, hedgehogs who specialize more "are—strange to say—harmed."[19] If, as Tetlock notes, "we normally expect knowledge to promote accuracy (a working assumption of our educational systems)," then we should find it "downright disturbing to discover that knowledge handicaps so large a fraction of forecasters."[20]

Why would this be so? Tetlock theorizes that hedgehogs have a greater need for closure and structure. Essentially, hedgehogs are more likely to shape the evidence to their existing ideas than to modify their ideas in the face of new evidence. We can also see in Tetlock's research at least a suggestion that the relationship between specialization and expertise may be more complex than we had thought. For hedgehogs who are also intensely specialized, the more information they have, the worse their forecasts. I believe that specialization, beyond a certain point, narrows people's scope of concern so acutely that they lose track of the big picture. French diplomat Aristide Briand famously observed that "war is too important to be left to generals." The military aspect of war is only part of it, and perhaps not the most important part. The specialist learns to wear blinders in order to focus better on what is straight ahead and not be distracted by the peripheral. But the periphery is where the world is, and where the rest of us live.

We have already discussed the importance of cognitive diversity in groups. But some individuals possess the ability to access a variety of cognitive tools and approaches. A hedgehog follows the rule of cognitive unity, a fox cognitive diversity. The fox is more likely to consider different perspectives, tangential evidence, and multiple sources. And so foxes are better predictors. Where specialization, in knowledge and in patterns of thought, suppresses exploration then we have the illusion of expertise.

The illusion of expertise, unfortunately, is sometimes more impressive and dramatic than the real thing. Tetlock notes that "hedgehog opinion was in greater demand from the media." Why? Because "simple, decisive statements are easier to package in sound bites. The same style of reasoning that impairs experts' performance on scientific indicators of good judgment boosts experts' attractiveness to the mass market-driven media."[21] So not only is the illusion of expertise commonplace, it often looks to the unaided eye deceptively real. This issue affects public thinking and policy making in many fields other than education, but it certainly skews public and even professional thinking about education.

The illusion of expertise often arises in academic work, as the previous examples suggest. But I believe that it arises disproportionately in the realm of teaching. It accounts in large measure for the myth of teacher professionalism.

We see illusory expertise in academic research as well. Some researchers do seek to constrain the scope of their specialty to essentially what they have already mastered. The preparation of researchers in doctoral programs is sometimes dominated by busywork, and some advisers urge their graduate students to narrow their dissertation focus to subjects that are "original" only because they are too small to have been noticed with the naked eye. (Doctoral education is a breeding ground for hedgehogs.) Arguably, whole fields or subfields have been so locked into their orthodox paradigms of scholarship that the repetition of designated jargon and ritual obeisance to the gods of the discipline completely overwhelms the prospect of real analysis and advancement of thinking. Many have argued, and I agree, that the pressure to publish has diluted the quality of both academic thinking and academic writing. As a result, much that is written in scholarly journals and books is nearly unreadable and deservedly unread. And this is much more the case in some disciplines than others because some disciplines have become essentially self-contained echo chambers utterly controlled by groupthink.

Still, there can be no doubt that the ideal of the academic researcher is realized in many places. The project as a whole, if not everyone engaged in it, is a success, and embodies the progressive model of expertise. Much could be done better, from graduate school on, but much is done well.

When it comes to teaching undergraduates, however, the picture is much darker. We have already seen this. Many college teachers, even when they do devote time and effort to improvement, make little progress. And here, the fox-hedgehog framework might help us to explain what sometimes happens. Most faculty members believe they are good teachers, at least so they say on surveys. But they tend to operate in a closed belief system much like that generated by hedgehogs, who see all of reality through the lens of their central concerns and wear blinders to shut out what they don't want to see. Thus it is possible for many teachers in higher education to believe, in effect, "I teach well, but my students don't learn much." Robert Zemsky, Gregory Wegner, and William Massy point out that "relatively few faculty understand how their students learn. Most have at best a passing knowledge of quality processes, and very few have the training to implement such knowledge. Most faculty equate quality with content—with the design specifications for the finished product, so to speak. Few are trained in the art and science of pedagogy. Great teaching is viewed mainly as classroom performance, which is discounted by saying that some professors have more standup-talent than others. Many professors think that little can be done to improve classroom performance; after all, good teachers are born, not made."[22]

Given these premises, most faculty members would have a difficult time explaining what would be evidence of *bad* teaching. In other words, they don't have any clear idea of what kind of information could *disconfirm* their beliefs in their own success. In the absence of clear feedback that points to the need for improvement, improvement doesn't happen. And persistence at a specialized task without improvement defines the illusion of expertise.

Maryellen Weimer, a scholar of pedagogy at Penn State Berks and for many years the editor of the *Teaching Professor*, poses the challenge to the claim of expertise in teaching quite explicitly: "What other profession exists without a viable literature supporting its practice? In what other profession can those who practice do so for years without expanding or updating their knowledge or skills? What other profession fails to use its literature to set benchmarks, identify best (or at least preferred) practices, and exert at least some pressure on those professionals who fail to meet standards?"[23]

No, I can't think of one either.

SECOND-ORDER ENVIRONMENTS

Bereiter and Scardamalia provide a framework that explains why academic research works and when it does and that also allows us to see the contrasting situation with most teaching. Most people work on a daily basis in what they call *first-order environments*. A first-order environment consists of the people, rules, and technologies of the workplace, with relatively stable conditions and demands. But to create a situation in which expertise can thrive, you need another level of operations: "*Second-order environments* are ones in which the conditions to which people must adapt change progressively as a result of the successes of other people in the environment."[24] An example they provide is auto racing: "Each team's advance in technology or strategy sets a new standard which others try to surpass, with the net result that, except for periodic changes in regulations, lap speeds keep going up and up. Adapting in the world of racing means adapting to a progressive set of conditions."[25]

Adapting to the world of research, at its best, also means adapting to a progressive set of conditions. The second-order environment here is created by the intellectual discipline, the framework of scholars reviewing the work of other scholars and seeking to raise the standards of discovery. As researchers test new ideas and confirm theories and hypotheses, their successes—and the failure to confirm a hypothesis is, from the perspective of the search for knowledge, a success—change the environment in which other researchers are formulating questions and seeking new knowledge. We should expect that, within reasonable bounds, the more cognitive diversity there is in a second-order environment, the more effective and creative it will be. The more foxlike an environment, the better it will solve problems; the more hedgehog-like it is, the more it will be prone to groupthink and the preservation of error.

The peer review system in a discipline is intended to expose people's work to cognitive diversity. There is much wrong with the peer review system in some disciplines, and it is always open to abuse. But at root it is an irreplaceable idea, a system for maintaining and continually raising the quality of inquiry and thinking in a discipline. We should be appalled at its abuses, but—if we are being honest and balanced in our judgment—we can only be amazed at its unparalleled accomplishments.

A large part of the training of college faculty in graduate schools consists of socialization to the second-order environment of the discipline. Here, again, there is much to criticize. But entry into that second-order environment is a prerequisite for doing good research, and while the socialization process can be done well or poorly, it must be done if research is to thrive.

What, then, is the second-order environment for college teachers? What is the process by which *as teachers* they must adapt progressively to the environment defined by the success of other teachers, and by the success of their students? It is obvious on any fair account of things that there isn't one. College teachers do not operate in a second-order environment at all. When their colleagues succeed—as many do—most teachers don't know it. And when they themselves succeed, their colleagues rarely know it. Indeed, when an individual teacher succeeds or fails with students, he or she may not be aware of it because all the feedback teachers get on the quality of their work is usually self-generated. A teacher could fail for years without knowing it. The privacy of teaching, protected in many faculty minds by the myth of academic freedom and insulated from inquiry by the logic of confidence, makes teaching an individual activity, conducted in secrecy.

Indeed, the preparation for an academic career that most doctoral programs offer specifically deters future faculty members from creating a second-order community around teaching. Mark Connolly of the University of Wisconsin–Madison interviewed over seventy students who were working on or had recently completed their degrees in science, engineering, or math. Most of these students had entered doctoral programs with the expectation that they would be prepared as both researchers and teachers: "But what many of my study participants really learned during grad school about teaching was how little it is valued. While not surprised to hear that academic success depends on becoming a first-rate researcher, many interviewees were dismayed by messages that being a good researcher is incompatible with being a good teacher—either because there is not enough time for pedagogical training (and, after all, it can be easily learned on the job) or because an obvious interest in teaching is a sign of a failed researcher."[26]

Connolly found that "study participants learned that admitting an interest in teaching exposes them to career-related risks seen and unseen, regardless of their research proficiency and productivity. As a result, doctoral students who identify as college teachers self-monitor more than those focused primarily on research."[27] To "self-monitor" in this case means to check any tendency to reveal a special interest in teaching: "Some sometimes overemphasized their genuine interest in research to pass themselves off as a kind of laser-focused doctoral students that advisors tend to favor."[28] Such a process is obviously not conducive to forming a community of scholars who pursue teaching in common and support one another in doing so.

Back in 1984, Paul Baker of Illinois State University and Mary Zey-Ferrell of Texas A&M University conducted a survey of over five hundred university faculty members and follow-up interviews with a hundred twenty. They sought to find out how faculty thought of their own roles and priorities in the university, and how these self-conceptions affected their relationships with others. They found that "the majority of faculty who see themselves primarily as teachers . . . do not have strong internal or external social ties in any work role area."[29] In contrast, those who identified as researchers "have strong internal and external social networks to sustain their research endeavors."[30] They were contrasting—without using the term—the presence and absence of a second-order environment when they concluded that "research has external groups that determine its objective worth, but teaching has no external system of credibility. Furthermore, no internal system exists that adequately assesses the quality of teaching performance."[31] I see no evidence that things have changed much in the thirty years since this study was done.

In chapter 5 we discussed the factors that conspire to keep teaching uncoupled from real quality control mechanisms. Where the reward system is already linked to faculty research activities, and the logic of confidence reinforced by superstitious reasoning insulates teaching from scrutiny, the second-order environment that already exists to promote academic research works to prevent the creation of a second-order environment around teaching. We have already seen that in the competition for faculty time research trumps teaching. The creation of a second-order environment for teaching would greatly increase the competition for time between teaching and research. Academic research thrives, in large measure, on a system of review and quality control that has grown up at the expense of teaching and that creates enormous pressure to keep teaching quiet, private, and unexamined.

Russell Edgerton was president of the American Association for Higher Education for eighteen years during the time it took the lead in creating a vital movement toward learning outcomes assessment and rethinking faculty roles. He became director of the education programs at the Pew Charitable Trusts in 1997. In a white paper he wrote on that occasion describing the nature of the challenge, he summarized "one of the great ironies of the academic profession":

> With respect to the work of research, faculty members belong to a genuine community, a community of scholars. The earning of a Ph.D. is, in effect, the rite of passage into a community of ongoing discourse about the advancement of knowledge in one's field. Every scholarly field develops journals, annual meetings and dozens of other ways to facilitate discussion about the findings and breakthroughs in the field. To be a scholar is to assume an obligation to share one's work with one's peers. . . . As a result, young scholars entering the field, as the saying goes, can "stand on the shoulders of giants," the great scholars who went before them.
>
> But with respect to the work of teaching, no such community exists. Teaching is a largely private act, something that takes place behind the closed doors of the classroom. Faculty talk to each other about the teaching in the elevators and gripe about their students over lunch. But they do not really engage each other in reflecting on their teaching practice, the way doctors reflect on their

medical practice, for example. So knowledge of good teaching practice rarely gets shared. . . . Although research is subject to elaborate systems of peer review, teaching is evaluated principally through student ratings, with faculty playing secondary roles. When it comes to teaching new faculty do not stand on the shoulders of giants; they start over from scratch.[32]

Edgerton also points out the effect of this double standard on the way faculty members—and others—think about teaching: "Treating teaching as though it were primarily 'private property' sends a powerful message. It says that teaching is not really considered scholarly work that requires scholarly judgment to help determine whether it is being done well. It says that teaching is easy work that students are qualified to judge, whereas real scholars are engaged in more difficult and important things."[33]

This helps to explain the paradox of effort and the myth of teacher professionalism. Faculty as researchers are engaged in a progressive development of expertise, supported by a second-order environment that serves as a framework for continually raising their goals and testing their practice. Faculty as teachers are working alone, with no clear definition of success and no significant feedback on the quality of their performance, no models of increasing excellence, no evidence. Thus the illusion of expertise is commonplace in teaching.

But it is worse than that. It is very hard to tell, in the realm of teaching, who the real experts are because there are no publicly acknowledged criteria by which to measure them. We cannot find evidence of persistent achievement among stock pickers, where the evidence of the results of their work is made public every day. We cannot find any credible evidence of achievement among most college teachers at all, because nobody gathers that evidence.

9 · TRIAL RUN

The Case of the Degree Qualifications Profile

Many hope that lessons learned from successful innovations can be expanded to new ways of doing education. The pattern has tended to be, however, that enclaves of reform, where they survive, persist as anomalies in a larger environment insulated against information that challenges the instruction myth and the status quo bias. This phenomenon, of course, has not escaped the notice of those who have advocated reforms over the years. Indeed, many of the private foundations that had sponsored powerful research and innovation in the 1980s and 1990s decided early in this century to simply withdraw from higher education or greatly decrease their activities for essentially this reason. The Pew Charitable Trusts alone, under the higher education leadership of Russell Edgerton, initiated and advanced dozens of projects that sparked widespread reform in higher education. But in the early 2000s Pew, along with the Annenberg Foundation and Atlantic Philanthropies, announced that they were greatly reducing or completely terminating their funding for higher education programs. Why?

Patricia J. Gumport, who is director of the Stanford Institute for Higher Education Research, conducted interviews with many of the personnel of these foundations to find out what caused their abrupt withdrawal. "Among the reasons," she says, "program staff said they were frustrated that their prior funding, whether for research or for programmatic initiatives, did not yield recognizable and sustainable changes in colleges and universities, and they thus concluded their funding was not an effective lever for change."[1] Mary B. Marcy, who was codirector of Antioch University's Project on the Future of Higher Education, summarized the situation this way: "Many foundations would say that the goal of most higher-education institutions is to remain the same, except with more financial support."[2] The pattern that the foundations saw was one of intermittent, sporadic, and unsystematic reform that left the core institutions essentially untouched. As Marcy put it, "Our pockets of innovations tend to remain pockets and have little effect on the overall fabric of higher education."[3] For one instance, while course redesign has proven beneficial in every way to most institutions that have pursued it, they have rarely taken its principles further than a few core general education courses. Reform of the "curriculum" has tended to be a readjustment of distribution requirements that are already so broadly and loosely conceived as to have no shape and point in no particular direction.

One of the tools that has been widely adopted to achieve leverage for change is the learning outcomes. All of the regional accrediting associations have mandated that colleges define the learning outcomes they hope their students to achieve and uniformly assess them. But, as we have seen before, this effort has not been notably successful.

One of the colleges that has participated in the Wabash National Study, which incorporates assessment extensively, is Hamilton College, a small liberal-arts college in Clinton, New York. Daniel Chambliss, a sociologist at Hamilton, and Christopher Takacs, a graduate of the college completing his doctorate at the University of Chicago, studied a cohort of about a hundred Hamilton students for about ten years, beginning in 1999. They came away with some interesting ideas about *How College Works* (the title of their 2014 book). They give us some insight on how the assessment problem looks from the inside at one of the Wabash colleges: "Honestly, after a decade of work, we came away skeptical of the entire assessment enterprise. We know, without doubt, that assessment as conventionally practiced is routinely derided by conscientious professors, including those at evidently excellent schools; that it frequently demands significant amounts of new work for both faculties and administrations, and that the evidence for its efficacy is, at best, mixed."[4] Their core criticism is that assessment doesn't seem to have improved the quality of higher education. It is hard to disagree. Assessment has been largely an appendix to accreditation, a bureaucratic process bolted on the Instruction Paradigm College. It has not changed most of them very much.

While many major foundations were abandoning higher education, one that did not was the Lumina Foundation, based in Indianapolis. It has in recent years pursued several projects seeking to leverage its investment into deeply rooted organizational change. Perhaps the most ambitious of those projects has been the Degree Qualifications Profile (DQP), an attempt to connect the assessment of student learning—an activity that at most institutions is diffused into different approaches in different departments and creates no coherent curriculum at all—with the core certifying process of all institutions, the granting of degrees. How can we ensure, they were asking, that a degree adds up to something significant?

THE DQP

To answer this question, Lumina recruited four of the most knowledgeable and thoughtful people working in higher education. Clifford Adelman, for many years one of the premier researchers in the U.S. Department of Education, is a senior associate at the Institute for Higher Education Policy in Washington, DC. Peter Ewell, whom we have encountered on several occasions already for his outstanding work on assessment, was then vice president and is now president emeritus of the National Center for Higher Education Management Systems. Paul Gaston, a professor at Kent State University in Ohio, has special familiarity with the work of European countries to collaborate on learning and assessment through the Bologna Process, which he explains in his book *The Challenge of Bologna*. Carol Geary Schneider was then president of the Association of American Colleges and Universities (AAC&U), the organization that has been engaged for the past twenty years in defining, clarifying, and advocating for the assessment of student learning outcomes. These four set out to design a framework for describing "what students should be expected to know and be able to do once they earn their degrees—at any level."[5] That framework, the DQP, was quite intentionally presented as "a tool that can help transform U.S. higher education."[6]

Acknowledging the increasing emphasis on the importance of a college degree, the authors of the DQP point out that "the press toward helping many more students earn degrees has not been grounded in any consistent public understanding of what these degrees ought to mean."[7] The DQP describes the curriculum leading to a degree not in terms of courses but in terms of what students should be able to do. It divides collegiate learning into five categories: Broad, Integrative Knowledge; Specialized Knowledge; Intellectual Skills; Applied Learning; and Civic Learning. Intellectual Skills are further specified as analytic inquiry, use of information resources, engaging diverse perspectives, quantitative fluency, and communication fluency. The DQP suggests levels of accomplishment in these areas for the three kinds of degrees most often granted by colleges and universities: the associate's degree, a two-year degree most often granted by community colleges; the bachelor's degree, the traditional "four-year" college degree; and the master's degree, the graduate degree that usually involves a year or two of work beyond the bachelor's.

While the DQP does not prescribe, except in the most general of terms, what students should study or learn, it does prescribe how the institution needs to think about that learning: "The descriptions of learning outcomes are presented through active verbs that tell all parties—students, faculty, employers, policymakers and the general public—what students actually should do to demonstrate their mastery."[8] In terms of Broad, Integrative Knowledge, for example, the student at the associate's level "describes how existing knowledge or practice is advanced, tested and revised" in various fields.[9] At the bachelor's level, the student "produces, independently or collaboratively, an investigative, creative or practical work that draws on specific theories, tools and methods from at least two academic fields."[10] In a specialized field, the bachelor's-level student "defines and explains the boundaries and major sub-fields, styles, and/or practices of the field."[11]

The DQP is not a detailed curriculum, but it provides a framework and set of criteria that could be used to evaluate and modify any curriculum. It is, if you will, a rubric for the rubrics that institutions should develop to assess their students' learning. The DQP as designed calls on institutions to change in several ways.

First, it calls upon institutions to assess and record the progress of every student, not just some or most; it embodies Chambliss and Takacs's suggestion to make the individual student the unit of analysis. To create such a record of each student's learning would create a new body of information about student progress and challenges that could seriously undermine the instruction myth—and in turn could support well-grounded confidence in some areas and concern and reform in others. Peter Ewell makes a point that we noted earlier, that "the underlying philosophy of assessment at most institutions . . . has centered largely on periodic inspection of samples of students."[12] Thus most institutions are reporting some isolated assessment information about the "average" student, but have no information that can feed back to the process of educating the actual students who attend there. The DQP, however, asks colleges to look at real work from every student. Ewell points out how this would change the institution's governing value in terms of assessment: "By insisting that all graduates master all of the described competencies, the DQP implies a significant shift in the underlying philosophy of assessment. In place of evidence-gathering activities added on to the teaching and learning process to 'check up' on its effectiveness, assessment activities are embedded within the process in the form of progressively more challenging exercises, performances, and assignments for demonstrating student mastery at multiple points."[13]

Second, the DQP asks institutions to base their degrees on evidence of student work, actual products of learning produced by students. Under the DQP, no one could earn a degree just by taking multiple-choice tests. Of course, many students produce a lot of work at most colleges. But the products of student labor, and the criteria on which they are evaluated, disappear behind the opaque veil of the transcript that drops like a shroud over the actual body of work. What students produce and the standards that are used to evaluate it are hidden in the classroom, and all that survives of them to determine the granting of a degree is the mystical emblem of the grade, powerful but inarticulate, controlling but uninformative. If an institution were to adopt the DQP it would have to publicly articulate the criteria for a degree and record the specific student performances that justify it. As Ewell puts it, "Assignments or examination questions designed to determine proficiency in particular DQP competencies . . . must require students to generate a product of some kind—a research paper, an oral presentation, a dance performance, a translation of a text from one language to another, an engineering design, and so forth. Merely identifying a 'correct' answer from a set of posed alternatives is not a production task."[14]

Third, just as the DQP would require institutions to go beyond the multiple-choice test, it would require them to go beyond the transcript. If the degree is a report of student work, then the institution must keep track of the student work in order to determine whether it meets the qualifications of the degree. Ewell says, "The DQP approach requires a comprehensive record-keeping system for posting, housing, and manipulating data on what students have learned."[15] I have characterized such as system as an *outcomes transcript*, a comprehensive record not of grades, but of student learning products assessed by publicly available rubrics.[16] Such a transcript, in the DQP framework, would point to a portfolio of student work that survives the individual class and documents the student's accomplishment of learning outcomes, a portfolio of the sort that Alverno College and other forward-looking institutions have already developed. Such a system would provide a record of progress for each student at the institution and would constitute a framework for defining what the student has accomplished and what challenges still need to be met. It would replace the logic of confidence and the myth of quality with a body of direct, understandable evidence of student learning.

The fourth way in which the DQP moves institutions toward significant learning is that, by creating a visible pathway to the degree defined not by classes but by student accomplishment, it would make institutions start to deal with the curriculum as a whole rather than as a collection of parts. As Ewell puts it, "Taking the vector of student growth and development on each DQP competency as the primary point of departure, in place of the more familiar standpoint of content coverage, is a far more deliberate approach to curricular design than what customarily occurs."[17] The DQP is quite explicitly not a list of courses; it is a matrix of competencies designed to emphasize their coherent and complementary nature. It makes room for the traditional major, specialized study in one domain. "But we also know that most students will change jobs and even fields many times during their lives. Therefore, the Degree Profile strongly emphasizes the kinds of crosscutting competencies that graduates need for continuous learning in complex and changing environments."[18] This means that the organization and sequencing cannot be left, as it too often is today, to random chance and departmental fiat. Furthermore, it cannot be simply a sequencing of content, a table of contents of what teachers should cover. It must be a sequential, actionable plan of student learning. Ewell puts it this way: "We believe that the courses constituting the curriculum should be intentional and cumulative and, further, should feature many connections demanding and developing these competencies in different settings. Course sequencing, therefore, is critical—to ensure that the series of courses a given student takes includes successive benchmark assessments that build toward culminating demonstrations of mastery. In this way, adopting the DQP makes assessment the centerpiece of any institution's curriculum, rather than simply one more feature of the courses that comprise it."[19]

A SLOW SLOG

The DQP is without question a transformative document, and its authors have designed it to promote rethinking the curriculum.

So, how is it progressing so far? I believe that the DQP is an inspiring and exciting document, that it embodies many of the qualities that have the capacity to break down the instruction myth and create new flows of information about student learning that will dislodge the status quo bias from its current control over institutional processes. And if this is so, we should expect that it will be very difficult for institutions to adopt it. We should expect that defensive routines will arise that will deter or delay its implementation. And we should expect that the clear and explicit elements of the DQP will be muddied and altered as organizational groupthink redefines its terms into something quite different.

It is too early to say with confidence. I still hope that the DQP will prove transformative in some places and will create models of change that will inspire others. But, so far, the news is, shall we say, mixed.

In October 2011, ten months after the DQP was published and made available at no charge to everyone on the Lumina web page, Indiana University–Purdue University Indianapolis (IUPUI) held its annual Assessment Institute. Trudy Banta, a professor of higher education at IUPUI and long a leader of the assessment movement, opened the conference: "During my opening remarks, I asked the roomful of 980 academics sufficiently interested in assessment to attend the Institute how many knew enough about the DQP to explain it, and only about 30 people raised their hands. Clearly, the word about the DQP and its potential to influence assessment has not yet reached a broad segment of higher education."[20]

Following an explanation and panel discussion of the DQP, the presenters asked for written questions and comments. Banta reports that "most of us on the panel were surprised at the number and intensity of the negative comments about the DQP."[21] One respondent charged that the panel was being paid by Lumina to "sell" the concept. Another claimed that it was an effort to standardize colleges that "undermines the greatest strength of American higher education—its diversity." Yet another asserted that the project was a Trojan horse, that "it becomes an institutional template for curricular and assessment reform." Most of the objections were patently inaccurate— the tool is free to everyone and goes to great lengths to explain how it can be adapted to different institutional missions.

The one "gotcha" that is especially worth considering is the charge that it is a template for reform. Because, of course, it is. The first sentence on the first page of the document setting out the DQP declares it to be "a tool that can help transform U.S. higher education."[22] The charge that an explicitly reformist project is, in fact, a covert attempt to cause institutions to reform is a defensive routine that delves deep into the files of classic non sequitur challenges. Like "When did you stop beating your wife?," it is a challenge that cannot be answered without the appearance of both guilt and confusion. It resembles the time-honored charge that learning assessment is a covert plot to change teaching. Too often, in the history of outcomes assessment, the challenge has elicited a denial: "No, no! That's not true! You won't need to change a thing." Thus has assessment been reduced to a formal exercise with little or no effect on the learning experience of students.

The DQP has been put forward as an unmistakable agenda for reform. Whether it comes to be understood that way, however, is still open to question. Too often, in conversations about change at colleges and universities, acceptance of the myths that lock us into existing routines has been made a precondition for engaging in the discussion. If we must acknowledge in advance that existing routines must persist, then we must reinterpret "institutional transformation" as harmless tinkering. If the unwritten cultural code of conversation contains the condition that we must assume in advance the myth of quality, but that the code itself is undiscussable, then we will assume in advance that calls for reform are not *really* calls for reform. If they turn out to be, we will be shocked, shocked that people who don't know the bounds of good taste and acceptable behavior have appeared in our midst. They must be the paid agents of outside parties aiming to impose their agenda and deny us autonomy. It is not quite that bad. But when academics at an assessment conference believe that the charge of advocating reform is itself a fatal condemnation of an idea—well, it's almost that bad.

Dozens of colleges and universities across the country are working with the DQP at one level or another. In reviewing the experience so far, Carol Geary Schneider of the AAC&U concludes that "what we are learning is that while the DQP was designed to be a promising beacon for transformative change, a seemingly growing number of influential leaders do not see it that way."[23] The DQP depends crucially upon shifting the focus from the content that teachers teach to the skills and knowledge that students learn. This means that its whole vision rests upon the task of generating reliable, visible evidence about what students are learning. Ewell finds that "too many institutions now engaged with the DQP stop short of the difficult work of developing the needed assignments, examination questions, and projects that enable the collection of meaningful evidence of student mastery."[24] Schneider believes that "this is not for lack of conscientious commitment by faculty members working to operationalize the DQP on campus, but rather because the level of educational intentionality and collaboration implied in the DQP assessment principles contrasts so much . . . with deeply-rooted campus norms. What I think we are seeing is that the habit of treating college learning as a set of separate, discrete, and even 'siloed' units—individual course, the majors, general education, the co-curriculum, and so on—works at cross-purposes to the DQP's conception of a more intentional and, ultimately, integrative educational experience."[25]

We might be forgiven, at this point, for saying—certainly with no pleasure—well, of course it does.

What we may be seeing with the DQP is essentially the same thing that we have seen with institutional approaches to learning outcomes assessment over the past three decades. An attempt to generate information that has the potential to identify the weaknesses of present practice and lead to their improvement, adopted often with the best of intentions, is processed through the decision-making apparatus of the institution and with the organizational routines through which the organization acts. The result is that the potentially transformative information about the mission of the whole institution is translated into obscure and ambiguous information about the parts that provides no particular direction. Schneider notes that "in order to document the outcomes described in the DQP, many campuses experimenting with the DQP have focused their assessment work on a specific subset of the curriculum, such as the business or biology program in a transfer context, or writing in general education, or quantitative reasoning in four or five disciplines. These are 'subdivide assessments,' meaning that they tackle only a subset of the five DQP areas of learning and, in the case of the Intellectual Skills area, take on only a couple of the five complex intellectual skills."[26]

She fears that "wide use of this practical strategy—the commitment to 'subdivide and get it done'—may mean that we will learn less than is needed from the various DQP assessment experiments under way."[27]

The college will approach a holistic vision of student learning in the DQP by breaking it up into the parts that currently define the curriculum. The DQP threatens to radically undermine the instruction myth and create a new environment in which everyone at the college will need to reexamine the way they teach, the way they assess student learning, and the way they set goals for their work.

Some of the regional accrediting organizations have discussed the possibility of using the DQP as a framework for the accrediting process. But none have done so. And these same accrediting organizations have required colleges to define and assess student learning outcomes for a decade or more.

What has happened with student learning outcomes is that different people see such requirements very differently. Through the lenses of the Instruction Paradigm, seen in the grip of the status quo bias, learning outcomes are lists of curricular topics. I vividly remember a meeting on my own campus nearly twenty years ago. I had explained as clearly as I could the idea of creating explicit student learning outcomes for each course and across courses. When the time came for questions, a senior professor, a man who had a good reputation both as a scholar and as a teacher, raised his hand and asked, "But don't we already do that?" I distinctly recall the sense of confusion and disorientation that struck me as I thought, "What on earth is he talking about?" But from his perspective, he did establish outcomes for his students, and he used them as the basis for assigning grades. That was his framework for thinking about student assessment at college. Like a student trying to understand Newton's laws of motion, he plugged in the nearest recognizable concept that had a concrete reality in his world and that reality became the meaning of the new concept.

There is a serious danger that the faculty and administrators in higher education will look at the DQP and say, "Oh, we already do that." If that happens, the DQP will become, for them, a summary of what they already do.

PART III LEARNING TO CHANGE, CHANGING TO LEARN

10 · SEEDS OF CHANGE

People and institutions change for all sorts of reasons. But designed change, purposeful change to achieve conscious goals, is almost always a product of the experience of conflict or contradiction, of a felt dilemma or incongruity. We change to fix something, to correct a problem, to return to equilibrium. I hope in this chapter to show that many of those in higher education suffer such a felt dilemma today, that they are torn by conflicting goals. Indeed, there is a certain cognitive dissonance that is almost built in to the job of professor.

In order to take up this question productively we need to guard against the fundamental attribution error—the error of attributing to individuals motives and actions that are really caused by the systems and situations in which they find themselves. Before considering how people can change, we need to consider their motivation and correct a possible misreading of the previous chapters.

It is easy, on a superficial reading of the evidence, to draw a caricature of higher education faculty that shows them as obsessively concerned with their research and disdainful of teaching. It is very easy to blame the teachers, and it often serves the interests of both reformers and administrators—who may be at odds about much else—to lay all the problems of the academy at the feet of the faculty. But this would be a profoundly destructive error. It is demonstrably the case that faculty tend to resist change as a practical matter. But we make a serious mistake if we assume that this is because of some quality or characteristic of most individual faculty members. If we look more closely at the reasons why people become college teachers and their beliefs about their own roles, we will see that the real picture is radically different and a good deal more complex.

WHAT DO FACULTY WANT?

I believe that most college and university faculty members embrace the Learning Paradigm. They sincerely espouse it as their fundamental theory about their role and their work. They want to be in the business of generating learning in their students. Indeed, by their own account, that is the primary motivation of most students who become college faculty members. Does graduate school change this? We have already seen that doctoral programs emphasize research and often discourage students from devoting effort to teaching. If you ask the teachers, however, the answer is fairly consistent. No, graduate school does not kill their desire to teach.

The Higher Education Research Institute (HERI) at UCLA has conducted a periodic survey of faculty since 1978. The 2010–2011 survey reported results from over twenty-three thousand full-time faculty members at 417 four-year colleges and universities. Of those surveyed, 86 percent agreed with the statement "faculty here are strongly interested in the academic problems of undergraduates."[1] And 88.2 percent said that "my teaching is valued by faculty in my department."[2] Furthermore, faculty seem to support their commitment to teaching with their time. Golde and Dore reported from their survey of faculty that "teaching occupies most of a faculty member's time," while, in contrast, "research absorbs very little faculty time."[3] They find an average of twenty-nine hours per week devoted to teaching activities, as opposed to nine hours per week given to research. The National Center for Education Statistics of the U.S. Department of Education administers the National Study of Postsecondary Faculty (NSOPF). In 2004 it surveyed over thirty-five thousand faculty members at over a thousand institutions. Overall, faculty reported that they spent roughly 62 percent of their time on teaching, 18 percent on research, and 20 percent on other activities such as administration, governance, and service.[4]

There are, of course, variations among academic disciplines in all of these surveys, and among institutional types as well, but overall there is no persuasive evidence to support the view that students who pursue faculty careers look down on teaching or that they dislike or avoid teaching. Quite to the contrary, the profile that emerges from graduate student and faculty reports on anonymous surveys is that students who prepare for careers as higher education faculty are quite self-consciously pursuing jobs as teachers, and once they become faculty members they value teaching and spend most of their time on teaching—much more, on average, than they spend on research. If you think this seems at odds with what we have seen earlier about the priorities and rewards of universities, then you are to be commended for paying close attention. It does indeed seem that way.

And here is something even more striking. David W. Leslie, an education professor at the College of William and Mary, analyzed the data from the 1992–1993 NSOPF, a survey of over twenty-five thousand full-time faculty at over three thousand institutions. He found that "full-time faculty . . . agree that 'teaching effectiveness should be the primary criterion for promotion.' . . . They also disagree, on the whole, that 'research [and] publication should be the primary criterion for promotion.' . . . This difference confirms a strong normative commitment to teaching as the principal value of the academic profession."[5]

These results, which apply in varying degrees to all institutional types, "present a paradox," as Leslie notes. We have already seen that research, in practice, is the predominant criterion for promotion and tenure at nearly all four-year institutions. We have also seen that it has been very hard to change this priority. Aside from its other incoherencies, this means that faculty at most institutions are promoted and retained on the basis of what they spend a small portion of their working lives doing, while the activities to which they devote a majority of their working lives are largely ignored in the reward system. And faculty, quite understandably, don't like this. When asked on anonymous surveys, outside of the department or faculty meeting that might inspire self-censorship, they believe that the opposite should be the case. A paradox, indeed.

We have seen one side of the paradox in some detail. We saw that the actual criteria for promotion are heavily weighted toward research and against teaching. We saw as well that most faculty members—the same faculty members who chose this work to become teachers and would prefer to be evaluated on their teaching—would like to shift more of their time to research. Furthermore, they have done so. The HERI report mentioned above, while reporting that faculty spend much more time on teaching than on research, finds that the historical trend is in the opposite direction: "For 20 years,

HERI has monitored faculty trends in order to identify areas that may show significant changes in the nature of . . . faculty work. . . . There has been a significant decline in time spent teaching: The proportion of faculty reporting they spent nine hours of more per week teaching (roughly a quarter of their time) is currently 43.6%, which is a considerable decline from a high of 63.4% two decades ago and from 56.5% just 10 years ago."[6]

Similarly, time spent preparing for classes has declined over the same period. So faculty are successfully shifting their time away from teaching and toward research. If they prefer teaching, why are they moving away from it toward what, on balance, they do not prefer? Is the entire profession suffering from multiple personality disorder?

"The overriding point," as Leslie puts it, "is that faculty are motivated to teach, spend most of their time teaching, prefer that they be rewarded for teaching effectiveness, but that institutions may actually reward them for something else. That something else is clearly percentage of time spent on research, which correlates with basic salary. . . . At the same time, and significantly from the point of view of what motivates faculty, percentage of time spent on research is practically not correlated at all with overall job satisfaction."[7]

So faculty do not disdain teaching—on balance they prefer it to research—and the shift of emphasis from teaching to research that has been going on for the past century or more reflects not faculty preferences but organizational incentives. As we saw in chapter 5, the faculty member's endowment, both material and reputational, is deeply invested in research as opposed to teaching. Loss aversion and the status quo bias create a situation where the risk of shifting emphasis to teaching is too high for an individual faculty member, even when such a shift would improve job satisfaction.

DISSONANT THEORIES

The espoused theory of most college teachers—sincerely held—is that teaching is their central job and that student learning is their most important product. But the theory-in-use that guides their behavior values research over teaching and guides them, as if by an invisible hand, to follow the organizational routines that prioritize research over teaching. In many cases, as

Chris Argyris points out, we follow the organizational theory-in-use without even being aware of doing so. We are just doing the best job we can in the context where we find ourselves, and that context shapes the job we do in ways that may be invisible to us.

The competitive nature of the job market in higher education no doubt reinforces this pattern of incentives in a way that we might not notice at first. The educational qualifications of new faculty have been rising for decades, and the time between the degree and the first job has been growing. As Schuster and Finkelstein point out, thirty years ago "faculty members often were being plucked from their graduate school program prior to completion of their dissertations."[8] By 1992 faculty were reporting a gap of two years or more between completion of the degree and being hired for the first position.[9] And those were just the ones who were hired for a full-time position; an increasing number of graduates have not been able to find tenure-track positions at all. This trend may have reinforced something that Leslie notes, that graduates just out of doctoral programs tend to emphasize research more: "Younger faculty tend to look for jobs where they will have more opportunity to do research, an indication that the marketplace may press younger faculty toward more research activity."[10]

Most prospective college teachers, like most young adults in other fields, need a job. But most graduate students have little experience teaching and less credible evidence of the quality of their teaching. Graduate programs are research-oriented, and the teaching opportunities for graduate students are constrained strictly by the needs of the program. As we have seen, most graduate students get little preparation for teaching and little expert mentoring or supervision. As Ann Austin puts it, "The use of TAs usually responds to departmental needs to cover courses or sections, not the development of future professors."[11] Thus even if a newly minted Ph.D. were an exemplary teacher, there would probably be no reliable record of it. So the candidates for faculty positions, having been socialized to the research orientation of graduate school, can demonstrate their competitive advantages in the job market chiefly by emphasizing their research accomplishments.

The initial faculty endowment, the job itself, is thus often founded on the research ability of the candidate, not the teaching ability. And in the up-or-out tenure system, survival—keeping the job—depends on promotion. Thus the growing endowment rests increasingly on the research foundation. The faculty member may or may not prefer research to teaching—and in most cases does not—but is locked in a system in which the one who fails at research can lose everything, while the one who fails at teaching will probably lose little or nothing. Keeping in mind the power of loss aversion in guiding our thinking about risk, we should expect that most new faculty members will see research as their bread and butter, so to speak. And because the tenure track tends to be the virtual endowment of nearly all prospective faculty members, we should expect that they too will lean toward research as the means to secure their prospects. Still, most faculty members expend most of their time on teaching. And the time that they invest in teaching, on average, seems to be more satisfying to them than the time they invest in research. If the framework, the organizational setting, were different, the outcomes would be different.

Of course, there are colleges that hire people primarily or exclusively as teachers. Community colleges stand out here because faculty normally have no research responsibilities at all. (As a full-time community college teacher, I did my writing in the summer or on sabbaticals because teaching simply consumed all the available time during the academic year.)

While community college leaders talk a great deal about the value of teaching, they have no more ability to influence it in practice than do most four-year college administrators. The faculty role carries with it the myth of academic freedom as autonomy in the classroom. Community college teachers want to believe that we are *real* college faculty, and that carries with it the privacy of teaching and the individual control of the classroom that is the rule in four-year colleges. This insulates teaching from improvement and isolates teachers from feedback in the same way as it does at four-year colleges. So at most community colleges, tenure is achieved with some but not a great deal of feedback on teaching, and after tenure promotion is essentially based on seniority. In states where faculty unions are pervasive, this tendency is often reinforced by contracts that exclude evaluation of teaching from the criteria for promotion. So the faculty endowment at the community college resides in sticking close to the department and protecting the privacy of teaching, even in the absence of research responsibilities. Still, it may well be possible that faculty at community college have fewer structural restraints on their ability to change than their senior colleagues. That is a hypothesis that should be put to the test, but rarely has been. The model of senior institutions is too powerful, and community colleges lack the status or power to resist that model.

The myth of academic freedom would suggest that faculty as individuals must have some sort of irreducible integrity in their academic decisions. But this claim is fraudulent on many levels, most significantly perhaps on the level of the basic decision as to how to spend one's time and invest one's effort. As Leslie puts it, "Faculty express an impressive normative unity about the value of teaching and the intrinsic satisfaction they derive from it. These values and satisfactions may even be strong enough to override the extrinsic incentives (money, status, etc.) that go to faculty who do more research and publication. Given a reasonable level of security and compensation, faculty—on the average—would prefer to teach and be rewarded for teaching than to seek opportunities for higher pay if it means doing more research and publication."[12]

As we have already seen, pre-tenure faculty at four-year colleges would certainly not have a reasonable level of security if they took the option of putting teaching before research. And the longer faculty work in a given department, the more they have invested in the status quo as the source of personal rewards. Thus, the endowment effect and the status quo bias trump the intrinsic satisfaction of the work, and research trumps teaching.

The people doing the work have a strong intrinsic investment in the quality of their teaching and would be open to change that could lead to improvement. But the organizational setting locks them into protecting the status quo because that is where their interests lie. Promoting student learning is not hard to sell to college and university faculty. But significantly changing the college or university to promote student learning is. In my experience, most faculty members feel constrained and limited in the ways they do their work and believe that the oppressive hand of the "the system" or "the administration" keeps them from doing their best work as teachers. While it is not quite that simple, we have to acknowledge that there is something to it.

In other words, most college faculty today are in a continuing state of cognitive dissonance, though they may not fully realize it. They experience a disorienting dilemma in the inconsistency between their espoused theory of their work and its value and the theory-in-use that organizational routines impose upon them. But because most routines are so familiar, they appear to be just the background for the problems that arise rather than their cause. So the sense of unsettledness tends to be projected on someone or something else. This dissonance may manifest itself as a sense of oppression by the administration or the system, a sense that the college or university is under the control of the enemies of education who do not understand how the process works. In some cases, this may lead to a kind of siege mentality in which faculty cling ever more closely to their departments and hold up the myth of academic freedom and the privacy of teaching as shields against the barbarians. But whatever the response, hardly any faculty members think that things are as they should be.

11 · HOW DO PEOPLE LEARN TO CHANGE?

How do reformers most often try to change colleges? By changing faculty attitudes and practices. Indeed, in the minds of many, changing colleges and universities means simply changing the teaching practices of faculty, and nothing else. So attempts to improve learning outcomes for students often consist of professional development activities that seek to help teachers to teach better. It should be clear by now that this will never be enough. But it is an important and essential effort. And it should be clear by now that the major source of faculty resistance to change is not their personal opinions or preferences but their conception of their role in the organization and their perception of the risk that changes entail.

But it is also true that the resistance to change by individual faculty members and departments is a major factor locking institutions into their present dysfunctional practices. So to change the structures, we need to get those who work in the organization to change their attitudes, beliefs, and practices—especially their attitudes and beliefs about change. And it is certainly true that many teachers could do a much better job of teaching even within the framework of colleges organized and structured as they are today.

Some argue that changing the way teachers teach is just too hard to be practical. Chambliss and Takacs, in their study of Hamilton College students, find that good teachers are the key to a good education. But they conclude that efforts to "retrain professors into using new methods" are hopeless: "It's often quite difficult to change the daily working habits, not to say the personality, of an adult, especially one who has succeeded in landing a nice tenured position at a respected institution."[1] Their proposal? Schedule the good teachers so that they teach a lot of students! And the bad teachers? "You could just minimize the damage: schedule his class at 8:00 A.M. and hope that no one shows up."[2] The proposal lacks seriousness—and seems to regard the poor souls who do show up at eight o'clock as unavoidable collateral damage. But while such an ad hoc policy might be theoretically plausible for a while at a small liberal arts college with extraordinarily acute and observant deans, it assumes the answer to a question that is not in evidence and that these authors never explicitly address in their book: how do you tell the good teachers from the bad ones? As we will see, this is not always easy from the perspective of an administrator. And, of course, such a suggestion is completely incoherent at most of the colleges that most of the students in the country attend: large, public institutions, where deans may not even know the names of most of the teachers in general education departments, much less have the slightest clue how well they actually teach.

Chambliss and Takacs make the fundamental mistake of assuming the structure and theory-in-use of colleges and then asking if we can just reform the system by changing the people. And the answer is clearly that we cannot. In the end, we must change both the structure and the people in concert. But they also too blithely discount the possibility of changing people's behavior. They seem to embark from the assumption (unsupported in their book) that college and university faculty are themselves impervious to learning, that they can never learn to do things better than they already do. This seems an odd perspective for an educator to take, but we can see how working in a college for many years might implant such ideas.

STAGES OF CHANGE

Can people change? And if so, how do people, as individuals, change? Not all change is the same, and changes we make in our personal lives differ in significant ways from changes we make in our work. But there are also similarities. And one of the similarities is that change isn't easy when it involves altering long-standing habits. About this, Chambliss and Takacs are entirely correct: "that's hard to do."[3]

Most people are trying to change something about themselves much of the time. About half of all Americans make New Year's resolutions each year to change something significant in their lives. In one study of the outcomes, 77 percent of those resolutions were successful after the first week, 55 percent after a month, 40 percent after six months, and about 19 percent after two years.[4] College and university faculty are probably neither more nor less likely than people in general to make resolutions (at the New Year or other times) to lose weight or exercise more. And they are probably equally likely to have serious lapses and make slightly revised versions of those resolutions the next year. Is losing weight or quitting smoking harder or easier than adopting peer instruction in your classes? The success rates in both types of changes would suggest that the level of difficulty isn't vastly different. And, as we have seen, most college teachers are sincerely motivated to make changes that could improve their teaching. So the way people make changes in their lives in other areas may help us to understand how faculty members can make changes in their teaching.

Three psychotherapists have made a careful study of how people make major changes in their behavior. James Prochaska is director of the Cancer Prevention Research Consortium at the University of Rhode Island; John Norcross is a professor of psychology at the University of Scranton; and Carlo DiClemente is a professor of psychology at the University of Maryland, Baltimore County. Their research has focused on kinds of changes that are demonstrably difficult for people to make, things like quitting smoking, losing weight, or escaping the grip of an addiction to drugs or alcohol, but their theory seeks to describe the process that people must go through to change any engrained habit.

Prochaska, Norcross, and DiClemente begin with the observation that the dozens of approaches to psychotherapy have all developed distinctive ways to help people change their habits. Each of these approaches seems to help some people, but none is effective with all. Psychoanalysis might help one patient, cognitive behavioral therapy another, and humanistic approaches a third. But none works for all of them. Furthermore, some people seem able to change on their own, without any assistance at all. Prochaska and Norcross sought out the commonalities of various therapies, attempting to construct a *transtheoretical model* (TTM) of ways of achieving change. One reason, they conclude, why different approaches work for different people is that different people are at different stages in the change process. Changing ingrained habits is usually not a one-off kind of operation. It requires a process that involves several discrete stages, and very often cycling through these stages more than once.[5]

Anton Tolman, professor of psychology and former director of the Faculty Center for Teaching Excellence at Utah Valley University, has used the TTM to better understand the way that both students and teachers in educational settings approach change.[6] He has developed a set of surveys that attempt to assess where students and teachers fall on the stages. These tools help to clarify how we can connect the stages of change with change in teaching practices.

Broadly speaking, people seeking to change begin at a stage when they don't think change is desirable or practical, moving to one where they seriously think about it. As thinking about how to change makes it a more realistic option, they begin to prepare to actually do something about it. Then, they take action to change existing habits or patterns of behavior. Having changed, they then need to maintain the new patterns of behavior against tendencies to relapse into old habits. So there are five (or six, if you parse them a little differently) stages to the change process.

First is precontemplation. At the *precontemplation* stage people don't intend to change in the foreseeable future, though others may recognize that there is a problem. Prochaska, Norcross, and DiClemente quote G. K. Chesterton to characterize the state of mind of the person in precontemplation: "It isn't that they can't see the solution. It is that they can't see the problem."[7] Precontemplators have not made a choice to change, even though they may be in therapy: "Usually they feel coerced into changing the addictive behavior by a spouse who threatens to leave, an employer who threatens to dismiss them, parents who threaten to disown them or courts who threaten to punish them."[8] Precontemplators can wish things were different, but don't seriously consider the possibility of doing anything about their situation. In the questionnaires that are used to identify the stage of change an individual has reached, precontemplators are identified by statements like "as far as I'm concerned, I don't have any problems that need changing" or "I guess I have faults, but there's nothing that I really need to change."[9]

Precontemplators often maintain their equilibrium by avoiding information that could disturb their denial and by refusing to seek out information that might undermine current habits: "Precontemplators avoid learning about the problems."[10] This is a case of the confirmation bias, a form of motivated thinking in which we notice evidence that confirms our existing practices or beliefs and overlook, sometimes literally fail to perceive, evidence that challenges what we want to believe. It is not so much a conscious choice, in most cases, as a working out of what seems at the time to be "common sense."

In applying this stage to college faculty, Tolman has divided it into two parts. The faculty member in the first level of precontemplation (PC1) is essentially in denial, doesn't believe he or she needs to change. The person in PC1 would say, "As far as I'm concerned, I don't really need to study pedagogy . . . ; I'm a content expert. Students need to be accountable for learning what I teach them."[11] At the second level of precontemplation (PC2), the teacher can see that change might be desirable, but doubts that it is practical: "While I think focusing on pedagogy is fine, I don't have the time or energy. . . . It takes all my time to keep up with my main professional area."[12] This distinction between PC1 and PC2 makes good sense to me. And in practice we often see this kind of softening of resistance, from the claim that change is not a good idea to the claim that it just isn't possible under the circumstances.

The longer people stay in precontemplation, the harder it is for them to change. "Research shows that problems are almost always treated more effectively when they are less rather than more severe, and when they are shorter rather than longer duration. The longer people wait to change, the more difficult change becomes."[13] It is harder for a lifelong smoker to quit than it is for someone who has smoked for only a year. And it is harder for a teacher who has lectured as an exclusive approach to teaching for the past two decades to try different approaches than it is for someone new to the job.

The second stage is contemplation. As people become aware that they have a problem that needs attention, they enter the *contemplation* stage. In contemplation, as the name suggests, they think about the possibility of making changes. They haven't made a commitment to do anything about their situation, but they are thinking about it. They begin to doubt their previous positive ideas about the problem behavior, but they also consider "the amount of effort, energy, and loss it will cost to overcome the problem."[14] They will agree with statements like "I have a problem and I really think I should work on it" or "I've been thinking that I might want to change something about myself."[15] The faculty member contemplating changing pedagogy might say, for example, "I have been thinking that it might be time to think about and evaluate how I teach and how to improve my teaching."[16]

As with the precontemplation stage, people can stay in contemplation for a long time. One group of smokers who were followed for two years remained in the contemplation stage for the entire time without ever taking action. This is a state called *chronic contemplation*: "Chronic contemplators substitute thinking for acting, promising that they are going to act 'someday.' Their motto is 'when in doubt, don't change.'"[17] If precontemplators avoid learning about their problems, contemplators can use the learning process as a medium of procrastination. If you keep reading articles you're too busy with "research" to do anything, say, to revise your assignments or change your assessments (or write your book—I've tried this one myself). One form procrastination can take is the quest for certainty. If we think we want to change but still have doubts, we can indulge in an indefinite search for "proof" that the change will work on every level. As we shall see later, there is good reason to believe that chronic contemplation is common among college faculty and staff.

The third stage entails preparation. In many cases, if change is justified, contemplators will sort out the conflicting inclinations and make a decision. The individual then enters the *preparation* stage. In preparation, we are not just thinking about change; we have decided and are preparing to act. Most people in the preparation stage take some small-scale actions. They may cut down on the number of cigarettes or start to weigh themselves more often. But most significantly, they formulate a specific intention to take major action—to stop smoking or drinking altogether, to make major revisions in their syllabi, or to participate in a learning group or faculty learning community. As we move from viewing the prospective change as something to think about to viewing it as something to do, it becomes a higher priority. After all, we can think about something any time, whenever we have a free moment. But to take action means to do something in particular at a specific time. The movement from contemplation to preparation involves making specific commitments to what you will do and when and where you will do it.

When we intend to change behaviors with a number of moving parts, so to speak, preparation can be a fairly involved process. If I want to lose weight and sustain the loss, I may need to work out a completely new approach to selecting, preparing, and eating food. This may involve negotiation with other people in my life and rescheduling other activities. Likewise, if I plan to change my teaching to promote learning outcomes and long-term transfer, I may need to read books, attend workshops, and work with colleagues. I will need to design new assignments and reorganize lesson plans. The teacher in preparation for major changes might say, "I have decided to improve my teaching to enhance student learning and have begun to try a few new ideas. . . . I need to set some goals for making these changes a regular part of my work and for learning more."[18] I won't make this effort until I have decided to carry through. But I can't carry through until I'm prepared, or I am setting myself up for failure.

The fourth stage is action. Preparation leads to action. "*Action* is the stage in which individuals modify their behavior, experiences, or environment in order to overcome their problems. Action involves the most overt behavioral changes and requires considerable commitment of time and energy."[19] Action is the stage at which the alcoholic stops drinking, the smoker stops smoking, and the dieter systematically alters his or her eating or exercise patterns. To count as entering the action stage, an individual must sustain a change for a period of time, more than a day, certainly. But the duration of action may depend on the kind of change being made. For a faculty member to change the way he or she teaches a class, the changes must persist at least for a standard academic term. People in the action stage can say things like "I am really working hard to change" and "Anyone can talk about changing; I am actually doing something about it."[20] A faculty member has reached the action stage when he or she can say, "During the last or most recent semester, . . . I began to make changes to one or more of my courses based on the pedagogical literature or what I have learned."[21]

The final stage is maintenance. Changing an established habit is not like switching on a light bulb; it entails an ongoing effort to substitute the new behavior for the old one. Thus the final stage in changing a habitual behavior is *maintenance*. Having made a change, we must consolidate and reinforce the new behavior, and this requires ongoing effort. So maintenance is not a static state: "Maintenance is a continuation, not an absence, of change."[22] Anyone who has ever tried to change a habit has probably realized that maintenance is the hardest part. Losing weight is not enormously difficult; keeping it off, however, is proverbially challenging. Finding an interactive alternative to lecture for one class is simple; implementing it every day for a semester is another story altogether. The podium calls the recovering lecturer in very much the same way as the dessert table calls the "successful" dieter. You may be able to change your habit for six months, but you have the rest of your life to relapse. The proverbial smoker captures the difficulty nicely: "Quitting is easy! I've done it dozens of times!"

I am fortunate to have never been a smoker. However, I used to lecture. Having made the decision to stop, what I found was that classrooms and students offer an ongoing temptation to teachers to fill time with their own talk. The conventional advice to recovering alcoholics is that they avoid bars. But it is often impossible for recovering lecturers to avoid classrooms. That is where you do your work. And students often find the low-pressure, passive role of listener both familiar and comfortable. "Go ahead," they encourage us explicitly or implicitly, "tell us how it is, fill the rest of the hour for us." They are the equivalent of our old drinking buddies, reassuring us that the old habits will make life easier on everyone. And, of course, there really are instances when teachers have to explain things, give instructions, and answer questions. Where to draw the line? It's not an easy question to answer, and the faculty member who is implementing new ways of teaching may need the support and input of colleagues to sustain productive changes. People who have reached the maintenance stage may well believe that "I may need a boost right now to help me maintain the changes I've already made."[23]

The teacher who changes teaching habits needs to learn new ones, and the ability to consolidate new learning and gain facility in new practices will be an important part of maintaining the new habits. For instance, many teachers have little experience really listening to students in a classroom setting. If the goal has always been to get the right answer or the correct information broadcast over the classroom airwaves, then student mistakes are neither relevant nor interesting. They need to be recognized so that they can be moved past. But if the teacher is to understand how students think, then the students' mistakes need air time, need to be heard and understood, because they are embedded in a framework of thinking and assumptions that the student uses to discover new truths, so they provide the foundation for any possible learning. Learning to listen, hearing students in a different way, finding out what questions to ask, and when to ask them are all part of becoming competent at *Teaching with Your Mouth Shut*, to use the priceless phrase—also the title of his book—of the late Donald Finkel from the Evergreen State College.[24] New practices can become habits. So maintenance of new habits that involve complex interactive skills may require ongoing change.

THE UPWARD SPIRAL

In describing the five stages of change, Prochaska, Norcross, and DiClemente have warned against the error of seeing it as a linear progression, in which one systematically moves past one stage and on to the next. As we have already seen, people can get stuck on one stage, in some cases permanently. Likewise, people who have moved through the stages can relapse. Thus, they present these stages not as a straight line but as a spiral: "People can progress from contemplation to preparation to action to maintenance, but most individuals will relapse."[25] Some can fall back from action to precontemplation; the fear of another failure can deter them from trying to change again. Usually, however, relapse is less severe: "The vast majority of relapsers—85% of smokers, for example—recycle back to the contemplation or preparation stages. . . . They begin to consider plans for their next action attempt while trying to learn from their recent efforts."[26] Of those who fail at their New Year's resolutions, 60 percent make a version of the same resolution the following year. Thus, "most relapsers do not revolve endlessly in circles and . . . they do not regress all the way back to where they began. Instead, each time relapsers recycle through the stages, they potentially learn from their mistakes."[27] This is good news for all of us, of course. It means that every time we try to change a habit, even if we are unsuccessful, we increase the prospects of success the next time.

When considering the various therapies that support people in changing their habits, one of the most powerful indicators of whether treatment will be effective is the stage that the individual has reached before treatment. One study, for example, looked at smokers with heart problems who were put in an intensive smoking cessation program. The program showed "no significant effects . . . with patients in the precontemplation and contemplation stages." At the same time, "of the patients who began the program in the action or preparation stages, an impressive 94% were not smoking at six-month follow-up."[28]

The authors have examined different therapeutic approaches and have categorized the processes of treatment that are used. They have found that different processes are effective at different stages. So attempts at consciousness raising through classical psychoanalysis may be very helpful in moving people into the contemplation stage and advancing the contemplation process, but probably aren't so helpful in moving people from preparation to action.

Likewise, if an individual engages in processes for reinforcing action such as stimulus control and reinforcement management when they are still in the contemplation stage, it probably won't work for them. As people move through the stages, they need to engage in the kinds of activities appropriate to their stage: "We have determined that efficient self-change depends on doing the right things (processes) at the right time (stages)."[29] Prochaska and Norcross have described the ideal relationship between the person trying to change and the therapist at different stages of the process: "With precontemplators, often the role is like that of a nurturing parent joining with a resistant and defensive youngster who is both drawn to and repelled by the prospects of becoming more independent. With contemplators, the role is akin to a Socratic teacher who encourages clients to achieve their own insights into their condition. With clients who are in the preparation stage, the stance is more like that of an experienced coach who has been through many crucial matches and can provide a fine game plan or can review the person's own plan. With clients who are progressing into action and maintenance, the psychotherapist becomes more of a consultant who is available to provide expert advice and support when action is not progressing as smoothly as expected."[30]

WHAT ARE THE REAL BARRIERS TO PROGRESS?

The stated rationale for not moving faster to change their teaching practice, in most cases, is time. And that is an interesting rationale because it is incomplete. To say that I don't have time to do a given task means that it is more important for me to do another instead. It is a statement of priorities rather than an absolute limitation. So when faculty, who already spend the bulk of their time on teaching, say that they don't have time to improve their teaching, they are saying something about the priorities that compete with teaching. And when we consider the stages of change in terms of time commitment, we can see that there is a difference between the contemplation and the preparation stage. In contemplation, I can dabble. I can read an article in July, talk to a colleague about it in September, and postpone any real investment of effort until the following summer. I can spread out my contemplation, making a list of articles to read or workshops to attend that carries me through the foreseeable future. But when I move to preparation, I need to set deadlines for myself. I need to schedule the work.

It's a little bit like writing an essay. I often tell my students that there are two difficult things about writing an essay. One is determining when you're finished—unless you have a clear idea of where you're headed you can just keep writing until you run out of time. But that won't result in a unified piece of writing that makes a clear point. The other difficulty is telling when you've started. Many students will change their topic a dozen times, finding that every time they start to put down some words they see that this wasn't really what they wanted to write about, so they start again. (Sadly, some are still doing this when they choose their dissertation topics in doctoral programs.)

The problem with this is that it wastes a great deal of time and conceals the real problem, which is that having a thought and writing an argument are, as it turns out, quite different experiences. For the writer without much practice at the craft, the discovery that writing isn't easy, certainly isn't automatic, sometimes comes as a shock. And beginning writers are especially prone to self-defeating thoughts: If I can't easily put down my thoughts on paper, thoughts that seemed so well-formed and complete when they first occurred to me, then I must not have the knack; I can't write. Or I can't write about this. So they abandon every idea that proves difficult to develop and set out on a feckless quest for an effortless process to easily produce a finished product in a single draft.

I urge students, and many of them resist vigorously, that they must often write a bad essay as a step toward writing a good one. I warn them that if they aren't writing a certain amount of indecipherable glop they probably aren't doing it right. At some point, you must resolve that you have begun a process that you are committed to carry through in the face of difficulties and trials. That requires you to adopt what psychologist Carol Dweck calls a *growth mindset*—the belief that effort will pay off and that it's worth trying. She contrasts this with a *fixed mindset*, in which you conclude that your abilities are set and unchangeable, so that if you can't do it easily, you won't be able to do it at all.[31] The student with a growth mindset sees difficulties not as a final judgment on her potential but as steps to improvement.

Likewise, faculty members who embark upon serious revision of their approach to teaching must reach a point of commitment, a point where they self-consciously acknowledge that the project has begun and will be carried through. This is the preparation stage. It marks the difference between someone who is thinking about change and someone who is changing. And it differs from the previous stages in another way. While the person in preparation may not actually devote more time to the change process than the person in contemplation—and, indeed, may even devote less time—the person in preparation has *committed* the time. Time spent in preparation is not just found or borrowed; it is scheduled. The individual knows in advance that she will spend the time, and roughly when. This means that even though the chronological burden may not be greater, the psychological burden is. Time committed is a more serious matter than time found. This may be in large measure what the professors mean on the surveys when they describe time as the great deterrent.

Another important difference between the contemplation and preparation stages is that contemplation is, or can be, a much more private experience. I can read about teaching and think about how I might teach differently on my own time, in my own head. But when I prepare to implement changes, especially significant ones, it usually involves at least the consent, if not the active support, of other people. Tolman puts it this way: "The move from pre-contemplation to contemplation is an internal process, but the move from contemplation to preparation or into action is mediated by the institutional environment. So they are willing to make that shift in their willingness to change internally—cognitively and emotionally—to a point." After contact with the institutional culture, "they're in a waiting game, this chronic contemplation, looking at the environment and wondering 'Is it too risky to stick my neck out or is it safe to do so?'"[32]

Faculty members who may want to change, even after they begin to attend to the evidence about how learning works and how teaching affects it, can move only so far on the path to change by themselves. There is another paradox at work here. The privacy of teaching, to a considerable extent, protects the freedom of the individual teacher to change, to innovate, to try different approaches. But often the teacher can exercise that freedom only in private. That is, you can do whatever you want as long as you keep it to yourself. But if you seek the help or support—or even the permission—of others, innovation can face the pressures of academic groupthink and departmental habit. That was certainly my experience in trying to change my approach to teaching. I could make a broad array of changes on my own. But to ask even for permission to do something differently would frequently trigger an apparently automatic impulse at the departmental and division level to shut down, postpone, and create roadblocks. After a while, I stopped asking permission. My suspicion is that there is a great deal more innovation going on at colleges and universities than anyone knows—and it is going on precisely because no one knows it. But beyond a certain point, innovations will either expand or contract. And many of the most powerful innovations in teaching are by their nature larger than a single class or a single teacher. Thus, yet again, academic freedom understood as privacy and isolation for every teacher becomes a straightjacket on the freedom to teach well.

12 · DIFFUSING INNOVATION BY MAKING PEER GROUPS

We have seen that people can learn how to change established habits of thought and action but that to do so takes time and often involves several attempts. And beyond a certain point, the ability of people to change their habits depends on the environment and the people around them. Beyond a certain point, people can change only if their organizations change. For organizations to learn means that they change their theories-in-use, alter the routine practices of the organization. In the case of teaching and curriculum in a college or university, the privacy of teaching creates an enclave of safety where individual teachers can contemplate change and, to a considerable degree, experiment with it. But changes made in the privacy of the classroom do not spread easily, and those who make the changes rarely get reliable feedback on their consequences. So the isolation of teachers tends to limit the amount of innovation and experimentation going on in the institution as a whole.

THE DIFFUSION OF INNOVATIONS

Scholars have studied how and why innovations come to be adopted in groups and organizations. Everett M. Rogers of the University of New Mexico has surveyed the field in his classic work *Diffusion of Innovations*. Rogers uses the stages of change that I explained in the last chapter as one framework for how people come to accept innovations. He also discusses the attributes of various innovations that tend to lead to their adoption—or not. I will not discuss all of these attributes, but two of them seem especially relevant to our thinking about change in colleges and universities: *relative advantage* and *compatibility*.

"Diffusion scholars," Rogers reports, "have found relative advantage to be one of the strongest predictors of an innovation's rate of adoption. 'Relative advantage' is a ratio of the expected benefits and the costs of adoption of an innovation."[1] People's perceptions of relative advantage explain, for example, why innovations that offer an immediate payoff are usually adopted more rapidly than preventive innovations. Extensive and persistent efforts are often required to get people to take actions today that will prevent harm in the indeterminate future by doing things such as quitting smoking, losing weight, getting vaccinated against potential diseases, or performing routine maintenance on their houses, cars, or teeth. This is true even though the long-term advantages of preventive changes often far exceed those of changes with short-term benefits. If the costs are immediate and clear but the benefits a bit vague and distant, it is easy to postpone action, to get stuck in chronic contemplation.

When we think about the relative advantage of moving from the precontemplation to the contemplation stage in terms of teaching innovations, the costs are low, usually some time devoted to reading and conversation. The rewards are also vague and contingent, but if one has seen examples of significant success or is dogged by conspicuous failure, then it is worth thinking about. But the faculty member moving from contemplation to preparation faces explicit costs in the near term: time dedicated to the task in the immediate future, a deadline for completion that threatens to undermine other tasks, and the real work of designing new assignments and assessments. And the commitment that the preparation stage entails also introduces the possibility of failure, thus making the project more risky. It is almost impossible to fail at contemplation. But a new method of teaching may fall flat, and often does if we judge by the testimony of those teachers who report that they tried an innovative method and then gave it up. So the relative advantage of contemplation is likely to appear much more positive than the relative advantage of preparation.

This becomes clearer when we consider the attribute of compatibility. "The basic notion of the compatibility attribute," Rogers points out, "is that a new idea is perceived in relationship to existing practices that are already familiar to the individual."[2] The closer the innovation is to what you are already doing, the more likely you are to see it as low-cost and simple. The shift from the blackboard or whiteboard to PowerPoint was an easy one for many faculty members because it was completely compatible with using their existing notes to deliver the same lectures they had already prepared. Thus, the new technology was low-cost if computers and projectors were available in the classroom. But if you were a math teacher who had been teaching algebra from the same syllabus for several years, the prospect of moving into a different course design, such as a math emporium where students work at their own pace, would mean you would have to abandon your familiar lectures, exercises, and tests, learn the new software, and prepare for much more frequent and detailed advisement and tutoring. A math emporium is much less compatible with a traditional math class than PowerPoint is with a traditional lecture.

Changes in the design of a course, foundational change, often involve what Rogers calls *radical innovations*: "The more radical an innovation, indexed by the amount of knowledge that organization members must acquire in order to adopt, the more uncertainty it creates and the more difficult its implementation."[3]

THE JUDGMENT OF PEERS

In an organizational setting, the judgments people make about relative advantage and compatibility are not purely individual judgments. Studies of the dissemination of innovations in vastly different settings, from technologically primitive societies to high-tech firms, reveal that innovations are mediated by social interactions. Rogers finds that "most people depend mainly upon a subjective evaluation of an innovation that is conveyed to them from other individuals like themselves who have already adopted the innovation. This dependence on the experience of near peers suggests that the heart of the diffusion process consists of the modeling and imitation by potential adopters of their network partners who have previously adopted. Diffusion is a very social process that involves interpersonal communication relationships."[4]

I think what people like me think I think. And this is especially so when I am a little unsure about what I do think, when I do not have a well-established belief, a clear mental convention to fall back on.

At conventional colleges and universities, where are your near peers? They tend to be those with the same second-order environment: the other people in your department. That means that the diffusion of innovations at colleges and universities tends to be within disciplinary departments more than between them. In the development of learning outcomes, for example, some departments move much faster and more seriously than others. This may in part be because some departments have a more sophisticated approach to assessment to begin with, but it is also in part because some departments contain individuals who are accepted as credible and who have modeled the use of learning outcomes. If there are no near peers to model the innovation, then that innovation may appear to be radical to the people in the department even though it would not appear so to others. If a department is completely reliant on "outsiders" for modeling an innovation, it is much less likely to adopt it.

People tend to trust people they perceive as like them. A faculty member is much more likely to move from contemplation to preparation if she can see instances of people like her who are engaged in preparation or action. But the criterion of "likeness" that often counts the most is a sense of parallel professional identity. Sara Brownell and Kimberly Tanner, biologists at Stanford and San Francisco State University, express surprise at the institutional sluggishness of most universities, especially in the sciences, echoing Derek Bok's recognition of the inconsistent behavior of faculty with respect to research and teaching: "In fact, it is somewhat perplexing that we as scientists are resistant to such change. We are well trained in how to approach problems analytically, collect data, make interpretations, form conclusions, and then revise our experimental hypotheses and protocols accordingly. If we are experts at making evidence-based decisions in our experimental laboratories, then what forces are at play that impede us from adopting equally iterative and evidence-based approaches to teaching in our classrooms?"[5]

They acknowledge the conventional explanation: lack of time. But they probe a bit more deeply. As we noted in the last chapter, time is limited but fungible. To say that you don't have time to do one thing implies that you are using that time to do something else. We discussed in chapter 8 the fact that the faculty sense of expertise resides in the research end of faculty work. Brownell and Tanner suggest that, at least in the sciences, the sense of professional identity—the self-awareness of being a professional, an expert— resides almost entirely in the research function: "If a scientist has a professional identity he or she feels could be put at risk in his or her discipline and among his or her peers by embracing innovative approaches to teaching, then professional identity becomes a critical barrier in efforts to promote widespread change in undergraduate biology education."[6] If one's near peers seem to define their roles in ways that devalue teaching, then pursuing innovations in teaching can lower one's status in the peer group. Indeed, conspicuous effort devoted to teaching can imperil one's status as a peer.

As we have seen, this sense of professional identity is formulated first in graduate school: "The first tension point between professional identity and pedagogical change efforts is that scientists are trained in an atmosphere that defines their professional identities primarily as research identities to the exclusion of teaching identities."[7] And as we saw earlier, graduate school prioritizes research in many ways, and not just for scientists. Brownell and Tanner's point could be applied in a wide array of academic disciplines: "Some faculty advise graduate students to hide their interest in teaching; these mentors worry that the rest of academia will not take such students seriously."[8] The result is that teachers learn, even in graduate school, to use the privacy of teaching to conceal their interest in pedagogy: "If graduate students and postdoctoral scholars fear the ramifications of admitting that teaching is part of their identity, an interest in teaching can be internalized as something illicit, to be kept hidden from peers and mentors."[9] To the extent that this takes place, the privacy of teaching both reinforces and is reinforced by this sense that teaching is the lesser role. Even new faculty members who put a high value on teaching will tend to conceal that evaluation—they might report it on anonymous surveys, but are much less likely to bring it up in a department meeting. This reinforces other faculty members in the belief that teaching has, at best, an ambiguous value in the peer group.

Thus Brownell and Tanner question whether the standard explanation for why faculty don't innovate more in teaching is valid—or at least whether it is the whole story: "Perhaps it is not only a matter of institutions needing to provide training, time, and incentives, but also a need for a disciplinary culture shift, such that there are both a sufficient level of status attached to teaching and a critical mass of individuals who have professional identities that include teaching. Some might argue that regardless of what institutions offer, most faculty will not change the way they teach, because they view teaching as accessory to their professional identities, derived not from their institutions, but rather from their disciplines, which are cross-institutional."[10]

The cross-institutional professional identity that animates much of a faculty member's thinking also entails a perspective on change. Keep in mind that the academic discipline is embodied in the second-order environment that defines success for the scholar, and that makes the quest for success a dynamic journey, the destination ever changing because the successes of others in the field change it. Thus advancing as a researcher in an academic discipline is an inherently communal activity, and an inherently flexible and changing one. For the researcher, keeping up in the field is not done just to make sure one's knowledge is current—that is just as important for a teacher—but is an ongoing effort to monitor whether the field has changed in a way that impacts one's own work, in a way that will change the trajectory of future research. So researchers must be willing to change on an ongoing basis, to incorporate the findings of others, to ask new questions, and to adjust their claims in light of new evidence.

The same should be true of teachers. They should monitor the success of others to see how to change and improve their own teaching. But generally they do not, except in the most casual and unplanned way. As we have seen, teachers lack the second-order environment that would support expert thinking and ongoing learning about teaching. Paul Baker and Mary Zey-Ferrell, whose study of faculty orientations to their work we discussed in chapter 8, suggest that something like the opposite happens in teaching. Keeping up with the field implies a commitment to change as the field changes. Therefore, keeping up with the field of teaching would mean constantly questioning and examining one's own practice. According to Baker and Zey-Ferrell, "In self-fulfilling terms, each faculty member maximizes a sense of personal teaching achievement by unwittingly endorsing pluralistic ignorance about the actual tasks of instruction."[11] The cost of keeping up with current knowledge is a cost the researcher has to pay in order to maintain the professional identity as an expert in the field. But that is because the second-order environment, in a way, enforces standards of currency on the faculty member. In the realm of teaching, however, there is something more like a pact of ignorance. Baker and Zey-Ferrell put it this way: "Our investigation suggests that it pays to be ignorant of both new pedagogical developments and the inadequacies of existing ones. If one has good student ratings it is best to leave well enough alone and spend time and energies where they will 'pay off.'"[12]

To a degree, an individual faculty member can prepare to implement changes in the classroom and can even implement them in private. But if the individual hopes to find out how well the innovations work, that raises questions of comparison with alternatives. For a faculty member to seriously engage in assessment involves working with others to define the standards of excellence and making changes public. The faculty member who fears being labeled, explicitly or implicitly, as "second rate" for working with others to develop common standards for assessment will prefer to be seen as doing so only under duress. I once spoke with the faculty planning committee at a state university about their efforts to create an assessment system. The conversation kept coming back to the accreditation requirements. At one point, I asked, "Well, how would you like to approach assessing learning outcomes if it were not an accreditation requirement?" The faculty senate president, by far the most vocal and self-assured member of the group, responded: "If it weren't for the accreditation requirement, we wouldn't do it at all." Later, a member of the group pulled me aside to tell me that the faculty senate president didn't speak for all of the people there. But none of them were willing to say so publicly. To improve one's teaching is intrinsically rewarding. But to be seen to work at improving one's teaching may be risky. And to be seen to work at improving the quality of teaching overall may be too risky.

Movement to the contemplation stage in terms of pedagogical change is relatively safe. But to move to the preparation stage risks exposure as less professional, less expert, less a master of the real work of the discipline. I am not suggesting, of course, that faculty members who face a decision as to how to spend their time are consciously aware of this trade-off. Rather, the prospect of committing time to the scholarship of teaching and learning rather than the scholarship of discovery, of designating time in advance to collaborative work on assessments and assessment standards just *feels* risky, somehow secondary and derivative, not completely professional. For many teachers who report that the barrier to improving their teaching is lack of time, all time is not created equal. Some expenditures of time feel different from others. And sometimes, these risky commitments of time also mean that a person must reject the model of near peers in the organization in favor of more distant peers who have much less in common with the individual. It is interesting to note that many of those teachers who have become public advocates for teaching have made their reputations as researchers and writers in their fields. A solid reputation as a researcher protects one from the doubts that might otherwise be triggered by advocating more attention to teaching.

So the connection between organizational change and personal change is more complex than it might at first appear. We should readily accept the testimony of faculty who report that lack of time, lack of resources, and lack of institutional support are significant barriers to pedagogical change. But we can also see why some institutions that have invested in providing those things for their faculty have sometimes not achieved as much innovation as they had hoped for. We can also see, again, why "top-down" innovation, no matter how enlightened and reasonable, may not catch on. The dissemination of innovations tends to happen not from the top down—and, really, not from the bottom up either. It is more of a sideways process, in which near peers embolden their colleagues in the faith that reallocating their time to new and different tasks is worth trying.

The conventional advice for promoting change includes the ideas that the leaders of the organization must support change, that experimentation—including the right to fail—must be protected, and that people must have the time and resources to learn new practices. All of this is true and valuable. But it is not the whole story, certainly not in the case of higher education.

How, then, can higher education create the infrastructure to support change? This is, of course, not a new question. Many institutions and organizations have made efforts to address the problems we have discussed through creating a second-order community around teaching.

PEER NETWORKS THAT ENABLE CHANGE

The second-order environments that support, assess, and reward faculty expertise tend to be, as Brownell and Tanner point out, cross-institutional: the national and international communities of practitioners that make up academic disciplines. Most of the professional organizations that represent these disciplines tend to advocate, at least in their public pronouncements, a very positive approach to pedagogical innovation. Where the resistance comes in is with the local incarnation of the discipline, the academic department. This institutional agent of the cross-institutional entity embodies the barriers to change most completely.

If we read the speeches of either the president of the college or the president of the disciplinary organization, we are likely to get the impression that academic change is the order of the day, that active learning, pedagogical innovation, and experimental approaches embody the new university world. This tends to be the espoused theory conveyed by the public face of education and research both. Indeed, at some institutions, if we read the tenure and promotion policies, we will come to believe that the scholarship of teaching and learning stands as equal to the scholarship of discovery in personnel decisions. But none of this makes its way into daily practice at most institutions. It is the cadre of near peers, not the leaders, that most directly shapes the expectations and possibilities of faculty members.

Some institutions have attempted to make academic departments more open to new practices. And this often works to some extent. But such strategies have not been very effective for the most part. We have already discussed several of the problems here. The competition among departments for resources and enrollments reinforces the tendencies to groupthink and defensive routines. If the character of academic departments is going to change, it will be by either decreasing their control over faculty careers or increasing their inputs from other sources.

One approach is to create a peer group of faculty outside the department by constructing interdisciplinary faculty communities that pay attention to teaching and learning. This is being done at many institutions. One template for such communities is collaboration directly around the act of teaching. One example of such collaboration is teams that do course redesign, where the redesign involves more than one department. Another is team-taught learning community courses, where from two to four faculty members teach a theme-based course that involves multiple disciplines. The Washington Center at the Evergreen State College in Olympia, Washington, has long provided information and support for the development of such programs. But the vast majority of institutions that offer learning community courses involve a distinct minority of the faculty in teaching those courses. I suspect that those involved come to have a very different attitude toward teaching than many of their colleagues, but they must still return to their home departments to be reviewed for tenure and promotion.

Communities can also be constructed outside the immediate teaching task through faculty learning communities (FLCs). An FLC is a group of faculty members, usually six to twelve, who meet on a regular basis to address some problem or issue. The idea has been developed most extensively at Miami University in Ohio. Milton Cox, the professional developer who pioneered the development of FLCs at Miami beginning in 1979, points out that "multidisciplinarity and community are the elements that allow FLCs to excel in teaching and learning pursuits."[13] There are basically two types of FLCs: cohort-based and topic-based. Cohort-based communities involve faculty members who are in a similar situation, such as new faculty or midcareer faculty. Topic-based communities address some problem or issue related to teaching and learning. In either case, these communities bring faculty from different departments together to explore issues in common. An FLC is a community of practice, a group of people who meet together regularly and get to know each other for a well-defined purpose. Like well-designed student learning communities, FLCs bring together teachers from different departments and different disciplines. The multidisciplinary structure insulates against the dangers of groupthink and self-censorship. The members of an FLC have a common object of study, but do not exercise the power of promotion over each other and do not determine one another's teaching schedules. They also do not share a common disciplinary culture, which invariably means they communicate more fully and clearly because they do not make as many assumptions about the prior knowledge and attitudes of the other people in the group.

Many institutions have followed Miami's lead in developing FLCs. A 2004 survey found 308 FLCs at 132 different institutions.[14] The number has certainly grown since then. They are a direct attempt to build second-order environments outside of the department structure, and usually focused on issues of undergraduate learning.

FLCs seek to create near peers for faculty members who are not members of the disciplinary community and so pose a counterweight to the forces of departmental self-defense that make innovation more risky. They can create a safe space to examine the governing values that are taken for granted elsewhere. Cox contrasts FLCs with other approaches to professional development: "Workshops and consulting can provide only surface or single-loop learning (acting to achieve a result without much deep reflection on value or appropriateness) for the participants, but an FLC provides, deep, double-loop learning (careful reflection on the appropriateness of actions with respect to outcomes and social structures) for the topics that the participants address."[15] He expresses the hope that "through FLC programs at some point we will have established sufficient connections in our institutions to support a learning organization and overcome the isolation in higher education."[16]

It appears to me that widespread participation of faculty in such learning communities changes the faculty culture precisely by creating these connections. Such active faculty groups are designed to intersect in a productive way with the process of individual change. By participating in an FLC, a faculty member is moving beyond the contemplation stage, is taking action and making commitments that are themselves a preparation for further change around whatever the focus of the learning community might be. Where the FLC is designed to produce a proposal for action or an experiment to be tried, the extended preparation period that the FLC offers lets participants chart a trajectory toward more change. The question remains whether transient groupings like FLCs can alter the behavior of faculty in the permanent structures that shape their work.

In some cases, campuses have created long-term connections across departmental boundaries. One obvious framework for such connections is the learning outcomes that cross the lines between classes and departments. This principle has been integrated most fully into the faculty design at places like Alverno College, a Roman Catholic women's college in Milwaukee, Wisconsin. Alverno's project began with a rethinking of the governing value behind the curriculum. Having decided to operate on the basis of what students learned rather than what teachers covered, they found that this meant the faculty needed to have a common understanding of the learning outcomes and the kinds of assessment evidence that they would accept. As Alverno's Marcia Mentkowski and Associates put it, "It was critical to have structured opportunities in which educators could talk in depth."[17] That led to ongoing, interdisciplinary faculty committees focused not just on departmental issues but on the eight abilities that were the core of the curriculum, college-wide institutes held three times a year, and faculty meetings and working groups every Friday.

One effect of these processes was to break down the privacy of teaching as a norm governing faculty expectations: "Faculty need to be engaged in a public discussion about teaching and learning and their practices. This opportunity allows for critical analysis, where faculty explore their own observations, ideas, and concerns about student performance." Part of this critical analysis needs to be "a sharp comparison between one's practice and the frameworks that represent and inform it."[18] In the conventional Instruction Paradigm College, there are no frameworks that inform faculty practice in general, across disciplines. There are merely routines that seal that practice and perpetuate it. The result is that the routines that govern day-to-day faculty practice have developed quite differently at Alverno than at most institutions. One of the routines that new faculty members become socialized to is open deliberation on the nature and meaning of their own teaching—not just in the department but with faculty from other disciplines and staff educational researchers as well. The instruction myth comes to be replaced with a routine practice of deliberative inquiry and reflection. This manifests itself in both group and individual exploration of how things work and what practices result in what outcomes. The faculty becomes a second-order community that knows what it is trying to do and can get better at doing it. And each faculty member develops closer peers in teaching practice than would be possible outside the department at most institutions.

Both FLCs and sustained faculty deliberation around learning outcomes have the potential to allow colleges and universities to learn how to change more productively. But that will happen only when such practices reach a critical mass that makes the default attitude one of openness and transparency around teaching.

13 · PROMOTING INNOVATION THROUGH SCHOLARLY TEACHING

All institutions of higher education, of course, have systems in place to monitor and, ideally, improve the quality of teaching. They must in order to meet accreditation standards. But for the most part these processes work haltingly if at all. Most institutions can give no systematic account of how their faculty are teaching, much less how well, and have no coherent plan for making it better. This seems odd in view of the fact that most of the quality control mechanisms are essentially borrowed from the research realm, where they seem to work reasonably well. But the differences are crucial.

Peer review is the primary means of quality control on faculty research. It is also an engine of productivity in that it creates a process by which faculty research is assessed on a continuing basis by people who are skilled in the object of the research but unbiased with respect to the researcher. It is not a perfect system, but overall it has been a successful one. The picture is very different with respect to teaching. Daniel Bernstein, a psychologist and former director of the Center for Teaching Excellence at the University of Kansas, points out that "historically, the *peer review of teaching* has typically meant only that a faculty member has watched a colleague lead a class."[1]

Why the contrast? Institutions do so much better at evaluating research than at evaluating teaching for two reasons: research is more important to them, and they have the apparatus for evaluating it already in place. Economists Dahlia K. Remler of Baruch College in New York City and Elda Pema of the Naval Postgraduate School in Monterey, California, in a 2009 paper for the National Bureau of Economic Research, examine the question of why institutions "reward research while selling education." They find that to the extent there is competition between institutions for share of the student market, it is much more powerfully influenced by research than teaching: "Empirically, whatever competitive forces are at work in the education services market, they appear to reward the research reputations of institutions of higher education far more than they reward their teaching reputations."[2] Perhaps as a result, institutions spend a good deal more money on evaluating their research than their teaching. It is hard to determine cause and effect here; perhaps the market emphasizes research reputation because there is so much evidence to support it, or perhaps institutions collect the evidence because it has such a high reputational value. Whatever the case, the empirical fact of the matter is that institutions have created an extensive apparatus for evaluating research: "In fact, the relative easiness of evaluating research performance could be due to the relatively large resources devoted to evaluating research. Specifically, there is an extensive *existing* system of peer-review for research, including journal rankings, academic presses and grant review agencies. . . . So, *given* that we have available all these ranking systems for research work, and that we lack similar systems for evaluating teaching, it *is* easier to evaluate research. More resources are devoted to the evaluation of research: consider the time and effort that academics put into refereeing papers and reviewing grants. In contrast, few resources have gone into the evaluation of teaching."[3]

As we shall see, this inequity of resources has serious and abiding consequences.

STUDENT EVALUATIONS: UBIQUITOUS AND UNINFORMATIVE

The overwhelmingly predominant forms of assessing the quality of teaching today, both for the institutional evaluation of teaching and for feedback to teachers, are student evaluations of teaching (SET). Andrew Delbanco of Columbia University summarizes a widely held view: "Our current method of assessing college teachers—mainly surveying students about how much they like or dislike them—is atomistic, impressionistic, and generally close to worthless."[4] John Cross and Edie Goldenberg, both administrators at the University of Michigan when they conducted their study, analyzed ten elite research universities with special attention to their use of contingent faculty. They found that "because the student opinions that are summarized in course evaluations are frequently the only pieces of evidence of teaching performance that can be compared across faculty members, they often assume unreasonable importance in hiring, retention, and promotion decisions. Given the compression that is characteristic of student scores, sometimes great importance is attached to even small differences."[5]

Pieter Spooren, Bert Brockx, and Dimitri Mortelmans of the University of Antwerp in Belgium recently conducted an extensive review of the research done to date on SET. They find that institutions use many different student surveys; there is "a surprising amount of variation."[6] Many of the instruments used are developed locally by the institutions using them, and "many instruments are developed without any clear theory of effective teaching."[7] The dominant motivation appears to be that "institutions need instruments that will allow them to gather information . . . for different types of courses as quickly as possible," while "surveys must also be highly economical."[8] Stated more simply, SET must be fast and cheap.

Research on SET is complicated by the great variety of different methods and by the fact that at most institutions there is no reliable way of telling how valid the surveys are. The only method of assessing teacher quality at many institutions is the student evaluation itself. Faculty in general accept the use of SET for the evaluation of teaching, but without much confidence in their reliability. So though faculty members may not object to the instruments for promotion and tenure decisions, they don't rely on them much to improve their own teaching. Spooren, Brockx, and Mortelmans find that "many teachers do not find SET very helpful for such formative purposes and . . . they tend to ignore the comments and suggestions that students provide."[9]

To the extent that it is possible to evaluate SET in terms of quality, the results are mixed. At the end of their extensive research review, the Belgian scholars conclude that "the utility and validity ascribed to SET should continue to be called into question."[10] In seeking to discover indications of the relative effectiveness of different groups of teachers, Cross and Goldenberg found little hard evidence: "Indeed, we are aware of no empirical demonstration of a positive correlation between evaluation scores and any objective measure of student learning."[11] Philip Stark, a professor of statistics at UC Berkeley, has surveyed the empirical evidence as well and reports that "the only controlled randomized experiments on student teaching evaluations have found that student evaluations of teaching effectiveness are negatively associated with direct measures of effectiveness: Evaluations do not seem to measure teaching effectiveness."[12]

In 2016 Bob Uttl, Carmela A. White, and Daniela Wong Gonzalez—psychologists at Mount Royal University in Calgary, Canada—undertook a detailed examination of all previous meta-analyses of SET, going back to the original data and applying the best statistical methodology. One thing they found is that many past studies that seemed to show some positive correlation between evaluations and learning used very small samples and often did not adjust their conclusions correctly considering the sample size. Furthermore, they frequently ignored the prior learning of students. As the authors put it, "Previous reports of 'moderate' and 'substantial' SET/learning correlations were artifacts of small study size effects."[13] The conclusion of this comprehensive meta-analysis was that "the best evidence—the meta-analyses of SET/learning correlations when prior learning/ability are taken into account—indicates that the SET/learning correlation is zero."[14] Taking all the evidence into account, it seems clear that "students do not learn more from professors who receive higher SET ratings."[15] Carl Wieman, who has conducted extensive research on the impact of pedagogy on learning as part of the Science Education Initiative, concludes that "there is no correlation between student evaluations and objective measures of learning, and we have seen no correlation between evaluations and the use of effective instructional practices."[16]

One clear conclusion from the research is that no single number, or set of numbers, is particularly meaningful in evaluating the quality of teaching. Even well-developed surveys need to be interpreted carefully, and they hardly ever provide direct and clear advice for improving teaching. There is simply no evidence that student evaluations alone, as the sole feedback to teachers on their teaching, can ever be very effective at improving the quality of teaching overall. Yet the tendency of many administrators is to use the simplest number to be found: the overall evaluation. Not surprisingly, this is probably the least reliable indicator of anything meaningful. As Stark notes, "Students seem to make snap judgements about instructors that have nothing to do with teaching effectiveness, and to rely on those judgements when asked about teaching effectiveness."[17] Uttl, White, and Gonzalez suggest that these snap judgments are often based on the student's interest in the subject and level of ability on entering the class rather than any characteristic of a particular teacher.[18] The more general the question, of course, the more likely it is to become a surrogate for something else in the student's mind, as Stark points out: "The survey questions apparently most influenced by extraneous factors are exactly of the form we ask on campus: overall teaching effectiveness."[19]

SET can potentially be useful when a well-designed survey is weighed along with other evidence in a thoughtful process guided by a coherent method. But usually the only other evidence that is combined with SET is a classroom observation by a colleague or administrator. Watching a faculty member teach a single class can, of course, provide some useful information. But in the absence of an understanding of how the class session fits in the whole design of the course and how representative the pedagogy demonstrated in that class is, it is hard to see how a single class observation can be very useful. Daniel Bernstein points out that "we would never evaluate research by watching someone do science in a library or take notes over a text in the library; nor would we ask the graduate students in the department to say whether the work has merit. Yet we consider that to be just fine to evaluate the intellectual work of teaching."[20]

Serious peer review of the sort done with academic research just doesn't arise as a possibility at most institutions. Those who could participate in such a thoughtful review process are held back by many factors, and the privacy of teaching is chief among them. This phenomenon is apparently not limited to North America. Gunnar Handal, a professor of higher education at the University of Oslo in Norway, notes that in terms of academic research, "without criticism of existing knowledge we would experience almost no scientific progress. Thus criticizing other researchers' reports and publications is an accepted activity."[21] In contrast, he points out, "we lack corresponding traditions in academic culture when it comes to teaching. Educators engage relatively rarely in systemic appraisal of their colleagues' teaching in the form of critical evaluation that is carried out publicly, as in the case of scholarly criticism. In keeping with the reigning culture, it is not wholly acceptable. University level teaching is more or less the private property of the individual instructor, and any commentary could be construed as meddling."[22]

Handal provides an example: "Among the questions we posed in an interview survey carried out among the participants in a faculty development course some years ago was this one: 'Do you often talk with colleagues about their teaching?' One of the participants answered in horror, 'No, that would be comparable to speaking to them about their personal hygiene.'"[23]

THE PROSPECT OF SCHOLARLY TEACHING

The privacy of teaching insulates it from the realm of serious professional activity. We use the phrase *scholarly research* so easily that the second term has become almost redundant. We can, for all practical purposes, exchange the words *scholarship* and *research* without any fear of causing confusion. If we speak of *scholarly teaching*, on the other hand, most people—in and out of the academy—will be a bit confused about just what we mean. The linguistic confusion is related to the academic practice: scholarship is public and subject to open analysis and critique. Teaching, on the other hand, is private and out of bounds in polite conversation. The scholarship of teaching and learning (SoTL) is an effort to change that. And it aspires to create a mode of scholarly teaching.

What I mean by *scholarly teaching* is a process in which the teacher becomes better at teaching through observing, assessing, and gathering evidence about how and what students are learning and refining the practice of teaching through progressive problem solving. The scholarly teacher is not just the subject matter expert who teaches but is becoming an expert teacher by learning systematically from experience—her own and others'—to continuously refine and improve the teaching process.

There are many scholarly teachers working in higher education today. Some teachers read SoTL publications and spend time studying the research on student learning. Most, however, do not take a scholarly approach in their teaching. Nira Hativa of Tel Aviv University in Israel conducted a survey of faculty at a large research university to discover how they learned to teach. More than four out of five reported that trial and error made a major contribution to their teaching. This ranked far higher than any other factor. More than half of faculty members also reported that the following factors made a major contribution to their teaching: self-evaluation, student feedback, and observing former instructors. Hativa found that "strikingly, although the large majority of all respondents experienced discussions with peers on matters of teaching, teaching as TAs, sharing teaching a course with peers, observing peers' classes, . . . only a small proportion of them perceived these experiences to have contributed much to their current teaching practices."[24]

We sometimes hear that the scientific method is just a refinement of trial and error. That, of course, is half true. A scientific experiment is certainly a trial of a given hypothesis, but an idea becomes an experimental hypothesis only when the experimenter can describe the conditions that would disprove it. Testing new ideas contributes to the growth of knowledge only when we can describe the standards of discovery in advance and hence record the new knowledge gained as a result. Random guessing and spontaneous efforts without establishing the criteria of success are neither scientific nor scholarly. Even in our informal and unsystematic learning, there must be an underlying theory at work or no learning happens. The adage "if at first you don't succeed, try, try again" assumes that we know what success looks like, that we have a clear and testable vision of what it is that we are trying to do. But the unsystematic and unstructured way in which many faculty think about teaching, sadly, seems to not fit this mold. As Hativa concludes, "This nonsystematic unplanned training is insufficient to generate the appropriate pedagogical knowledge of the ability to apply it in actual classroom teaching. It appears that knowledge thus acquired may just as likely promote university teachers' misperceptions and misconceptions regarding students and teaching."[25]

THE PEER REVIEW OF TEACHING

Teaching can never be genuinely scholarly unless it becomes an object of public feedback and discourse, unless it is subject to something like peer review. Nearly all the SoTL publications I am familiar with are peer reviewed, in the sense that disinterested outsiders read articles submitted for publication and evaluate them for acceptability. What I mean here, though, is not that the research about teaching needs to be peer reviewed, but that the teaching itself does. Hence alongside the growth of SoTL we have seen a movement to create credible and authentic peer review of teaching.

Before he came to the Carnegie Foundation as president, Lee Shulman was a professor of education at Stanford University. Beginning in 1985 he directed the Teacher Assessment Project (TAP), which sought to improve the quality of teacher evaluation and also use assessment to improve the quality of teaching. Most of the research that TAP sponsored dealt with K–12 teachers. But an interesting application of the question to higher education arose. Larry Cuban, whose work I have referred to in previous chapters, was an associate professor at Stanford, due to be promoted to full professor. He made an unusual request—so far as I can tell, an unprecedented one. He asked if he could refuse tenure. His rationale, as related by Shulman, was as follows: "I don't want tenure because as soon as you give me tenure you give up your obligation to provide me with an intelligent review of my work. I refuse to work in an organization that does not take responsibility for reviewing the quality of my work regularly and providing me feedback on it."[26] The university agreed that if Cuban would accept tenure, they would establish a process for post-tenure review every five years. A committee was duly constituted, of which Shulman was a member. As he describes it, "At our first meeting, Larry proposed putting together a portfolio of his work. . . . Three months after that discussion we received a rather large box of materials: annotated copies of syllabi of courses he had designed and was teaching; a videotape [remember, this was the 1980s] of one or two sessions of courses he taught; and commentaries on how that videotape represented both the best things he did as a teacher and some of the enduring dilemmas he confronted as a teacher—ones he was still working on."[27]

The box also contained student evaluations and samples of work the students had done in the classes. The committee met and discussed its contents and posed some questions. Cuban took some time to address those questions. They met three times. "What was clear," Shulman concluded, "was that it was not only Larry Cuban who profited from the experience; each of us benefited. [Psycholinguist and committee member new to the faculty] John Baugh reported that he learned more quickly about teaching at Stanford than he ever would have learned in the normal ways in which new faculty could possibly learn."[28]

While nearly all the original contents of Cuban's portfolio were already in existence, what he did was to organize and select materials that would illustrate both his successes and challenges as a teacher. Shulman noted, "One of the reasons that my own portfolio has remained incomplete, although I've got all the parts around, is that I am not part of an ad hoc community organized to discuss my portfolio."[29] But the experience led Shulman to ask, "What would happen if we as teacher educators organized ourselves to review each other's work in this way? If we supported each other in this way, what would that do for us and our students?"[30]

In the 1990s, the American Association for Higher Education sponsored the Peer Review of Teaching Project, under the leadership of Pat Hutchings. In 1991, Russell Edgerton, president of the AAHE, Hutchings, and staff member Kathleen Quinlan set out a rationale and format for *The Teaching Portfolio: Capturing the Scholarship in Teaching.* They noted the limitations of the existing dependence on student evaluations: "What is 'peer reviewed' is not the process of teaching and its products (the learning that the teaching enabled) but the observations and ratings submitted by students and assorted others."[31] They were also fully cognizant of the distance that most institutions had to go to create genuinely scholarly teaching: "In truth, the teaching portfolio is a technology yet to be invented for a culture that on many campuses doesn't yet exist—a culture of professional inquiry about good teaching."[32]

One of the initial participants in the Peer Review of Teaching Project was Daniel Bernstein. His background at the University of Nebraska had prepared him admirably for the work, but coming to this national project on teaching from the frame of reference of his prior academic work was still a significant adjustment. He had come to Nebraska in the 1970s, and had begun his career as an innovator in teaching. He completely redesigned the basic psychology course in line with the pedagogical ideas of Fred Keller, a behavioral psychologist at Columbia University, who developed the "personalized system of instruction." This was a form of what is often called mastery learning. In most conventional instruction, the teacher teaches a body of material, the students are tested on it, and then, whatever their performance on the test, they move on to the next unit. In the Keller Plan, students who did not demonstrate mastery on a test (which often required 90 percent or better) would work with a tutor and retake versions of the test until they could demonstrate mastery. Lectures were moved to the background and used mainly for motivation; study, mentoring by tutors, and retesting moved to the foreground. Bernstein developed his own version of the Keller Plan and implemented it in basic psychology courses. He then compared the performance of students in different versions of the same course. (In other words, Bernstein was doing SoTL in the 1970s—nearly twenty years before Ernest Boyer "invented" the scholarship of teaching.) And when called before the college "grade inflation committee" to explain why his students were getting higher grades than expected, he was able to demonstrate that students in these courses did better because they learned more. In other words, he was innovating productively, doing real scholarship on the teaching, and making the results public.[33]

While the work of scholarly teaching was demonstrably successful, Bernstein found that it appeared to slow the progress of his career. In the 1980s he turned in a serious way to research, getting grants, publishing much more regularly, teaching little, and eventually becoming the editor of one of the premier research journals in his field.

But by the late 1980s, he had reached the top of the ladder and was able to step back and evaluate his priorities: "I very consciously said, 'OK. I'm a full professor. I can do whatever I want now. What do I want do to?' And what I decided was that I wanted to really focus on teaching."[34] This return to a major focus on teaching led to grants for professional development projects at Nebraska, conducting workshops on other campuses, and involvement with the growing national network of academics who were also concerned about teaching. And to the AAHE's Peer Review of Teaching Project.

Even faculty members deeply immersed in the effort to improve teaching have often been insulated from other faculty members with the same interest. The goal of the AAHE project, to create a culture of professional inquiry about good teaching, really called for a major transformation of the privacy of teaching, the creation of a genuine second-order community around teaching that would inevitably break down the instruction myth and the myth of teacher professionalism.

Bernstein's work with the AAHE project led to the creation of a project of the same name—the Peer Review of Teaching Project—at the University of Nebraska, which is still active today. The repository of course portfolios at Nebraska contains over 450 portfolios from many universities and invites comment from anyone who cares to review them. The project web page offers examples of teaching portfolios and of formats and review criteria.[35] In addition, several excellent books have been written on the teaching portfolio and the peer review of teaching, including *Making Teaching and Learning Visible: Course Portfolios and the Peer Review of Teaching,* by Bernstein and his former Nebraska colleagues Amy Nelson Burnett, Amy Goodburn, and Paul Savory.

A well-designed teaching portfolio can open up the possibility of three kinds of substantive peer review. First, it can allow faculty from the teacher's department to conduct a serious and well-informed review of the whole range of teaching practices. Second, it can allow faculty from other departments and disciplines to understand how the individual is teaching and how it is working. Third, it can allow faculty and others from outside the institution, perhaps those teaching the same subject elsewhere, to understand what a teacher is trying to do in a different institutional context and to bring a new perspective to the review. The Nebraska project describes different kinds of portfolios with slightly different purposes, adaptable to the needs and situations of different teachers. But the core idea is common to all forms of teaching portfolios: that teachers will systematically reflect on their teaching and gather evidence by which it can be reviewed.

Bernstein, Burnett, Goodburn, and Savory summarize the value of a course portfolio in this way: "A *course portfolio* captures and makes visible the scholarly work of teaching by combining inquiry into the intellectual work of a course with an investigation of the quality of student understanding and performance."[36]

It should be clear by now that serious feedback is as essential to teachers as to students. And that is the core value of the peer review of teaching. As Bernstein and his colleagues point out, "In our model, peers participate in all stages of the course portfolio process. Internal peers from your department, college, or campus respond to your initial writing about your course and read and review the resulting course portfolio that you create. They then provide suggestions to improve your teaching as represented in your portfolio. In some cases, external peers from other schools read and assess your portfolio, either to help you develop your teaching or to evaluate your teaching. By sharing your teaching with many different peers, you receive helpful feedback that can strengthen your course design, teaching methods, and classroom assessments."[37]

Such an approach to the peer review of teaching opens up the teaching process to a whole new level of scrutiny, and likewise ensures a rich flow of feedback to the teacher that would raise the quality of his or her thinking and practice in almost every case. The price to pay, obviously, would be to abandon privacy, to make teaching, as Lee Shulman puts it, community property.

The book and the website are peppered with testimonials from faculty members about the transformative effect of genuine peer review. It appears that for faculty who engage in it, it is a powerful experience, and one that can significantly improve their teaching. But for those who have not yet participated, and for their department chairs, it can appear to be yet another drain on their valuable time.

At most institutions where teaching portfolios are in use, they are entirely voluntary. So what we often have is a pattern of frequent portfolio development in some departments and none in others, or intermittent portfolio use across departments. Today, the teaching portfolio is a technology that has been developed and refined that still awaits, on most campuses, the development of a culture of inquiry about good teaching.

In recent years, work has continued on the intellectual framework for genuine peer review of teaching. Scholars have articulated the idea of a Teaching Quality Framework (TQF) that could be implemented across an institution. Noah Finkelstein, Daniel Reinholz, and Joel Corbo of the University of Colorado Boulder have collaborated with Daniel Bernstein to articulatea TQF and begin to implement it at UC Boulder. The TQF, as they envision it would entail "1) a campus-wide, cross-disciplinary *structure* for defining teaching quality and associated tools for assessing teaching quality, and 2) a *process* for contextualizing the structure to each disciplinary unit and enacting it across campus."[38]

Some institutions have attempted to incorporate peer review of teaching into the tenure and promotion process, as a TQF would certainly do. In other words, they have begun to treat teaching in the same way as they do research, as a professional activity that can be meaningfully evaluated, and for which excellence can be reliably recognized and rewarded. The core difficulty seems to be, however, that paying serious attention to teaching takes more time for the evaluators, with no corresponding reduction of other commitments. In some cases the written policies are simply not followed, or the box gets checked but the work doesn't get done. In others, departmental pressure has led to rolling back the official policies.

Many institutions have accepted the use of teaching portfolios and some form of peer review as an optional mode of professional development, as formative assessment—or feedback—aimed at improving teaching. But some have argued that peer review can be acceptable in the modern university only if it is limited to the improvement of teaching and excluded from any reward or promotion system. Many faculty members view with horror the prospect of using student learning outcomes in any way as a part of faculty evaluation. Of course, the assessment of faculty research has always combined formative and summative assessment, feedback, and evaluation. When an academic journal rejects a manuscript, it includes the reviewers' comments, which often point to directions for revising or rethinking either the article or the project to make it more successful in the future. The periodic reviews of tenure-track faculty may simultaneously deny promotion while specifying the kinds of publications or research that would justify promotion in the future. And when faculty respond to student work, they usually assign a grade and make suggestions for improvement on the same paper. Today, SET is used both as feedback to faculty and as a tool of evaluation. So there is apparently nothing distinctive about teaching that makes feedback and evaluation incompatible. There is no inherent conflict between the two functions. In fact, in most serious endeavors both are necessary.

Yet for most institutions raising teaching to the level where it is evaluated as serious intellectual work seems an impossible idea. Faculty and administrators do not, for the most part, present arguments against the wisdom or utility of assessing teaching in the same way we currently assess research. But the whole range of defensive routines come into play to deflect such an idea. As one professional developer at a major university put it to me, when they are presented with the comparison with research "colleagues never have a good answer for these parallel observations; they just shrug and say it's too high a standard or there is not enough time to do it or that they just don't think it is worth that much consideration."

And it is not, at least at the institutions that I have any evidence about, that faculty are generally happy with the way teaching is currently evaluated. Most faculty believe that the heavy, sometimes exclusive, reliance on SET leads to simplistic and misleading reviews, and sometimes explicitly bad decisions. And, as pointed out above, most faculty make little use of student evaluations to improve their teaching.

Daniel Bernstein has had, as we have seen, a long career as a researcher as well as a faculty developer. "I am not," he points out, "anti-research." But he is also deeply invested in teaching. "It's just that the balance of effort and consequences is way out of line," he says, "even in small institutions with a traditionally student-oriented mission. It's a matter of people asserting that all published research, by its nature, no matter how derivative or unimpressive, should somehow count more than the very best teaching. That's the part that loses me."[39]

In the evaluation and review of teaching, superstitious reasoning comes to the fore. The widespread use of student evaluations as the chief means of assessing and reviewing teaching has been accompanied by grade inflation. Stuart Rojstaczer and Christopher Healy, whose work on grades we discussed in the first chapter, conclude that there is probably a connection. But efforts to address this connection have been confounded: "Efforts at employing even soft external guidelines on grading practices are almost always rebuffed by both instructors and university leadership, and often equated with a lack of faith in the integrity of the faculty."[40] In the spirit of the instruction myth, "the integrity of the faculty" tends to be equated with the myth of academic freedom and the privacy of teaching. A similar dynamic is no doubt at work in terms of efforts to achieve more valid peer review of teaching.

Even if faculty are not happy with what they are doing, the prospect of changing present practices, especially when it involves intruding on the privacy of teaching, threatens damage and loss. Just exactly what the nature of this loss would be is unforeseeable. It is the monster in the closet, known only by vague sounds and dreamy imaginings. But this very vagueness makes it all the more frightening. Rather than invite the attack of potentially devastating changes, it is safe to stick with the familiar, the predictable. Don't open the closet door *because* you don't know what is behind it.

14 · THE TEACHING INVENTORY AND PORTFOLIO

As we have seen, many colleges and universities are fully engaged in pursuing innovation. They want to try new things and be seen to be trying new things. But after decades of such innovations we see precious little improvement. They are experimenting without, apparently, learning much from the experiments. The problem is that these "innovative" institutions are not engaged so much in scientific experimentation as educational alchemy. The reasoning about what works and what doesn't is largely superstitious reasoning, repeating rituals without understanding their real effects. Hoping by repeated attempts at doing something different to transform students who enter as leaden learners into graduate gold, they mix their potions and repeat their incantations, following the traditions of their craft. And so these institutions produce a great deal of activity, expend vast resources, and cause not a few explosions and fires. And occasionally, they encounter, in the bottom of a flask or a mortar, a nugget of gold. This confirms their faith in the potential of alchemical magic for a time, even though they seem not to be able to reproduce the transformation at will. So they try something different. In the end, the alchemy of innovation offers no promise of consistent growth either in theory or practice. Hence institutions continue to get bigger, but without getting consistently better.

Like the work of the alchemist, the real work of higher education is carried on mainly in secret. The classroom, like the alchemist's chamber, is a private space, a den secured by conjurers' spells, a black box, and what goes on inside is invisible to the uninitiated. And as with alchemy, concealment generates a superstitious deference and admiration from the laity. For a while.

How can we move from the alchemy of innovation to the science of improvement? One way to approach this question is to use the contradiction between institutional theory-in-use and espoused theory as a point of leverage. There is an underlying cognitive dissonance at nearly every conventional institution. And the tension created by this cognitive dissonance generates much of the energy and even rancor that is released in disputes over personnel or curriculum or policy. That tension is a potential source of energy to promote improvement if it can be tapped into in the right way. Maintaining the rules and habits that protect the instruction myth depends on suppressing information about what is really going on at the institution. The alchemist, like the magician, maintains his reputation by keeping his methods hidden. If that information can be revealed, it will unleash a new dynamic in pedagogy, planning, and policy.

Paul Ramsden, then with Griffith University, and Elaine Martin, of the Royal Melbourne Institute of Technology, conducted a study of Australian universities. They surveyed administrators at thirty-two different universities, then surveyed 1,489 faculty members at six different institutions. They followed up with interviews of about 40 faculty. On the large faculty survey, 95 percent of faculty said that teaching should be highly valued, while only 37 percent said that it was. Faculty endorsed by large majorities ideas for "removing obstacles to enjoying teaching, such as excessive workloads" (83 percent), "taking greater account of teaching in the promotions process" (77 percent), "providing academics with more time to develop and introduce innovations in learning and teaching" (74 percent), and "allocating the university budget so teaching is treated equally with research" (71 percent). One of the purposes of the study was to discover whether faculty ideas on university practices differed from the "official" university position. Reviewing the overall results, the authors concluded that "they demonstrate two important discrepancies: between what universities say they do to recognize good teaching, and what the majority of their academic staff perceive they do; and between the value that most staff would like teaching to be given, and the value which they believe it is in fact given."[1] It is hard to believe that the results would be dramatically different if the same study were conducted at North American universities. What it vividly demonstrates is what we have seen in other anonymous surveys of faculty, that faculty in general value teaching but do not feel authorized to act on this belief.

It is tempting to see the problem as one of an intransigent faculty that needs to be compelled to change against its determined resistance. But the situation is more accurately described as an intransigent faculty that is afraid to change because they fear losing what they have. If this is the case, the most effective route to change may be not compulsion but liberation, giving faculty the freedom to do what they want to do anyway but have been prevented from doing by the structure and culture of their workplaces. Many college and university administrators, quite reasonably given their situations, believe that faculty are intractable resisters. "Yet," Ramsden and Martin conclude, "university teachers, as the survey showed, are not against change. They are in favor of a more professional approach to teaching, valid methods of evaluating teaching and more accountability for good teaching. Preferred methods include peer review, research-based approaches to teaching improvement, and proper training in teaching."[2] The question is not how we can make faculty change; it is how we can let them change.

We should approach that question realizing that any answer we come up with will be fraught with controversy and will inevitably encounter resistance. The very nature of these institutions, as I have described it here, ensures that proposals that promise to unmoor them from their controlling myths and assumptions will trigger an onslaught of defensive routines and efforts to deflect, distract, and derange the argument. And, as we have seen, neither individuals nor organizations can change established habits easily in most cases. This is predictable and inevitable.

The hard truth is that you can't change without changing. It strikes me that in many cases, once we pare away the rhetorical obfuscations and distractions, the arguments against ideas to promote student learning boil down to "You can't do that! It would be different!"

In this chapter I will discuss the need to undermine the instruction myth, to shake the working assumption of most institutions that "excellence" consists of making sure that students are taking classes and moving through them in the prescribed sequence. The instruction myth is the filter that excludes or obscures feedback that would raise doubts about the governing values currently in place. It protects and is protected by the privacy of teaching. The first requirement for learning is feedback. Thus, changing the system so that faculty and the institution get feedback about what goes on in classes and what the consequences are is essential to designing change that will improve results.

At the same time, the privacy of teaching has been a feature of faculty work for decades. We cannot simply and directly make everything transparent. What we could do, what institutions could do today if they wished, is to make the *collective* practices of teachers transparent, while still allowing individual teachers control of their own classes.

THE IMPORTANCE OF FEEDBACK FOR IMPROVING TEACHING

Neither individual teachers nor colleges and universities as institutions can improve core processes without clear feedback on how teachers are teaching and how students are learning. If I don't find out whether my answers to the test questions were right or wrong, I won't do any better the next time I'm tested, even if it's the same test. In learning a new skill or refining an established one, if I don't see the consequences of my performance, then I won't improve. The old bromide that we learn from our mistakes is true, but only if we receive feedback on our performance that allows us to see what our mistakes were. If I don't recognize it as a mistake, I won't correct it.

Many people in many settings repeat the same mistakes over and over again, not because they aim to fail, but because they literally don't know what they're doing. And when they do fail, not understanding the cause, they tend to fall back on Harvey Hornstein's rule of repeated action: do the same thing you did yesterday, but do it faster and better. That is why coaches and directors find that video recordings of games or performances are such effective teaching tools: they show the student what she really did, rather than what she thought she was doing. The first time you watched a video recording of your golf swing or tennis stroke, or of you delivering a public talk, you almost certainly had the reaction, at least once, "Do I do that? I didn't know I was doing that!" Over many years of teaching writing, I have seen repeated confirmation of the insight that the single most effective editorial intervention with most students is simply to have them read out loud a problem passage.

Many beginning writers are prevented from revising their work because, while they know what they meant, they don't know what they have said; they have written it, but they have never really read it. They may look at the words, but they read what they intended rather than what they executed. Reading aloud helps them to hear the words rather than just reimagine the ideas. Growth in any skill depends on getting—or generating—reliable feedback.

Probably the most severe critique we can make of traditional lectures is that they are sealed against effective feedback. When the professor talks for an entire class period and never listens, he insulates himself against information that could help him to teach more effectively. I think this explains in large measure why so many college professors consider themselves excellent teachers. Just as students are terrible at estimating how much they have learned, teachers are terrible at estimating how much they have taught in the absence of feedback. All methods of teaching that camouflage the failure of students to learn will tend to sink to mediocrity, while leaving their practitioners content with the subjective sense of success. Today, colleges and universities as institutions have isolated teachers and denied them the feedback they need to improve. Like the students in the lecture hall, the teacher at the podium is flying blind, denied the information that would allow her to improve.

The lack of feedback combined with the lack of preparation for teaching of most college faculty will tend to push the faculty overall toward middling or worse performance, and not just for the reasons we have already discussed. We have already seen that many faculty members, like many students, tend to overestimate the quality of their own performance and that the absence of a second-order environment around teaching inhibits efforts at improvement. But the tendency to overrate one's own performance is probably not equally distributed and is probably related to the knowledge and ability of the teacher with respect to teaching.

Two Cornell University psychologists, Justin Kruger and David Dunning, conducted a series of experiments to test whether an individual's competence at a task was related to that individual's ability to assess his or her own performance. They reported their findings in their 1999 article with a provocative title that also summarized their conclusions: "Unskilled and Unaware of It: How Difficulties in Recognizing One's Own Incompetence Lead to Inflated Self-Assessments." They conducted a series of four studies in the domains of humor, logical reasoning, and English grammar. What they found was that those who were least competent at a given task were most likely to overestimate their own abilities. Those in the bottom fourth of the performance distribution overestimated their performance by an average of 50 percentile points—a truly massive miscalculation. In part, this seems to be caused by the fact that those who are less competent don't know what competence looks like, and hence have more difficulty in recognizing it in others as well as themselves: "Incompetent individuals lack the metacognitive skills that enable them to tell how poorly they are performing, and as a result, they come to hold inflated views of their performance and ability."[3] Thus, "those who performed particularly poorly relative to their peers were utterly unaware of this fact."[4] Poor performers, literally, don't know what they are doing.

Dunning and Kruger found a somewhat counterintuitive contrary effect among the high performers. Those in the top fourth in terms of performance tended to *underestimate* their own performance in comparison with their peers. Or, to put it another way, they tended to *overestimate* the average performance of their peers. The researchers attribute this in large measure to a *false-consensus effect*: "These participants assumed that because they performed so well, their peers must have performed well likewise."[5]

Thus, both the less skilled and the more skilled suffer from "a dual burden." For unskilled individuals, "not only do they perform poorly, but they fail to realize it." On the other hand, "extremely competent individuals suffer a burden as well. Although they perform competently, they fail to realize that their proficiency is not necessarily shared by their peers."[6]

To the extent that these are tendencies of most people, they have special relevance for the quality of teaching in a feedback-free environment. We should expect that the least competent teachers will overestimate their own abilities the most. At the same time, the most competent teachers will tend to overestimate the abilities of their peers. Professional developers frequently report that voluntary programs for faculty fail to reach those who need them the most. And the conventional wisdom among most faculties is that individual teachers are competent to judge their own needs. It is hard to tell whether people believe this, but it is easy to accept the conventional wisdom because it is rarely challenged in public. It camouflages the weaknesses of those most in need of improvement, and deference to the etiquette imposed by the instruction myth camouflages the camouflage. Nobody talks about it, and it would be rude to talk about why nobody talks about it. Teachers who are in the precontemplation stage of changing their teaching can rationalize inaction on the double grounds that action would be pointless and, anyway, they are doing a fine job already. Thus, the privacy of teaching will tend to further insulate the weakest performers from improvement, and will likewise make it easier for even excellent performers to rationalize that the system works fine.

Dunning and Kruger discovered something else that is relevant here. In one of their studies, the one concerning logical reasoning, after they tested the entire group they put half of them through a training program that taught them how to solve logic problems of the sort on the test. They found, as they had expected, that as people become more competent at a task they also do a better job of evaluating their own performance. Thus, it is not just a matter of people with low metacognition also lacking skill. The lack of skill appears to actively impede the development of accurate self-reflection, and an increase in skill appears to increase the capacity for judging one's own performance. In the absence of feedback that corrects people's misconceptions about their own performance, those who perform poorly will often fail to realize it because their lack of ability camouflages their failure. However, with feedback that can identify deficiencies, those with low ability can increase their ability and at the same time increase their capacity to monitor their own performance. With feedback, they really can learn from their mistakes, rather than just ignoring them and covering them up.

WHAT KINDS OF FEEDBACK?

At the heart of the system that has grown up around the privacy of teaching and the instruction myth is obscurity about what people are actually doing, what I have characterized as "the fog of learning."[7] Teachers do not know what other teachers are doing. So, in the minds of nearly everyone involved, the issues are framed not by the current practice of most real teachers but by personal recollections—intermittent, emotionally charged, and uninterpreted—and by the strongly expressed views of the most ardent defenders of "faculty interests." The absence of information about educational practices and results sustains the instruction myth and the myth of quality while camouflaging declining standards and mediocre performance. Effective feedback would allow institutions to direct their attention where it is needed and to correct deficiencies.

Probably the greatest barrier to a credible feedback system on undergraduate learning is the entrenched power of the departments. Departments, recall, are fundamentally designed as protective shields for graduate training in research. Departments structurally favor the academic discipline over the students, and the students of their discipline over the students of other disciplines. That is not to say that most teachers favor the discipline over the students. But as agents of the department they tend to emphasize what is distinctive about the department, and that is the discipline. The resistance to feedback is rooted in the idea that what is feedback for one department is not relevant to another. Outsiders don't understand what is involved in microbiology/comparative literature/sociology/history/recreational science. Therefore, outsiders cannot judge what we do, and feedback generic enough to apply to several departments really doesn't say much about our distinctive role. Leave us alone to do our job.

There is some truth in this, of course. But there is also a good deal of exaggeration. And there is hardly any truth at all in the idea that good pedagogy is radically different in different disciplines. Of course, content matters. But people learn different content is very similar ways. So while the object of study in hospitality management and algebra is very different, the way the student tunes his or her mind to these very different subjects is very similar. No one should suggest that every subject be reduced to generic skills. But neither should anyone suggest that effective teaching in any discipline is hidden in a black box, incomprehensible to anyone but postdoctoral experts. If that were true, the only people who could "learn" would be those who already understand, which would make education pointless.

The kind of information the system needs is information about its processes and their results, about what people are doing and what the consequences are. So every institution should create systems to make that information available.

THE TEACHING INVENTORY

In terms of educational practices, the first thing we need to know is what they are, what the teachers are doing. The most striking thing about the current situation is that most college administrators, to say nothing of teachers, have very little information about what is going on in their classrooms. Ask them how many students are taking which classes, how many complete them, and what grades they receive, and you will get answers immediately. But what the students are experiencing, how they are taught in those classes—that is largely a closed book. Some colleges are getting information about the overall distribution of pedagogical practices. For instance, institutions that administer the NSSE or for community colleges the CCSSE get results that indicate how much their students are reading and writing in their classes, how long they are studying, whether they are working in groups with other students, and related information. But this is generalized information that can't be localized to specific classes or programs unless the surveys are specially targeted. So they may find out that there are problems, but not where the problems come from. At many institutions that do administer these surveys, many faculty members simply ignore the results because they see them as irrelevant to their daily work. They are about others, not about me. And the Dunning-Kruger Effect makes it likely that those who should pay the closest attention to such evidence will be the most likely to ignore it.

I have asked dozens of deans and provosts what they know about the pedagogical practices of their faculties. The answer has almost always been that, beyond the small scope of classes they have personally observed, they don't know and don't have any way of finding out how their teachers are teaching. At the urging of Carl Wieman, the American Association of Universities and the American Association of Public and Land Grant Universities polled their membership on whether they collected data on the teaching practices that teachers used in science and technology courses. Wieman asked the same question of those in attendance at a meeting of presidents and chancellors of institutions belonging to the Association of American Colleges and Universities. The results were unanimous: "No institution reported collecting data on the teaching practices in use in its courses."[8]

In the realm of pedagogy, it is not a judgment but a simple statement of fact that institutions do not know what they are doing. In the age of big data, at institutions that frequently boast of their commitment to "data-driven decision making," there are no data at all about the core practices that define the institution. They do not know what students are learning, to be sure. But it is worse than that. They do not even know how teachers are teaching.

There is a simple, quick, and essentially free way of finding out: an inventory of pedagogical practices. Carl Wieman, when he was working in the

White House Office of Science and Technology Policy, suggested that universities receiving federal research grants should report their pedagogical practices. That suggestion went nowhere in the face of serious resistance from the presidents of major research universities. Since then he has collaborated with Sarah Gilbert, director of the Carl Wieman Science Education Initiative at the University of British Columbia (UBC), to develop a Teaching Practices Inventory or TPI.[9] It is essentially a checklist of teaching practices covering the range of subjects that have been found in research to have a significant effect on student learning, including course information, supporting materials, in-class activities, assignments, feedback and testing, and collaboration. For example, the inventory asks teachers how many tests they give and how many assignments of various kinds, what portion of questions require the students to produce an explanation, how and how often they ask for feedback from students, in what portion of classes they lecture, how often students work in groups, and a variety of other matters. The questions are all based on careful research, and generate a profile of effective pedagogy.[10]

They have tested the inventory in over two hundred courses at UBC and report that the instructor can complete it in less than ten minutes. It can produce a report of the distribution of teaching practice by individual faculty members, individual classes, departments, colleges, and universities. Wieman and Gilbert propose that this inventory be used to evaluate faculty because it reports faculty activities that have been linked clearly to better student learning. While I think this is an excellent idea, and would be a vast improvement over reliance on student evaluations, I also think that an inventory of this sort could be a powerful tool to provide feedback to the faculty and the institution.

The TPI specifically may not be appropriate for all classes, but it seems to me an excellent template to be used where possible and adapted where necessary. It is designed for use mainly in math, science, and engineering classes at research universities. It includes questions about teaching assistants, for example, and would have to be adjusted for colleges that don't use teaching assistants extensively. It could probably be applied directly to most social science classes, though it has yet to be tested in such classes. Wieman and Gilbert report that it doesn't seem to work in, for example, small seminar classes and performance-based classes. So different tools will need to be developed for different contexts. But the research on which the TPI is based applies generally to nearly all college classes, and it would not be daunting to develop parallel tools appropriate to different kinds of classes and even for cocurricular experiences.

Several groups and individuals have worked on similar questionnaires that reflect how teachers are teaching. One of the most promising is the Postsecondary Instructional Practices Survey (PIPS), developed by Emily M. Walter of California State University, Fresno and Charles R. Henderson, Andrea L. Beach, and Cody T. Williams of the Mallinson Institute for Science Education at Western Michigan University.[11] While developed mainly by science educators, this survey of twenty-four questions could be applied in any course or discipline. It seeks to identify whether instructors are practicing student-centered pedagogy and could be used, like the TPI, to identify strengths and weaknesses in a teacher's approach, to set goals for improvement, and to compare teachers between disciplines and within disciplines.

Another means, and a complementary one, of providing a rudimentary inventory of teaching practices would be to ask the students. The great weakness of student evaluations of teaching (SET), as we have already discussed, is that they usually provide context-free opinions about the quality of teaching. But such surveys could provide context, could ask students not only what they think of the teacher but what they did in the class. The NSSE is a foundational model for how to do this. And there is a classroom-based version of the NSSE that could be applied widely. Many of the questions in the TPI and the PIPS could be asked of students as easily as of teachers and would provide much more information about what actually happened in class. The PIPS, for example, asks teachers to rank themselves on a scale of one to four on how descriptive of their teaching the following statements are: "I structure class so that students regularly talk with one another about course concepts," "I require students to work in small groups," "I structure problems so that students consider multiple approaches to finding a solution."[12] Such questions could be asked of students as readily as of teachers, and if they were asked of both the resulting information would be much more valuable as an indicator of how teaching really happens in a class. With just a few additional questions, the SET could ask students how they spend time in class, whether they did collaborative work, what kinds of assignments they did, how much they read, and how much they wrote, spoke, or performed. Such information could be easily aggregated by course and program to put together a profile of how teachers are teaching, which could complement the teachers' own accounts of their teaching. Both differences and similarities would be revealing.

The individual teacher's report could be included as part of a teaching portfolio and kept largely private. But the aggregate report should be made public. And such a tool could inform students and parents about the institution if uniformly required as part of the accreditation process. Such an inventory could also provide an initial baseline that would allow the institution to track its progress, to keep an ongoing record of whether it was improving in pedagogical practices.

Such a teaching inventory would provide a glimpse into how teachers, in general and in specific programs, were teaching. In most cases it would be the first time that such information was collected. We could see at a glance, for example, whether students were mainly assessed by multiple-choice, short-answer, or essay exams or by performance. We could see whether most teachers lectured most of the time and whether their lectures were interactive or monologic and whether most teachers involved students in group work. We could see whether some departments or schools tended to lean toward a different set of pedagogical practices than others. And after a few applications, such an inventory would show us whether pedagogical practices change over time, and how. If teaching matters, these are things we should know. Indeed, the information generated by such an inventory would instantly be a better tool to evaluate a faculty member, a program, or an institution than any of those widely used today.

A teaching inventory would be a step toward changing the faculty culture. The privacy of teaching and the instruction myth cast people back on their own experience in their assumptions about how most teaching is done because there is no reliable evidence of actual practice. In Ramsden and Martin's study in Australia, recall, 74 percent of faculty wanted to introduce innovations in their teaching. Yet, even when significant innovation is going on, it is largely invisible.

We have seen that groupthink thrives in an environment in which people who might have a different point of view censor themselves because they feel isolated and fear retribution. This is why gathering anonymous information about teaching practice has the potential to reveal the existence of enclaves of diversity and to reduce the motivation for self-censorship. We have also seen that the Dunning-Kruger Effect leads poor performers to overestimate their effectiveness and hence avoid rather than seek out opportunities for improvement. Concrete feedback on general practices and the range of practice will tend to reveal rather than conceal where improvement is needed.

And if departments were to have direct evidence of how their teachers were teaching, it would undermine the power of defensive routines in deflecting ideas for change.

William Massy, a former vice-provost at Stanford who has grappled with the dynamics of departments for years, has proposed an idea that would almost certainly change the framework that departments use to think about teaching: the Departmental Teaching Improvement Portfolio. He proposes that "the data in the portfolio would cover course design and redesign activities, together with the evidence that led to the design choices and the results obtained from implementation. Because compilation would be a collective departmental responsibility, most, if not all, faculty would be expected to contribute and learn about others' contributions. The fundamental objective would be to develop information and human capital that can be used by everyone, currently and in the future, to further the cause of student learning."[13] Now imagine that the department had the data from the Teaching Inventory for every faculty member. This would allow the Teaching Improvement Portfolio to be evidence-based from the outset and to track developments in pedagogy and course design through time. Such a portfolio at the department level, of course, could be easily generated at an institution with a Teaching Quality Framework (TQF), as described in the last chapter. Today, departmental groupthink derives much of its power from ignorance. If nobody knows what is really happening, the pressure to go along with the conventional wisdom is powerful. But if the department really has such an evidence-based portfolio to support the discussion, they could have a real conversation. It would make departments smarter about teaching and learning.

Of course, in some places a teaching inventory would reveal very little diversity of practice, very rare instances of experimentation or innovative practices. Where this is the case, it is important to know it. I suspect that at most institutions the teaching inventory would reveal a good deal more diversity of practice than is visible on the surface and would thus lead to a ferment of inquiry and activity concerning the alternatives. Most colleges and universities are conducting SoTL research in secret; they are trying out a range of new approaches but hiding the fact—from themselves as well as from others. But those that are stuck in conventional practices in a serious way need to know that, so that they can compare their performance with other institutions that are notably different.

Perhaps the most important effect of something like a teaching inventory is that, if done regularly, it would be a powerful support for faculty at the contemplation stage to move into planning. If many people are changing their practice, how risky could it be? Just by creating feedback about the fact of change, such a system would encourage improvement.

Faculty engaged in research are accustomed to receiving feedback on their research and writing. From undergraduate papers through the dissertation and perhaps postdoctoral fellowships and articles, a faculty member's sense of his or her work as a researcher is densely informed by the reactions, ideas, and suggestions of other people. When it comes to teaching, however, most live in a bubble, a feedback-free environment—free not just of information about their own teaching but of information on the norms and behaviors of other teachers. The default assumption is often that nearly all teachers must teach as I was taught. A teaching inventory has the potential to dislodge the naïve assumptions about common practices that hold many teachers in place.

As we have already seen, the differences within most colleges and universities are much greater than the differences between them. Still, the range of options available at a given institution is important. The teaching inventory would tell us much more about the actual educational experience available at most institutions than is available to anyone today—even to the presidents and provosts of those institutions. More significantly, information about how teachers are teaching their classes would allow the institution to weigh evidence about the outcomes of those classes, to connect learning success with teaching practice.

15 · THE OUTCOMES TRANSCRIPT AND PORTFOLIO

Gathering and feeding back to the institution reliable information about how teachers teach would be an important step toward breaking down the instruction myth. But it would be a partial step. The other half of the equation is how and what students learn.

The most important document for most students, today, is the transcript of grades. It is important because it determines whether they will be granted a degree or leave college without one. It is the document that—not just for students but for employers, parents, foundations, and government—defines "success" in college. The transcript of grades, as we have already seen, is a deeply flawed document. It provides a global evaluation of all a student's work in classes, but it does not contain any information to contextualize that evaluation or to indicate exactly what was being evaluated. And as average grades have risen over the past thirty years or so, the effective range in which they are usually assigned has narrowed. Thus sometimes small variations in average grades take on vast significance in the minds of students. Yet as grades have risen overall, they have actually become less important to employers as an index of ability. Hence the enthusiasm for badges and other confirmations of competence that could serve the purpose that the transcript of grades no longer serves—if it ever did. Overwhelmingly, institutions have attempted to measure their performance by the number of students completing courses, getting instructed, as measured by their grades. As Jon F. Wergin, a professor of education at Virginia Commonwealth University, has pointed out, "In an attempt to become more accountable and to mollify its critics, Western higher education has embarked upon a highly dangerous course of chasing measures of quality that may have little to do with quality itself."[1]

For decades many educators have argued that what is called for is a more specific indicator of what students have learned or can do as a result of their college experience: explicit statements of learning outcomes for each student. At one level, this effort has been largely successful. Nearly every accredited college and university has spelled out and published a set of student learning outcomes. They have done this, for the most part, because each of the regional accrediting organizations has made it a condition of accreditation. On the other hand, different institutions make quite different use of these learning outcomes. In many cases the team of accreditors that visits the college is deluged with data on student learning outcomes, while most of the students at the same institution have never heard of such things. At the high end, some institutions are attempting to identify the competencies or abilities that students should achieve and documenting their achievement. But overall, learning outcomes have been approached, as Peter Ewell put it, much more with an eye to accountability than to improvement. This is one reason why the Lumina Foundation developed the Degree Qualifications Profile (DQP).

STUDENT LEARNING OUTCOMES ARE MORE IMPORTANT THAN GRADES

Student learning outcomes have two major advantages over course grades as indicators of students' progress. First, they mean something in particular. And in theory and aspiration, they mean the same thing to everybody. Grades mean different things to different people. Ohmer Milton, Howard Pollio, and James Eison, in *Making Sense of College Grades*—still, after nearly thirty years, perhaps the best analysis of the grading phenomenon—point out, "A grade is a unidimensional symbol into which multidimensional phenomena have been incorporated, a true salmagundi. Translated this means a given grade can reflect level of information, attitudes, procrastination, errors or misconceptions, cheating, and mixtures of all of these plus other ingredients; all of this was noted in the literature over fifty years ago as well as today and is well known but ignored. The lone letter symbol is a conglomerate which specifies none of its contents."[2]

There are programs in which faculty develop common grading standards and attempt to apply them. These are promising, but are also few and far between. And even if the faculty in a single department or course sequence do have common standards, those standards are lost to the world as soon as the letter is engraved on the transcript. Grades usually do mean something, and often something worth knowing, to the instructor who gives them, and perhaps—or perhaps not—for the students who receive them. But that meaning is lost for everyone else.

Student learning outcomes, on the other hand, need to be defined by specific rubrics that will be used not by a single teacher but by every teacher who assesses a student's performance in terms of that outcome. These rubrics apply across different courses and in many cases across different disciplines. And the criteria for accomplishment—the rubrics themselves—are public, not private. A student rating on a learning outcome makes a specific claim about what the student has done and can do. For institutions that are moving toward incorporating the DQP and others that have adopted a digital portfolio of student work, the faculty rating of the student is connected to actual student work that is preserved as evidence of achieving the learning outcome. At the very highest level of assessment, faculty write narrative evaluations for students to explain their learning progress, thus making specific and explicit the value of the learning experience. This is the practice, for example, at Alverno College, which organizes its curriculum around the abilities that constitute the intended learning outcomes, and provides narrative evaluations for each student, dispensing with grades altogether. Alverno has also been an exemplar of authentic assessment, assessment that is based on student performance, not just tests. But even if institutions do not go that far, by recognizing and recording student learning, they would raise the quality of assessment and of the degree. For institutions that have sought to define specific competencies that will be required for the degree, standard assessments and performances are required of all students who want the competency confirmed. So there is a range of sophistication, but learning outcomes are always more specific than grades.

The second area in which learning outcomes have a significant advantage over grades is pedagogy. End-of-term grades rarely function as feedback to students to guide future learning. Assessments of learning outcomes—when the student finds out what they are!—almost always do. Grades are vague but permanent. Because a grade is linked to a specific class, the grade cannot be changed without retaking the class. This is both time-consuming and difficult—often impossible. Thus, most students do not see grades as feedback, both because they do not provide any specific information on how to improve and because their finality fairly well excludes the possibility of improvement. For the student who has a C in chemistry or European history, it matters not at all how much she learns or what she does afterward. She could win the Nobel Prize in chemistry or publish works of insight on history; the C will remain on her transcript until the day she dies—and longer. As certain as taxes and as permanent as death, your transcript will survive longer than you do.

The transcript of grades consists of a series of evaluative snapshots frozen in time. Even for the student who graduates "on time" after four years (and they are in the minority today), his freshman grades report his performance in discrete classes four years ago, yet stand as evidence of his current knowledge and abilities. This is a fiction that nobody believes but everybody accepts; it is part of the instruction myth.

Unlike grades, learning outcomes can be evaluated many times in different contexts. Alexander Astin points out that "to generate grades, the professor needs only to compare students with *each other* at a single point in time, whereas to assess the learning that is taking place that professor needs to compare individual students with *themselves* at different points in time."[3] This is even more the case when we look at the whole progress of the student through the curriculum. The student who fails to achieve satisfactory performance in analytical reasoning or written communication can do so later in the same class, or failing that, a different class. If learning were the focus, faculty would spend more time assessing student progress than student status. And in a growing number of cases a student can be assessed on some learning outcomes outside of class, in service or extracurricular activities where many students do their best work. End-of-semester grades are pure evaluation, usually without any element of feedback, simply because the task they are evaluating can never be done again. Learning outcomes in one class can serve as feedback to students, pointing to how they can improve their performance in future classes, where the same abilities will be assessed again, and in life outside of class.

An increasing number of institutions are moving toward a portfolio of student work that includes products of student learning. These portfolios vary greatly in their value. Some are little more than digital scrapbooks of student assignments. The best, however, are organized as evidence of student progress in the institutional learning outcomes, with samples of student work that demonstrate the growing mastery of these outcomes. The framework of student learning outcomes, combined with the substance of a digital portfolio of student work, promise an alternative to the transcript of grades, a record of actual learning more specific, credible, detailed, and relevant to students' goals.

The portfolio of student work also serves the purpose of keeping the outcomes honest, of providing concrete evidence of the student learning asserted in the outcomes. Some faculty members, especially in the arts and humanities, have expressed the fear that learning outcomes will become reductionistic, a kind of process checklist separated from the substance of learning. Because most learning outcomes are not discipline-specific, some fear that will shift attention to skills and away from knowledge. A well-designed portfolio of student work can ensure that the range of important learning that the institution values can be represented by solid evidence of real accomplishment.

Accreditors and reformers have adopted the idea that if colleges and universities take learning seriously they need to be able to say what they want students to learn and find out whether they have learned it. Hence all institutions are required to define student learning outcomes and assess students' progress toward those outcomes. But it follows that if learning outcomes really are significant evidence of student learning, the institution must record and preserve that evidence. If the college preserves the transcript of grades but discards the report of learning outcomes, students will pay attention to grades and ignore learning outcomes. And it is perfectly reasonable that they should do so. At a minimum, institutions should preserve the equivalent of a transcript of outcomes assessments for each student, parallel to the transcript of grades. The DQP strongly suggests this. As Peter Ewell notes, "The DQP approach requires a comprehensive record-keeping system for posting, housing, and manipulating data on what students have learned."[4]

Of course, to develop a comprehensive record-keeping system for learning outcomes an institution would have to ensure that all faculty were directly involved in assessing learning outcomes. That means it could not be relying simply on taking a statistical sample of students and giving them some sort of test. It would have to have teachers assessing learning outcomes, inside or outside of classes, using common rubrics. That is the ideal that the DQP points toward, and for very good reason. That means that every teacher must have a stake in measuring and reporting student learning. Late in 2016, an administrator at one of the most elite research universities in the country reported at a conference that at his institution 50 percent of the faculty had defined learning outcomes for their classes in their course syllabi. His point was the vast improvement over just a few years ago. No one will challenge this institution's accreditation, but clearly there is a double standard at work. If he reported that only 50 percent of the faculty were assigning grades, they would lose their accreditation. An institution that assesses learning outcomes for only a sample of students, or for only those faculty who decide to take the time, can provide a report to accreditors, and perhaps some feedback to its planning process. But it is, by definition, not providing feedback to its students or to its faculty. Thus, those who are supposed to be central to the process do not profit from it; the learners learn nothing from this exercise.

AN OUTCOMES TRANSCRIPT

Alexander Astin concludes that "the profit of any educational institution is learning, so one might expect that college faculty would regularly gather data that reflects what their students are learning and how they are growing and developing during their time in college. Such data would not only be collected, but also be expected to occupy the attention of the faculty at least as much as any other information about students or the institution."[5] Recording student performance on learning outcomes would be no more complicated than recording grades in classes, which today is remarkably simple, almost always done online by clicking a box. Ideally, of course, such evaluations would be accompanied by narratives of student progress by faculty and documentation of it through a portfolio. But the basic record of accomplishment could be as simple as the current transcript. With the transcript of grades, institutions already have the ability to keep personal information private and aggregate the overall data in a variety of ways. It is a simple matter to report the average grades and distribution of grades for each individual teacher, for a course, for a department, and for a college. The same thing could be easily done for learning outcomes, and the software to do it is readily available. A number of private companies have developed systems for easily recording learning outcomes, using the rubrics internally developed by the college, and then aggregating the results in any way the institution wishes.[6] Several such systems have the capacity to automatically generate an outcomes transcript for every student, and also to store and aggregate all the outcome data. Such data can then be organized horizontally (How are all the students in Algebra 1 performing on the whole array of learning outcomes?) and vertically (How are the students who took Algebra 1 last year performing on quantitative reasoning learning outcomes this year?). Such systems already exist. But certainly, if there were a demand, the supply would quickly follow.

What is interesting about some of these programs is that while they are widely used today by colleges and universities, they are rarely—if ever— configured in such a way as to provide comprehensive feedback to students or faculty on their overall learning outcomes profile. They are more commonly used for accreditation data than for student feedback or program planning. If learning outcomes really are important to institutions, why do they not preserve the data on student learning that these outcomes generate and use them in their planning and decision making?

The record of student progress toward achieving significant learning outcomes offers a tool that both the student and the institution could use as powerful feedback on what works and what doesn't for learning. For students, performance on learning outcomes—unlike course grades—indicates specific strengths and weaknesses and allows them to direct their efforts and plan their activities to improve future work. And a record of learning outcomes assessment would help advisers to direct students toward courses and activities that will directly serve their needs. Advisement at many institutions is based largely on averages and guesswork. Rarely do counselors or faculty advisors have much credible information about the students' real learning needs or strengths. Learning outcomes assessments based on reasonably specific rubrics would guide advisors in guiding students toward courses and programs that could address their needs. For the institution, the overall profile of student performance on the whole range of learning outcomes indicates strengths and weaknesses in the curriculum and in teaching that can allow the institution to plan with a real index of success—something that most lack today.

And if the institution is conducting a teaching inventory, it can aggregate outcomes data in a way that links them with pedagogy; thus, it can create an ongoing source of information on the outcomes of programs and teachers. Learning outcomes information is specific enough that it can point us to weaknesses and inconsistencies in the system. One of the objections made to learning outcomes, of course, is that different teachers will employ different standards—because they will fail to understand the rubrics, fail to understand the rubrics in the same way, or ignore the rubrics. These are possible weaknesses in the use of learning outcomes. They are guaranteed deficiencies in the system of letter grades, where there are no common rubrics at all.

But while there is no way of testing for these inconsistencies and hence correcting them with letter grades, it would be an easy matter to both test for and address the problem in terms of learning outcomes. If two professors, for example, assign the same students significantly different rubric scores on the same outcome, then that suggests that the teachers are using different standards or that different assignments are not really assessing the same outcome. Or it may suggest a weakness in the rubric or inconsistent performance by the student. With that feedback, that there is an apparent inconsistency in the way outcomes are being assessed, it makes sense to get some professors together and test the rubrics for consistency. Good rubrics should not be static; we should always be developing and improving them. A rubric for learning outcomes is not a set of rules; it is a language for communication. So a rubric needs to be tested with teachers and students, and revised when it can make the exchange of information more effective. The rubrics should become a framework for an ongoing conversation, one that will change both teachers and students, as they learn what is meaningful and valuable to one another. Learning outcomes are much more powerful tools for learning than letter grades because where grades camouflage and conceal differences in standards and confusion about goals, learning outcomes reveal these things and hence make learning—individual and organizational—possible.

The institution with a comprehensive learning outcomes database could look for correlations that suggest patterns. It would make sense to start looking in places where prior research already directs our attention. Do students taking certain groupings of classes do better in some learning outcomes than those taking different combinations? We even know, from course cluster analysis, some of the groupings to look for. Do students who move vertically through the curriculum in certain patterns maintain and improve their performance better than others? Do certain courses or departments seem to produce "spillover effects"? That is, do students taking some classes do better in learning outcomes not assessed in those classes but in other classes they are taking at the same time? Much of the information we could gain from a comprehensive database of learning outcomes would point to connections, both positive and negative, that would rarely be noticed within a single department or course but that could be significant for the design of the curriculum and for advising students. Indeed, if advisors had access to learning outcomes results, it would empower them to provide much more specific and useful advice.

And if we had even a reasonably accurate description of how teachers were teaching, we could look for relationships between pedagogy and outcomes. Do students who take classes where they write more than average do better on communication outcomes in subsequent semesters? Do students who take classes with more active learning approaches show better or worse transfer of outcomes in subsequent classes? Where there is a reasonably clear contrast in pedagogical approaches between sets of classes, it would be an easy matter to track the learning outcomes results in subsequent experiences. An outcomes transcript could be a tool for validating and revising the teaching inventory, refining it to reveal and hence promote the best pedagogy.

A student's learning is not contained by a class—or if it is, we're in trouble, because the learning is unlikely to survive the end of the class. Today, the individual class and its individual teacher frame nearly the whole experience of the student as student. The master question for the successful student is "What does this teacher want?" The answer to that question provides the key to the fungible reward that the class offers: the grade. What a global learning outcomes transcript creates is an alternate frame for the student's educational experience. No longer is the learning contained by the class; the class is contained by the larger frame of learning outcomes. So what happens in one class is relevant to what happens in the next. And even the general education curriculum, which is today a hodgepodge of miscellaneous and unconnected requirements, could become an actual curriculum, a coherent path with a destination.

If faculty are in fact assessing students in terms of defined learning outcomes—and nearly every college president and provost will tell you that they are—then it is hard to see why institutions would not collect and aggregate that information to create a flow of feedback to faculty and students. Well, perhaps it is not so hard to see. For to do so would undermine both the privacy of teaching and the instruction myth by revealing gaps and inconsistencies in the learning experience of many students.

An outcomes transcript combined with a portfolio of student work would provide more credible evidence of accomplishment to employers and other institutions, as well as the general public. It would make the degree more meaningful. Employers increasingly doubt the value of both the degree and grades as an indicator of much anything. In 2014, the polling firm Hart Research Associates was commissioned by the Association of American Colleges and Universities (AAC&U) to conduct a survey of employers across the country who hire college graduates. The employers endorsed most of the standard learning outcomes that the AAC&U has defined by a large margin. But fewer than half found the college transcript useful in evaluating job candidates. Only 9 percent found it "very useful." In contrast, 80 percent said that they would like to see an electronic portfolio of student work "summarizing and demonstrating accomplishments in key skill and knowledge areas."[7] For most employers, the instruction myth is no longer persuasive. They are much more interested in substantive learning outcomes than in college grades, and are especially interested in the concrete evidence for the learning outcomes, such as a digital portfolio might contain.

Dissatisfaction with the traditional transcript has been growing for years, and several experiments are under way to find alternatives. The American Association of Collegiate Registrars and Admissions Officers and the National Association of Student Personnel Administrators, an organization of student affairs professionals, have joined together in the Comprehensive Student Record Project, funded by the Lumina Foundation. The eleven institutions involved are all developing alternatives to the transcript that reflect more than just grades in classes. Frequently they involve portfolios of student work and evidence of student accomplishment outside of classes, in research, service, and cocurricular activities.

One of the more interesting examples is the University of Central Oklahoma's (UCO) Student Transformative Learning Record (STLR—pronounced "stellar"). UCO has long been committed to the goal of transformative learning, rooted in the work of Jack Mezirow and other scholars of adult learning. Transformative learning is more than content knowledge, it is learning that changes students at a metacognitive level, making them more self-conscious and intentional learners. UCO has embodied this goal in the six tenets that they present as the goals of undergraduate education: discipline knowledge; global and cultural competencies; health and wellness; leadership; research, creative, and scholarly activities; and service learning and civic engagement. The first tenet, discipline knowledge, is assessed through the traditional transcript of grades. The other five fall under the purview of STLR. They began with the AAC&U's VALUE Rubrics (it stands for Valid Assessment of Learning in Undergraduate Education). STLR assigned to the VALUE learning outcomes "badges" for each tenet that students can earn either through course work or through work in other settings such as community service or cocurricular activities. The student has an online dashboard that shows his or her badging in each of the tenets, which reflect accomplishment at three levels: exposure, integration, or transformation. The dashboard is also linked to the student portfolio that contains the artifacts of student work demonstrating the learning.

The portfolio is developed using the Integrative Knowledge Portfolio Process (IKPP), developed by Melissa Peet and her colleagues at the University of Michigan. Peet found from focus groups that students at Michigan, while they reported "extraordinary" learning experiences, "could not describe what they had learned, why it was valuable to them or how they might apply the knowledge and/or skills they had gained once they left the university."[8] IKPP uses collaborative student groups and a formal process of interviews and goal setting to help students to "synthesize learning from various experiences and understand the relevance and potential application of that learning to the world beyond the classroom."[9] With STLR, and very much unlike the traditional transcript, students can demonstrate progress with "tagged" assignments in classes, out-of-class activities, and self-designed projects.

The university began bringing new students into the process in 2012 and it continues to expand. So far, the evidence is that students who have participated in STLR have been more likely to stay in college and have earned higher grades than those who have not. For instance, from the fall of 2015 to the fall of 2016, those who had created at least one learning artifact assessed by the STLR rubrics had a retention rate of 77.7 percent, while those who had not participated in STLR at all had a rate of 57.9 percent.[10] In addition, according to Jeff King, executive director of the Center for Transformative Teaching and Learning at UCO, "STLR engagement darned near eliminates the achievement/retention gap that exists among first-generation, low-SES, and underrepresented students."[11]

Other institutions are experimenting with alternative transcripts and student portfolios, in many cases using the AAC&U VALUE rubrics. We see a variety of alternative transcripts in the making and many formats for student portfolios linked to these transcripts. In most of the cases that I have seen, the supplementary transcript is far more useful than the transcript of grades because it carries real information about what students have learned and how they have progressed over time.

Like the teaching inventory, the outcomes transcript can be an engine to drive improvement in undergraduate education by undermining the instruction myth and disabling the defensive routines that surround and protect it.

16 · CHANGING THE FACULTY ENDOWMENT

Colleges, of course, hope for great teachers. But they do very little to produce them or reward them. Their efforts, as a practical matter, are overwhelmingly devoted to producing great researchers. They pay lip service to teaching, but they rarely if ever sacrifice research possibilities for the sake of making teaching better. And even institutions that do not invest much effort in research seem to have achieved no clearer focus on teaching, for the reasons we have discussed.

The myth of the unity of research and teaching leads to a serious category error that undermines the capacity of people to think coherently about education. If research and teaching are in the same category, then it makes sense to give those with the greatest demonstrated expertise the most control. However, teaching and research are not in the same category. They are different and essentially unrelated activities. Institutions have given tenured faculty, administrators, and department chairs almost complete control over undergraduate education. These people are for the most part accomplished and successful researchers, serious experts in their academic disciplines. But many of them know little or nothing about how undergraduates learn, how teaching advances or impairs learning, or how to make teaching better. The assumption that expert researchers are also expert teachers is without foundation and leads to a situation where smart people do foolish things because they don't even know what questions to ask, much less how to answer them.

As we have seen, the status quo bias is rooted, in large measure, in the fear of loss. Because most of us are loss averse, we value what we already have—what we have the potential to lose—more highly that what we haven't yet acquired. This is the endowment effect, which we discussed in chapters 3 and 4. This sense of endowment begins to develop in graduate school and then is reinforced by the conditions of working at a college or university.

This is not to suggest that colleges and universities should not be engaged in research. Of course, many of them should. But the systemic requirement that all faculty members do research on an ongoing basis and that that research be published has in the end failed to serve either teaching or research very well.

HOW THE EMPHASIS ON RESEARCH HARMS TEACHING

The emphasis on research in graduate school damages teaching in two ways. First, doctoral education at large doesn't do much to prepare students to become teachers. Second, the preparation of the scholars for research careers tends to diminish their chance of becoming effective teachers. By creating an endowment in research early in the academic's career, graduate education tends to reinforce the hedgehog-like focus on narrow research questions. The weight of the evidence suggests that hedgehogs are not as good at research as foxes. That is to say, the best researchers need to have a breadth of perspective and a range of attention that lets them weigh evidence in a way that remains relevant beyond the specific confines of their immediate studies. The best researchers are interdisciplinary. But whatever we think about researchers, there is simply no doubt that effective teaching calls for the foxlike flexibility necessary to communicate with people very different from yourself.

A doctoral student fresh from her dissertation on literary theory is not well placed to address the concerns, doubts, and challenges of undergraduates. The new faculty member who has been immersed for five years in the strictly quantitative analysis of historical or political movements often needs to relearn how to talk to non-mathematicians or risk completely losing his students.

We have already seen that students are often actively discouraged from investing time and effort in teaching by a reward system and a method of socialization to the work that places research above teaching. William Massy summarizes the results of one of the faculty surveys we have examined: "Some respondents characterized teaching awards as 'the kiss of death' for assistant professors: The correlation with gaining tenure is negative, perhaps because the winners put so much time into their teaching."[1] The result is that graduate students and beginning faculty are pressured to reduce the time and effort they expend on understanding their students.

Cognitive diversity—the fox's access to a range of mental tools—is an advantage for anyone, but for a teacher it is a necessity. The teacher's central project is connecting with minds that embark from quite different premises and finding common ground with them. This is not controversial. Almost everyone recognizes that the good teacher must be able to explain a complicated subject in "language that students understand." We less often attend to the fact that before a teacher can talk to students in their own language, she must listen to them speak it. And I am not talking about learning the latest slang; I am talking about understanding the cognitive frameworks that students use to build their understanding of the world. The excellent teacher must play quite different roles, understanding the subject like an expert, and comprehending the framework that a novice will use. The excellent teacher must be at once the master and the beginner, the expert and the novice. She must see not only how to avoid errors, but how to make them, so that she can guide others in finding out how to avoid and correct them. The pure hedgehog-researcher, the subject matter expert who has no time for error or confusion, is often a skilled incompetent as a teacher, a smart person doing a bad job. One of the reasons that it is not easy for institutions to create a career track for teaching is that the academic preparation of most new faculty members does not prepare them to teach, and in fact prepares them not to teach. This leads to a couple of significant questions.

HOW SHOULD WE PREPARE TEACHERS?

First, does it make sense to require the doctorate of college teachers? It is very hard to see how it does, as the doctorate is presently configured. The Ph.D. in most conventional disciplines makes little sense as preparation for a career in teaching. (I may have a bias here because I taught for over thirty years without a doctorate and found myself—and my students, I suspect—none the worse for it. I have attempted to base the views I present here on more solid evidence, though.) Efforts to create a more teacher-friendly doctorate have so far foundered. So, second, if the doctorate as presently designed is not a qualification for teaching, how should it be redesigned? A degree that truly prepared students to become teachers would be a different kind of degree than today's Ph.D.

There is a long-standing belief in many sectors of higher education that a master's degree is not sufficient preparation for college teaching. And as presently configured that graduate degree has many of the deficiencies of the doctorate, but is shorter. But, frankly, shorter might be better in many ways. It is hard to believe that seven to ten years fussing with a narrow dissertation topic will make anyone a better teacher. Two or three years devoted to thoroughly understanding the discipline and its pedagogical challenges would make a good deal more sense, especially if the graduate studies were integrated with supervised teaching practice. A master's degree is generally accepted as qualification for teaching in community colleges and often for teaching lower division courses at four-year institutions. If such a degree were configured specifically to prepare teachers, it might be able to meet needs to which today it is not applied.

Institutions are already increasingly forced to rely on faculty without doctorates. While nearly 60 percent of all full-time college teachers, at all levels, had the doctorate in 2003, only slightly more than 17 percent of part-time teachers did. Even among public research universities, where nearly 74 percent of full-time faculty had doctorates, fewer than 36 percent of part-time faculty did.[2] Ronald Ehrenberg, an economist and director of the Cornell Higher Education Research Institute, predicts "it is likely that the share of undergraduate instruction done by faculty with doctoral degrees will be declining in the future because the increasing scarcity of faculty positions that are full-time tenure or tenure-track positions will likely dampen the already decreasing interest of American students in pursuing doctoral study."[3]

I do not make a very original point in suggesting that the doctorate needs to be either replaced or reformed. The Carnegie group made several excellent suggestions that one hopes will be widely followed. "In a contest," they wrote, "where research so easily trumps teaching, we envision developing each novice scholar into a powerful teacher and researcher simultaneously through repeated practice that moves the student along both trajectories."[4] Some institutions are attempting that, and we should wish them well.

Alternatives to the traditional dissertation are much talked about and are being tentatively tried in some places. Teaching tends to be emphasized more in some fields than in others.

Michael Palmer, a professional developer at the University of Virginia, and some colleagues have conducted surveys of research universities to find out what kind of preparation they are providing graduate students. They gathered information either from surveys, interviews, or examining the institutional web pages from 268 institutions that are involved in preparing doctoral students. More than half of the institutions (56.7 percent) offered TA preparation programs. About 35 percent had some program to certify teaching ability, either at the institutional or disciplinary level. Over half offered some courses in higher education pedagogy. A few institutions (5.6 percent) offered a minor in teaching.[5]

It is difficult to tell just what these programs entail. And it is often difficult to tell how many graduate students profit from them because they are often voluntary. Some of them are limited to nuts-and-bolts approaches to grading and lecture. Others are much more sophisticated and involve real preparation for research-based teaching. But Elizabeth Chandler of the University of Chicago reviewed specific courses in pedagogy offered at thirty-one research universities. Some were graded, some pass/fail, some not evaluated at all. Looking at the syllabi for these courses she could find no clear coverage of the idea of pedagogical content knowledge, the question of what knowledge and learning is essential for undergraduates: "Competency in choosing content that is pedagogically appropriate for undergraduates . . . appears to have been somehow lost, forgotten."[6] So something is going on, but it is hard to tell how deep it goes or how seriously it should be taken. It seems clear, however, that the vast majority of graduate students are still not receiving any serious preparation for teaching.

Linda von Hoene of UC Berkeley reports that about seventy-five universities now grant some sort of certificate for teaching. She received responses from forty-seven for her 2010 survey. For many of these, the University of Michigan and the University of California, Santa Barbara are two examples, seeking the certificate is voluntary. At UCSB the Certificate of College and University Teaching requires that students serve as teaching assistants at least twice and teach at least one course as the instructor of record. Students begin to build a teaching portfolio, and program staff review the teaching and the portfolio. Some of the certificates involve course work, some only workshops. Some appear on the transcript, some do not. Of the institutions that von Hoene surveyed, only six offered certificates before 1995, so there has been considerable growth in such programs. But the great majority of them are voluntary, and many are competitive and reach only a relatively few students.[7] It is hard to assess how such certificates affect the job prospects of applicants.

What we need for the next generation of faculty is a degree that is designed to prepare teachers. Idaho State University in 2009 replaced its old Doctor of Arts program with a Ph.D. in English and the Teaching of English. According to Jessica Winston, director of graduate studies, "the program trains conscientious, reflective, and versatile scholar teachers whose primary career goals lie in college-level teaching."[8] Students study pedagogy and learning. As is conventional in almost every graduate program, the students serve as teaching assistants and teach lower division classes. But in addition each doctoral student serves two internships, pairing with a senior faculty member to design a course and teach it. Students are encouraged to do internships with two different professors. The internships get doctoral students to apply what they have learned about student learning and course design, and to do so with the advice and support of an experienced teacher. It also ensures that every student will engage with a senior faculty member on issues of teaching and learning, not research. This is probably beneficial both to the students and to the senior faculty.

The capstone of this Ph.D. program is, of course, the dissertation. But the dissertation is designed to moderate the research requirement and connect it with the teaching role. As is the case with any program, the dissertation should be a work of original research in the field. However, as Winston puts it, "our dissertations are not books and are not aiming to be books."[9] The department believes that doing research in the field will help to prepare students as teachers, but they do not assume that that process will be automatic. Doing the dissertation involves reflecting on and articulating the relevance of this research to the teaching process. Part of the dissertation is a chapter exploring why the dissertation is relevant to the teaching of English. Thus, the teaching question becomes part of the research question. And the object of research becomes not just content knowledge, but explicitly pedagogical content knowledge.

The program handbook projects a four-year graduate program leading to the degree (that is, four years after the master's degree).[10] The idea of a doctorate that has the explicit objective of preparing good teachers is an idea whose time has definitely come.

Even if the degree is not called a teaching degree, every doctoral program that purports to prepare students for faculty positions should prepare them to teach. It should not be a mark of high status and academic respect for programs to focus exclusively on research. It should be seen for what it is, the conquest of skilled incompetence reinforced by groupthink over good sense and rational practice.

There is a place for the pure research degree, which would be appropriate for students who do not intend to become faculty members at all but plan to go into full-time research in labs or research institutes. But such degrees should be the exception, not the rule, and clearly identified as exceptional. If the doctorate is required for college faculty, a doctorate should entail preparation for teaching. And this should not be an option, an add-on, but a central requirement of the degree.

Students considering a doctorate should ask whether the degree will prepare them to become excellent teachers, and should insist on an answer. Parents of undergraduates, and undergraduates themselves, should ask the institutions they are considering what assurance they can have that the faculty have professional training for teaching. Today we can have some assurance that a first-grade teacher in the public schools has some training in how to teach but no such assurance about a professor at a research university. The absurdity of this situation goes unremarked because we have for too long passively accepted the myth of unity. The great and powerful universities in this country, when asked the teaching question, have answered the research question instead, and everyone has proceeded as if that was all right. It is not all right; it never was, and today it urgently requires correction.

TENURE AND THE FACULTY JOB

As we have seen, the most highly valued faculty endowment is tenure. This makes sense in terms of what we know of the endowment effect. The granting of tenure constitutes a promotion, usually accompanied by an increase in salary, so it directly increases one's endowment. But it also entails a guarantee of future employment, and hence secures the whole endowment against the future possibility of loss. As long as tenure is available, it will be an irresistibly attractive option that will tend to shape the thinking of all of those who believe that they might possibly be able to achieve it. It will constitute an endowment inherently more attractive than any other to most people because it projects the security it provides into the future and thus insures against potential loss.

For all the reasons we have discussed, tenure as presently constituted at most four-year colleges is based almost entirely upon research accomplishment and hence inherently invests the faculty endowment in research rather than teaching. All the happy talk and beautiful brochures notwithstanding, that is the current state of things. I believe that tenure as presently constituted creates an irresistible and pervasive bias for the status quo and against reform in the interest of student learning. Time and again we have seen that tenure as presently constituted blocks, deflects, and suppresses change. Institutions, foundations, and governments have been trying for over eighty years to find a way around this barrier and have consistently failed. They continue to fail today.

So if we are serious about student learning, there are really only two alternatives: eliminate tenure or reconstitute it. There is a serious argument in favor of eliminating tenure. And many institutions that have achieved notable results have done so without tenure, institutions such as the Evergreen State College in Washington, Olivet College in Michigan, and Southern New Hampshire University. However, I think that the structural factors arrayed against such a proposal are powerful. All institutions should be engaged in seriously reexamining tenure and seeking alternatives to present arrangements. But it is hard to see how tenure will be quickly abolished at institutions where the single most powerful decision-making group is the tenured faculty.

I am no friend of tenure, and would not regret its passing. I have no intention to defend it. However, I am not persuaded that it need be the lynchpin of obstruction, or that its elimination is essential for reform. There are three points we need to keep in mind when we consider the future of tenure.

Tenure and Student Learning

First, some institutions have eliminated tenure without achieving much measurable educational improvement. I refer here primarily to proprietary institutions that hire faculty on an as-needed basis. However, they have not produced notably better educational results. Where they have had success, it has been through the more systematic use of assessment. This, however, is unrelated to the presence or absence of tenure. So the absence of tenure, per se, does not seem to lead to better results, nor should we expect that it would.

It is true, of course, that in the absence of tenure it would be easier to dismiss obviously unqualified teachers. This seems, on a neutral view of things, to be a good idea. However, it is not at all clear that we should put much weight in this prospect. Firing bad teachers is not a reliable route to improving teaching overall. Most poor teachers could be much better ones if they put their minds to it and had proper direction. Teaching is not a genetic endowment; it is a skill that can be learned. The key to improving teaching overall is improving teachers, not removing them. I think there is a good argument to be made for loosening the constraints of tenure to make it easier to remove conspicuously and persistently incompetent teachers. But I don't think that will by itself bring about a significant increase in student learning overall.

The Rise of Contingent Faculty

Second, colleges and universities have been rapidly shifting the burden of undergraduate teaching away from tenured faculty and onto contingent faculty, those hired yearly or on multiyear contracts. A considerable majority of college students are taught by nontenured instructors, and a very large portion by instructors not on the track to tenure. According to Schuster and Finkelstein, "The transformation is remarkable: from 1969 to 1998, a decline by one-half in faculty members occupying tenure-eligible positions and a sevenfold increase in faculty reporting non-tenure-eligible appointments."[11] So a large-scale shift has been taking place for years toward increasing the role of contingent faculty and decreasing the role of tenure-track faculty in undergraduate teaching.

But we need to take even the most reliable estimates of the dimensions of this shift with a grain of salt, because they are very rough estimates that probably understate the size of the shift. John Cross and Edie Goldenberg, whose work I mentioned in the chapter 13 with respect to student evaluations of teaching, conducted a detailed analysis of the use of non-tenure-track faculty at ten elite research universities. Perhaps their most striking finding was that even the institutions themselves did not know just how many contingent faculty they had: "We found that most universities . . . do a poor job of tracking their own [non-tenure-track] faculty. Even those staff specifically charged with the maintenance of institutional data are unable to respond to basic questions about the number ... employed, in which departments, how long ..., what their duties are, and what their average salaries and benefits packages are—statistics that are readily available for the regular tenure-line faculty."[12]

Cross and Goldenberg conducted interviews at each of the ten universities that they studied and encountered more than twenty-one different terms to describe contingent faculty; often different terms were used by different people at a single institution to describe the same employees. As a result of this data chaos, they found that "no university in our study was able to provide student-oriented teaching data by faculty type—that is, how many students are taught in classes led by tenure-track faculty, non-tenure-track faculty, and graduate students."[13] The only ultimately honest answer to the question of how heavily higher education relies on contingent faculty is the one that Cross and Goldenberg settle for: "Nobody seems to know."[14]

It is hard to say that tenure improves teaching, but it is equally hard to claim that it hurts it. It may be that we just can't make any valid generalizations on the question. Cross and Goldenberg conclude that "whether the increasing use of [non-tenure-track] faculty in lower-division teaching strengthens or weakens an undergraduate curriculum remains for us an open question."[15] We may be left with the tentative conclusion that tenure, like research, is essentially irrelevant to the quality of teaching. This is an argument neither for nor against tenure.

Tenure and Academic Freedom

Third, the traditional defense of tenure is rooted in its role of protecting academic freedom. As we have seen, the idea of academic freedom has become encrusted with mythic growths that damage undergraduate education without doing anything substantial to promote the real interests of free inquiry and open discussion. But we can certainly reject the myth of academic freedom without endangering the thing itself. Indeed, a clear-eyed look at the real value of freedom of expression for faculty will help us to correct some problems in present arrangements. As we have already seen, the ideology of academic freedom survives alongside a highly restrictive informal "speech code," in many departments, where the standards of departmental groupthink lead to self-censorship by most of the faculty. I suspect that most faculty feel considerably less free to openly take stances that contradict the departmental orthodoxy than to speak out against the administration or express politically unpopular opinions—especially if those opinions are consistent with the dominant political stance of the department.

The real threats to academic freedom are much more threatening to the growing majority of faculty who lack the protection of tenure. Neil W. Hamilton, a professor at the University of St. Thomas School of Law in Minnesota, has written extensively on academic freedom. He notes that contingent faculty "get scant collegial support from their tenured colleagues, and they are much more vulnerable to coercion from students, full-time faculty colleagues, administrative leaders, and forces outside the university."[16] If tenure is the means to the end of academic freedom, it is a flawed instrument because it fails to protect the freedom of most academics, and the cohort to whom tenure is irrelevant is growing far more rapidly than the cohort of those protected by tenure. If the freedom of faculty to follow the truth as they see it is an object to be sought, tenure has become largely beside the point. If tenure remains a rigid and inflexible guarantee of employment for a smaller and smaller minority of the teaching faculty, it becomes increasingly divorced from its own putative rationale.

And this goes to the core issue behind many recent challenges to tenure. Hamilton points out that there is an implicit social contract between society and the "peer-review professions." Some professions—such as medicine, accounting, law, and the academy—rely on specialized expertise to carry out work that would simply not be possible for those with less training and practice. Hence, we grant those professions an exemption from the open competition in the marketplace in which most businesses and individuals operate: "The public grants a profession the autonomy to regulate itself through peer review."[17] This includes the right to monitor their own work, to control entry to the profession, and to set the standards for performance. In return, the public expects that the professions will maintain high standards of performance and of ethics, advance the core work of the profession, and "restrain self-interest to some degree in order to serve the public purpose of the profession."[18]

Academic tenure is perhaps the most notable example of a grant of professional independence. But if we differentiate teaching from research, it becomes clear that the profession has not lived up to its end of the bargain. Faculties, as Hamilton puts it, "do not undertake responsibility for assuring the quality of their members' work."[19] The privacy of teaching and the absence of genuine peer review mean that the academic profession has defaulted on its responsibility to maintain high standards. It has done this through the categorical legerdemain that we have already described: given the dual responsibilities of academics for teaching and research, it has created a peer review system for research and then proceeded as if it applied to teaching as well.

"The burden is on the peer-review professions," Hamilton points out, "to justify constantly why occupational control of the work serves the public good."[20] The teaching profession in higher education has appealed, in a circular way, to its own putative expertise as a justification of the right to privately conduct the work of education with no meaningful review at all. As David Leslie of the College of William and Mary puts it, "Preserving the tenure system in its traditional form has become difficult because it is widely perceived as a job preservation scheme—not unlike 'featherbedding' in some industries—and not integral to the protection of academic freedom."[21] When other professions have tried job protection without justifying the quality of their work, they have found their options increasingly limited by law and regulation. The public will not regard the practice of tenure as self-justifying. This means that if it is to continue, it will need to be justified. But the attempt to justify it can be carried on openly only if institutions conduct real peer review, not imitation peer review insulated by the instruction myth.

To respond to such issues with the rhetoric of rights and academic freedom is increasingly beside the point. Resolving the challenges to tenure will require taking responsibility for the quality of teaching, something that faculties and institutions have for decades avoided doing. It is long past the time that tenure as traditionally practiced should simply be taken for granted.

CAREER LADDERS FOR TEACHING

There are two possible ways of changing the current deplorable situation. Get rid of tenure and replace it with a career ladder for contingent work that promotes improvement, or significantly reconfigure it. In either case, if our goal is to improve undergraduate learning, then the reward system must create strong incentives for improvement in teaching. The faculty endowment needs to be linked to high performance and improvement as a teacher. A career ladder for teaching can be constructed with or without tenure, but if it involves tenure then the criteria for tenure need to be changed. The foundation for such a reconfiguration, here as elsewhere, needs to be a new level of honesty. Administrators and faculty members alike need to have the courage to abandon the instruction myth and face the facts.

They need to recognize, for example, that what the formal promotion and tenure policies say is relevant only to the extent that they are followed in practice. Many institutions assert in their policies that promotion will be based 40 percent on teaching, 40 percent on research, and 20 percent on service. As we have seen, this is a convenient fiction. Such assertions, by embedding numbers in the statements, often create an illusion of concreteness, with no referent in the real world. (Forty percent of *what*? If forty out of one hundred units are about teaching, what are the units? Some would say time, but if so then nobody makes any effort to actually measure such things, and when they do they find that such a distribution is completely wrong. Faculty spend more time teaching but get less credit for it in promotion calculations. The numbers are pure fiction, anchored to no observable reality.) More significantly, the implication that teaching and research receive equal credit and attention in promotion decisions is nearly always false. It is an ancient and venerated falsehood, but no less false for that.

Furthermore, given present arrangements, I would submit that giving equal credit for teaching and research is not only not done, it is not doable: it is impossible. As we have seen, there is vastly more evidence available in the system about research than about teaching. And without investing time and effort in creating new structures of review and evaluation, there is no way to get a comparable quantity of evidence about teaching. What most committees do today is to weigh hard quantitative evidence about research along with soft qualitative evidence about teaching. The impressions about teaching are as light as a feather, and can be explained away by the slightest breeze of an argument. The numbers about research are anvil-solid, to be moved only by persuasion of many horsepower. It is hard to imagine, given the information available to a committee, how they could possibly give as much attention to teaching as to research.

A Tenure Track for Teaching

How, then, could we construct a Learning Paradigm tenure system? How can we change the effect of promotion and tenure processes to raise the status of teaching and the prospects of undergraduate students? It is fairly obvious. If present arrangements, in effect, grant tenure based almost exclusively on research productivity, a tenure system that served the interests of undergraduates would grant tenure largely or exclusively based on teaching effectiveness. If one could become a full professor by spending all one's time becoming the best possible teacher, not only would we raise the quality of teaching, we would make higher quality teaching visible, conspicuous. (And we might save tenure, at many institutions.) We would create the framework of a genuine second-order environment around teaching, a group of professionals whose work was defined by progressively solving the problems that arise in teaching undergraduates. Such teachers would not work in private; it would become their modus operandi to study one another's successes and failures, to help one another build on the successes and avoid the failures. Such teachers would not be cut off from one another but would be a community of practice finding the meaning of their work, and new meanings for their work. Such teachers would not avoid research, but their research would be about their teaching, about the way their students were learning, about what worked for learning and what didn't.

If our point of departure is the mythology that sustains the Instruction Paradigm, then such a proposal will seem anti-academic and destructive. But if our point of departure is a clear view of the reality of higher education as it is today, such a proposal will seem an obvious correction of a long-standing inequity, setting on an even footing a system that is leaning so far in one direction that it is about to fall of its own weight.

Several institutions have created designated positions to recognize and encourage excellent teaching, but those who take those positions are nearly always tenured faculty who received tenure through their research. Some have also created positions within disciplinary departments for faculty who will specialize in teaching the discipline, and often take a role in supporting other faculty in improving their teaching through coaching or instructing them in current thinking about pedagogy. These experiments are praiseworthy and valuable. But for the most part they do not change the fundamental path to tenure for any significant number of teachers.

David Leslie suggested that traditional conceptions of tenure have not been thought out in terms of faculty work: "There is not one 'faculty job'— there are many different faculty jobs. Individual faculty may be asked to (or may choose to) take on new 'jobs' over the course of their careers. Tenure might be modified to enable both institutions and individuals to renegotiate their relationship periodically without sacrificing the important protections offered by tenure."[22] Thus, Leslie suggests, "appointments should be made on the basis of differentiated tasks and roles. Some faculty might be hired only to teach, others only to do research, and so on."[23]

This is being done today, and done at a major research university. The University of British Columbia (UBC), in Vancouver, Canada, has for some years granted tenure to faculty in the "teaching stream," which is distinguished from the "research and teaching stream." In 2011 UBC created the position of professor of teaching. Individuals in the teaching stream can progress from the position of instructor to senior instructor to professor of teaching. As the guidelines for the position point out, "This new rank reflects the commitment of the University to provide educational leadership, outstanding teaching, and curriculum development, and to recognize and reward it when it happens."[24] Tenure is granted on promotion to senior instructor in the teaching stream. The rank of professor of teaching "is designed to mirror the position of full professor, which is the highest academic rank for the research and teaching stream."[25] Thus UBC has created a career ladder in teaching to parallel the career ladder in research/teaching.

Candidates for promotion in the teaching stream must present a dossier that includes a teaching portfolio such as we discussed in chapter 14. It must include evidence of not only excellent teaching but also educational leadership activity, which might include work with curriculum and pedagogical development and contributions to the scholarship of teaching and learning. Simon Bates, professor of teaching in the Department of Physics and Astronomy, is the director of the Centre for Teaching, Learning, and Technology. He reports that there were seventeen professors of teaching as of 2015, with seven more in the process of seeking promotion in the teaching track.[26] UBC is home of the Carl Wieman Science Education Initiative, and Wieman's work helped to direct attention, especially in the sciences, to the importance of teaching. Of course, Wieman's work is available for anybody at any university to read. Yet, so far as I can determine, only UBC has followed it to its logical conclusion in this respect.

Part of the review process in the teaching stream is the selection of four "referees" by the candidates. Two of these will be from UBC, but outside of the candidate's department, and two will be external to UBC. Using outside evaluators has the potential to increase the credibility of the process by bringing in an element of disinterested peer review that is harder to achieve on the campus. The use of reviewers who are outside the department, but not outside the discipline, has the potential to correct the pressure for groupthink while bringing in people who are members of the same second-order community as the candidate.

The great potential of the teaching track as career ladder is that it shifts the source of the faculty endowment from research to teaching. Time expended on developing, applying, and testing new pedagogical approaches accelerates progress toward tenure and promotion rather than slowing it down. Hence, loss aversion reinforces the motivation of faculty to become better teachers. For faculty members on the teaching track, the relative advantage of investing time in improving teaching becomes much more positive, and hence they come to see it as in their benefit to seek innovation rather than to deflect it with defensive routines.

The idea of a teaching-based tenure track has the potential to change the faculty endowment in such a way as to channel new energy into improving teaching and learning. If we understand the deadening effect of the faculty endowment in research on the prospects of improving teaching, then this appears to be one of the most transformational steps an institution could take. At the same time, its effects would be felt gradually as teaching professors were promoted in the institution.

Making Research-Based Practice and SoTL a Condition of Employment and Promotion

Today, one of the problems with doing peer review of teaching is that most faculty lack both knowledge of and experience in critical intellectual work about teaching. Maryellen Weimer from Pennsylvania State University–Berks has done extensive work with SoTL. She notes that "there is no guarantee that colleagues in the discipline are pedagogically savvy—that their views of teaching are anything but eclectic, idiosyncratic and uninformed."[27] But, she points out, even those who follow SoTL are often constrained by their exposure only to research on teaching in their own disciplines: "Good discipline-based scholarship is seen by a very few when it is relevant to very many."[28]

Different disciplines face different teaching challenges. However, these differences tend to be exaggerated by those who are rewarded and recognized only as specialist researchers. When it comes to teaching, work in other disciplines often sparks more creative and effective approaches. Faculty whose chief concern is effective teaching are less likely to be limited by the disciplinary chauvinism that besets so many of their departmental colleagues and are more likely to seek out alternative approaches to teaching and learning informed by research and experimentation done in other disciplines.

While colleges and universities will not instantly produce large numbers of faculty on the teaching track, it is clear that they could and should immediately change the criteria for hiring and promoting faculty. Any faculty member hired for a teaching position should be required to have studied learning and done SoTL research. Institutions should explicitly lower the expectations for publications while simultaneously raising expectations for documentation of teaching and SoTL research, introducing full-fledged peer review of teaching and making the time available to do it by lowering research demands. The first step toward such adjustments would be for institutions to acknowledge and abandon the fiction that teaching and research are equally rewarded now and try to design a system in which they really are equally rewarded. If such changes are too frightening for currently tenured teachers, they could still be introduced for new hires, both on and off the tenure track.

Even before implementing full-fledged peer review, use of a research-based teaching inventory should be incorporated into the promotion process. Orientation to the inventory and to its foundation in educational research should be part of the orientation that all new faculty receive—tenure track and contingent alike. Wieman and Gilbert's TPI, described in the last chapter, generates an "ETP score," which stands for "extent of use of research-based teaching practices." The ETP score a faculty member receives in the first year provides a benchmark of pedagogical practice against which a faculty member should be measured in subsequent years. And minimum levels of performance on such an inventory should be considered a prerequisite for promotion. By any standard, the score on a research-based inventory of pedagogical practices is a more valid and reasonable basis for judging a faculty member's teaching performance than student evaluations alone.

The widespread use of a tested and validated teaching inventory has the potential to change the system by raising the standards of peer review in teaching. And even a few tenured faculty who model serious peer review can change the culture. Today, the factor that most powerfully militates against real peer review of teaching is simply that it takes too much time away from research. So even teachers who spend the lion's share of their time on teaching are not realistically evaluated on the quality of their work. If a few faculty modeled the process, in a given department, of a serious course portfolio and serious peer review, it would open up the possibility of giving other faculty the option of highlighting their teaching work. And if new faculty were more familiar with the research and practice of teaching than senior faculty, it would change the conversation in departments.

Supporting Teaching for All Faculty: The Teaching Sabbatical and Research Release

There are several ways that institutions could free up faculty time for improving teaching. One is to adapt the traditional idea of sabbatical leave to the need for better teaching. Traditionally, the sabbatical is time freed from teaching responsibilities that allows a faculty member to do more research. Why not reverse the priority, and grant faculty time freed from research responsibilities to work on improving their teaching? The faculty member might have a reduced teaching load, but with the explicit understanding that any research done during the leave period would be SoTL research aimed at improving his or her teaching. As with the conventional research-focused sabbatical, the faculty member would propose a plan of activities, but in this case, it would be directed at meeting explicit goals for improving courses, assignments, assessments, and pedagogy. The *teaching sabbatical*, clearly understood as a sabbatical *from research* to *improve teaching*, would be one way of addressing the pervasive complaint that there just isn't enough time to work on improving teaching. And it would be a way to bring the teaching-and-research faculty to a higher level of understanding and competence with respect to teaching, and to prepare them for meaningful peer review of teaching.

It is commonplace to grant faculty members time released from teaching duties to either do research or perform some service to the institution. For example, officers of faculty bodies—senates and unions—are frequently released from a part of their teaching responsibility to carry out administrative duties. Why not release faculty from research responsibilities to allow them to improve their teaching? Participants in faculty learning communities are often released from teaching one or more classes to allow them the time to do the work of the learning community. And this makes good sense. Indeed, it is reasonable to reduce the teaching load of teachers to allow them to focus more attention on improving their teaching. For the average teacher, release from a class will probably generate more available time than would release from research responsibilities. But the psychological pressure of research demands is probably greater than that of teaching, simply because of the high priority given research in the promotion process. To explicitly and officially postpone research deadlines or reduce the quantity required would free up time and effort and allow faculty to redirect their attention to teaching.

Reducing research demands on tenure-track faculty will not always be easy or straightforward. A research project, once under way, sometimes has a mind of its own. It is not always possible to drop it in the middle, or even take a break. But in at least as many cases, time away from such a project would improve the quality of the work. Today, many professors drag the research plough, heads down and shoulders hunched, not because they are tilling good soil but because they feel the tenure committee's whip on their backs. Taking a break now and again would be more likely to help than to hurt the quality of research in most cases. It might reduce the quantity, but that would be an entirely desirable trade-off.

The goal should be to develop in every faculty member who teaches the capacity to seriously and intelligently review the quality of teaching—his or her own as well as that of peer faculty members. What we should aspire to is a system in which every faculty member is credibly evaluated on the quality of his or her teaching, with the kind and quantity of evidence that make the evaluation persuasive. If this were the case, we would be moving toward a system in which the teaching of all faculty members, including those involved with disciplinary research, was reviewed in earnest and with reasonable expectations for improvement. If this happened, many faculty members would shift a good deal of their time and attention to teaching because they would be rewarded for doing so.

17 · CREATING A MARKET FOR EDUCATION

Colleges and universities in the United States operate in a free market—sort of. Unlike in K–12 education, students are free to attend any institution that will accept them. Furthermore, most people value higher education, and the institutions are vigorously attempting to attract students. So higher education seems to be a competitive market. In many areas of our lives competition leads to rapid innovations in technology and customer service. Why not education? The answer is linked to many of the factors we have already discussed, but also to the peculiar nature of the market for higher education.

Higher education has developed into a strange kind of market in which quality is hard for customers to discern; competition persists, but in a way that fails to advance educational excellence. And it is a regulated market; accrediting associations determine which institutions will be able to accept federal funds, and the federal government both authorizes the accreditors and provides a large share of the resources. These regulators play a vital role in shaping the market in higher education.

THE HIGHER EDUCATION MARKET: COMPETITION BY IMITATION

Many people assume that competitive markets encourage innovation and differentiation. And often they do—look at your phone. But Yale economists

Paul DiMaggio and Walter Powell pointed out over thirty years ago that some markets promote imitation rather than innovation, encourage the homogenization of processes and products, which they call *isomorphism*. They define this as "a constraining process that forces one unit of a population to resemble other units that face the same set of environmental conditions."[1] Under institutional isomorphism, "organizations tend to model themselves after similar organizations in their field that they perceive to be more legitimate or successful."[2] What determines whether an organization will try to innovate or imitate? DiMaggio and Powell theorized that certain characteristics of the organization and the environment promote isomorphism. Among these are ambiguous goals, an uncertain relationship between means and ends, greater reliance on academic credentials in choosing and hiring staff, professionalization of staff, and fewer visible alternative models of organizations. It seems fair to say that when an organization is driven by processes rather than products, and when it isn't clear just when it is achieving its goals, it is easier to imitate the market leaders than to compete with them. By these standards, contrast, say, the computer industry or energy production—where we have seen rapid innovation in recent years—with education. Ambiguous goals nearly define the current theory-in-use that governs most colleges. We have seen that they attend to the ritual classifications that govern organizational processes, and through the instruction myth they substitute processes for outcomes. The split between the espoused theory and the theory-in-use of these organizations essentially severs their internal governance from their asserted goals, thus makes it almost a complete mystery whether they are achieving those goals or not. Because they essentially substitute means for ends—counting instruction as an accomplishment and giving little organizational attention to the learning that instruction is supposed to produce—they are completely befuddled as to means and ends. These institutions rely heavily on academic qualifications in hiring and promotion, and in the realm of teaching and learning, the academic qualifications they rely on often have little or no relevance to the quality of work that gets done. And as to available models, colleges and universities are essentially imitating one another and have been doing so for centuries. Institutions that adopt the instruction myth and invest their efforts in maintaining the ritual classifications that obscure outcomes will quintessentially fit in these categories, and so we should expect a high degree of organizational isomorphism. And that is what we find.

Colleges and universities preach diversity and innovation but practice homogeneity and isomorphism. The fundamental strategy of nearly all conventional, nonprofit institutions is imitation of high-prestige models. The late J. Douglas Toma, a professor of higher education at the University of Georgia, notes that "while universities and colleges represent themselves as distinctive, differences are modest—matters more related to look and feel. They prefer the security that comes with following standard approaches, pursuing similar goals in roughly the same manner."[3] The coin of the realm, the thing institutions compete for, is prestige: "Prestige is to higher education as profit is to corporations."[4] This is not to say that all institutions are alike; they fall into a limited set of categories based on resources, students, and history. But all are connected in a kind of ladder of prestige, with those at each level emulating those above them. "They are eerily similar in vision . . . ," Toma points out, "seemingly obsessed with 'moving to the next level.' Their common goal is legitimacy through enhanced prestige—and with it access to greater resources, recognizing that the most prestigious institutions also tend to be the wealthiest."[5]

In 2008, Toma conducted a study of the thirty-eight colleges and universities in the greater Atlanta area, to determine what their institutional strategies for improvement were. He concluded, "The foundation of competitive strategy is differentiation. But universities and colleges, like those in the Atlanta market, tend to differentiate only to the extent that they must, with the comfort that comes with conformity and thus legitimacy proving compelling."[6] Indeed, he found that "as they seek legitimacy and autonomy through reference to others, organizations across types become more homogeneous over time, eventually adopting the innovations of leading organizations as these become prevailing wisdom. . . . Institutions, as across the Atlanta market, tend not only to develop parallel aspirations but also to pursue them through similar strategies."[7]

The isomorphic market for higher education is on prominent display in the annual *U.S. News & World Report* rankings of colleges and universities. Since 1983, *U.S. News* has been ranking colleges and universities by categories (national universities, regional universities, liberal arts colleges, and the like). These rankings of institutions assume a common standard because they rank the fifty top-performing schools in each category in numerical order. The rankings are based on a complex set of criteria, including such factors as selectivity, faculty salaries, faculty degrees, student-faculty ratio, average SAT or

ACT scores, alumni giving, and graduation rate. Thus, the standards are resource-intensive: colleges that spend more (high salaries, small classes, vast recruitment) will do better. The statistically largest factor (25 percent) is reputation, as measured by a survey completed by administrators at comparable institutions. In other words, what the standards reward most highly is more of the same: spending more money on the same things other institutions spend money on. They also reward the judgment of those—administrators at other colleges—who hold a strong bias and have partial and incomplete evidence. Selectivity, of course, is a measure that is based exclusively on the experience of students who have not yet attended the college—the ratio of those who will attend the college in the future to those who have applied but will not. If the students at a college learned more, that would be invisible in the rankings. As higher education scholars Robert Zemsky, Gregory Wegner, and William Massy point out, "U.S. News does not measure the quality of the educational experience. The data U.S. News so arduously collects tell nothing about what actually happens on campus or in the classrooms."[8]

It deserves emphasis that academic prestige, as identified and reinforced by U.S. News and other ranking organizations, is largely an illusion. The best study of the relationship between prestige and outcomes is the one by Alan B. Krueger and Stacy Berg Dale that we discussed in the first chapter. They went to some lengths to differentiate the advantages of the student from the advantages of the college and found that the selectivity of the college the student attended was less important than the selectivity of the colleges she applied to. This is entirely consistent with the large body of evidence we have already discussed, which shows that the differences in performance of students between different colleges pale in comparison to the differences within any given college. The idea that one can secure one's future by attending a high-prestige college is largely an illusion.

But it is an illusion that colleges and students alike largely embrace. James Monks of MIT and Ronald G. Ehrenberg of Cornell conducted a study of how the rankings affected a group of selective private institutions. They found that when rankings go down, colleges tend to accept a larger proportion of their applicants, hence making them less selective. The reverse happens when rankings improve: colleges can accept a smaller proportion of their applicants and thus become more selective. Since administrators at other colleges follow the rankings, these effects produce a kind of self-fulfilling prophecy: "The factor that receives the largest weight in the *USNWR* rankings is the survey of higher education administrators. Hence an improvement (or decline) in an institution's rank may lead to future movements in its rank in the same direction because administrators are increasingly aware of how other institutions fare in the rankings."[9]

An isomorphic market such as higher education will sometimes promote innovation, but innovation in a single direction. When market leaders adopt a new way of doing things, those seeking to ape their success will tend to follow their example. When Harvard adopted the elective system in the 1860s, other institutions followed the example, though usually in a less extreme way. As high-prestige institutions have offered online courses and MOOCs, others have followed suit quickly. Such a market will promote widespread imitation of high-prestige models. What such a market will not produce is the kind of competition that pursues, identifies, and rewards successful innovations.

The isomorphic market tends to reinforce the disabling myths that inhibit real innovation in undergraduate education. This is because the basis of reputation is overwhelmingly faculty research rather than teaching. Those institutions at the top of the pyramid are most likely to place the highest relative priority on faculty research in hiring, promotion, and tenure policies. This has been a major reason for the ratcheting up of research demands over the past century. Of course, in the realm of academic research there is a genuine competitive market. Institutions compete for grants, public and private, to support research projects. And they compete for faculty, trying to hire the best researchers. But this probably has little or no relevance to the quality of undergraduate education.

Institutions advertise their research to potential students and their parents, taking advantage of the myth of unity, which most of the public accepts. When university presidents and publicists perpetuate the myth, it reinforces the self-fulfilling prophecy that makes imitation the substitute for real competition in teaching and learning. And it encourages institutions to compete for the wrong things and to play, essentially, a bait-and-switch game with potential students: come to us because we have great researchers, and then if the teaching fails you, that's just bad luck.

Students may believe that they are making informed educational choices when they decide what institutions to attend and what programs to pursue, but for the most part they are not. The information on which they base their choices is largely irrelevant to their real hopes and prospects. What matters far and away more than anything else to students—the quality of the teaching and learning that will happen in college—is nearly invisible. Carl Wieman, writing in 2017, puts it clearly: "In the context of higher education, it is next to impossible for prospective students to get any meaningful information on the quality of teaching at the institutions they are considering."[10]

Institutions use other factors that are irrelevant to student learning to attract students: sports and amenities are important in some students' choices. Overall, the market for higher education exhibits competition by imitation. As in most isomorphic markets, the relationship between the actual practices and processes that the institutions pursue and the kinds of goods customers might want are obscure at best.

ACCREDITATION AS QUALITY CONTROL IN THE HIGHER EDUCATION MARKET

Of course, higher education has not ever been a completely free market. It was regulated by the churches that founded most American institutions for decades; public colleges and universities have long been regulated by the states, and since the end of the nineteenth century the whole system has been explicitly regulated by regional accrediting organizations. The seven regional accreditation groups periodically review the performance of every college and university. (There are only six regions, but one of them—the Western— has different commissions for community colleges and four-year colleges.) With the growth of higher education since the Second World War and the increase in federal aid, accreditation has become even more important because the federal government generally extends its largess only to accredited institutions. Specialized and professional programs—law, medicine, engineering, and the like—are also accredited by the disciplinary or professional associations that constitute gateways to the professions. But these accreditors are especially important for graduate programs and for professional majors. Most undergraduate education tends to fall under the purview of the regional accrediting associations.

These are voluntary associations of colleges and universities. Given the status of accreditation as the gatekeeper for federal revenue, we might question how genuinely voluntary they are. But their members are the colleges and universities themselves. They are governed by boards chosen from the member institutions. And their expenses are paid by the member institutions.

In spite of the obvious objections, the evidence does not show that accreditors have been passive or that they have ignored issues of student learning. In fact, all the accrediting associations have moved far beyond most of their member colleges in promoting innovation. They began thirty years ago calling for assessment of student learning outcomes, and that is now a standard requirement in all six regions. Paul Gaston of Kent State University of Ohio, in his extensive review of the history and practice of accreditation, concludes that "far from being an impediment to innovation, regional accreditation may be the broadest and most generative platform within higher education for motivating and sharing innovative ideas and practice."[11] The accrediting associations hold meetings at least annually in which they highlight innovative ideas and pedagogical advances. Some of the associations have done a great deal to publicize and promote new thinking about education.

We should make the disclaimer that the accreditation process probably affects the thinking of only a minority of the regular faculty. It is hard to know for sure. But at many institutions those directly involved in the accreditation process, those who read the standards and attend the conferences and meetings, are much better informed than many of their campus colleagues about both learning theory and accreditation requirements.

The accreditation agencies have moved impressively to require institutions to assess student learning outcomes. They have been much looser about what institutions need to do with and about those assessments. There is widespread agreement—not only among colleges and universities but among employers—about what skills and knowledge are important for college graduates to achieve. Yet the accreditation agencies have proceeded as if there were much more controversy over this matter than there really is. As Carol Geary Schneider, past president of the Association of American Colleges and Universities (AAC&U), points out, "Across all the regional accreditors, quality is 'assured' via a set of procedural requirements."[12] The result is that "the regional accreditors and their institutional members are keeping their goals for higher learning to themselves, hidden behind an accreditation smokescreen labeled 'institutional autonomy.'"[13]

This problem is reinforced by the fact that members of accrediting teams are all, or almost all, taken from institutions that are in isomorphic competition with the institution being evaluated. Faculty and administrators on accreditation teams will tend to take it for granted that if things are done the same way they are on their home campuses, it's probably all right. Thus accreditation teams tend not to challenge the myths that they themselves must accept in order to do their jobs. As Andrew Kelly and Frederick Hess of the American Enterprise Institute put it, "Because the accreditation process is run by higher education institutions themselves, *accreditation rewards congruence with the traditional model.*"[14]

THE FEDERAL ROLE: THE CREDIT HOUR AND LEARNING

The U.S. Department of Education has considerable sway over the accreditation agencies and over institutions of higher education. The department must recognize an accrediting agency for schools it accredits to be able to accept federal financial aid. So the accreditors pay close attention to federal policy in these matters. One of the major goals of both the accreditors and the federal regulators, of course, is to separate serious colleges and universities from "diploma mills," institutions that make a profit by essentially selling degrees in which students invest little time and achieve little learning. This is a worthy and important project and was a major impetus in the creation of the accrediting agencies at the end of the nineteenth century. One of the key tools for verifying that institutions are serious is the student credit hour, a tool of regulation that has become problematic in several ways as it has grown in importance.

As I explained in chapter 2, the credit hour—or "Carnegie unit"—emerged early in the twentieth century as a means, first, of certifying the validity of high school diplomas for college admission and, second, of certifying the full-time status of college faculty to establish eligibility for pensions. Since then, as the federal role in funding higher education has grown, the credit hour has had the vast advantages that it is already there and is easy to count.

Because the credit hour is a measure of time rather than learning, it has an ambiguous meaning. It is used by institutions, accreditors, and government agencies as if it were a measure of learning and thus has become a virtual embodiment of the instruction myth. As we saw in the first chapter, Eduardo M. Ochoa, assistant secretary for postsecondary education in the

U.S. Department of Education in the Obama administration, put it this way: "At its most basic, a credit hour is a proxy measure of a quality of student learning."[15] That is not what credit hours were created for, and the only reason they have become such a proxy for regulators and educators is that they already exist and are easy to count. But, as a matter of fact, hours in class are not a reasonable proxy for the quality of student learning at all. The claim ignores reality and makes the instruction myth federal policy.

Institutions themselves do not consistently accept credit hours as such a proxy—from other institutions. When just 41 percent of college graduates attend a single college and nearly a quarter attend three or more, when a majority of college students attend community colleges, the transfer of credit between institutions is of vital importance.[16] As Amy Laitinen, director of higher education for the New America Foundation, points out, "Countless dollars and hours are wasted every year as transfer students are forced to retake courses or never given credit for what they have learned due to the flawed currency of the credit hour."[17] The reason is, of course, that colleges and universities themselves recognize that the credit hour is not a measure of learning, hence they do not necessarily respect credit hours accumulated at other institutions: "In other words, through its everyday actions, the higher education system itself routinely rejects the idea that credit hours are a reliable measure of how much students have learned."[18]

During the last couple of decades, the credit hour has come under increasing pressure from advancements in technology. The advent of online courses makes it impossible to even pretend that hours in class are of any real significance. The credit hour is, as Laitinen puts it, "archaic, a nonsensical basis for regulating online programs in which the whole notion of time in the classroom has no meaning."[19] All that online courses do is reveal what was already the case, that we have no real quality control or index of accomplishment for college classes.

In 2009, the inspector general of the Education Department concluded that three of the regional accrediting agencies had failed to provide sufficient oversight of the process of assigning credit for online courses. The result was a long discussion about the credit hour among the Education Department, the regulators, and the institutions, which in 2010 brought forth from the department something it had (remarkably!) never produced before: a written definition of the credit hour. That definition was embedded in a long set of new rules, coming to over 140 pages, three columns of small print to a page.

Fortunately, the definition itself is relatively brief—if not, as we shall see, entirely transparent.

The Department of Education defined a credit hour in three ways, intending that the three definitions would be equivalent. First, it could be defined as "one hour of classroom or direct faculty instruction and a minimum of two hours of out of class student work for approximately fifteen weeks for one semester," or the equivalent hours adjusted for a shorter term. Second, it could mean "at least an equivalent amount of work" as done in the time just described in "other academic activities," such as labs, studio work, or internships. Third, it could refer to "institutionally established reasonable equivalencies for the amount of work required" under the first definition, "including as represented in intended learning outcomes and verified by evidence of student achievement."[20]

Begin with the second two possible meanings of the term. Both of them are defined in term of their equivalence to the first. That is to say, the adequacy of an alternative to the standard time-based meaning of the credit hour depends on the alternative requiring an amount of "work" equal to that in the first, standard definition. And how much work is that? Well, we have no idea. The amount of time is three hours per week per credit: one in class and two outside of class. Obviously, two different people could do very different amounts of work in those three hours. What is the standard of "work done in an hour" employed here? There is none.

This problem with verifying time spent brings us to an issue with the primary definition, the one that is the anchor and reference point for the other two. It defines a student credit hour as one hour spent in class and two spent outside of class for each credit. By that standard, a student taking a three-unit class would spend three hours in class and six hours outside of class each week, for a total of nine hours. And a student taking a full-time load of fifteen credits would spend at least fifteen hours in class each week and at least thirty hours outside of class, for a total of forty-five. I think that is a noble ideal. But we really do need to acknowledge that it is a complete fiction, one with no basis in fact whatsoever.

The figure of two hours out of class for every hour in class is simply imaginary. It is presented as a minimum, as if every student in every class must invest this much time or the institution cannot grant credit. It is not a minimum, a norm, or an average. It is a convenient fiction. There are some students who study for two hours or more for every hour of class time, but they are in a tiny minority in light of all the available evidence. According to the 2006 University of California Undergraduate Student Experience survey, completed by more than 6,000 UC students, the average student attended class for 15.67 hours per week and studied for 12.72 hours per week.[21] On the 2015 NSSE, which surveyed over 150,000 colleges seniors, nearly 70 percent reported taking four or more classes, and they reported an average of 14.57 hours of studying—not the minimum of 24 we should expect.[22] The best empirical evidence, *even evidence based on students' own self-reports*, tells us that most students spend *less* time studying outside of class than they do attending class, not twice as much time. To suggest that two hours outside of class for every hour of class is part of the *definition* of a credit hour is to make the credit hour itself a convenient fiction, even as a measure of time. If this rule were enforced as written, nearly all the higher education institutions in the country would lose their accreditation.

The formal, legal definition of the credit hour imports falsehood and magical thinking into the accreditation process. How can this happen? It can happen through a kind of administrative legerdemain that incorporates the foundational myths of the academy into their regulatory process. The federal rule we are discussing mandates that accrediting agencies "must conduct an effective review and evaluation of the reliability and accuracy of the institution's assignment of credit hours."[23] But the agency can meet this requirement if it "makes a reasonable determination of whether the institution's assignment of credit hours *conforms to commonly accepted practice in higher education*."[24] And there we have it. Commonly accepted practice in higher education, not only here but on many other topics we have examined, consists of replacing ends with means, outcomes with processes, and never examining the outcomes at all.

Indeed, the declining credibility of the credit hour is almost certainly the product of aspects of commonly accepted practice in higher education that we have already discussed. The myth of unity has allowed for the widespread substitution of research for teaching and the subsequent deemphasis of student learning. Alexander C. McCormick, director of the NSSE, has examined the decline in student study time over the past fifty years. He concludes that "the sharp decline in study time roughly coincided with the increasing emphasis on scholarly productivity in faculty incentives and preferences, as well as increased federal R&D support."[25] Hence we have good reason to believe that the decline in student out-of-class study time "involves the erosion in the importance of teaching in both the faculty reward structure and faculty preferences, coinciding with expansion of the research enterprise."[26] The myth of unity has facilitated the decline in the credibility of the credit hour. And it has likewise supported the rise of high-prestige models for imitation that increasingly value research over under-graduate learning, and hence skew the isomorphic market toward increasing incoherence.

The rule had the effect of discouraging innovation and encouraging insti-tutions to retreat to commonly accepted practice. This was not, of course, the intention of the Education Department, so Assistant Secretary Ochoa in 2011 issued a "Dear Colleague" letter attempting to clarify the intent of the rule. The new regulations, he insisted, "are completely consistent with innovative practices such as online education, competency-based credit, and academic activities that do not rely on 'seat time.'"[27] The credit hour, he asserted, "is an institutionally established equivalency that reasonably approximates some minimum amount of student work reflective of the amount of work expected in a Carnegie unit."[28] However, since no one is in a position to credibly define what that minimum amount of student work is, we are left with no solid ground but the fear of punishment by the well-intended regulators. Elena Silva, Taylor White, and Thomas Toch of the Carnegie Foundation, in a 2015 report on the status of the Carnegie unit, conclude that the current regula-tions "encourage colleges and universities to offer traditionally-paced pro-grams structured around Carnegie Units."[29] And I would add that they also encourage accreditors to fall back on the "accepted practice" excuse far more often than they should. A complete absence of results becomes acceptable progress when it is accepted practice.

In 1934, early in the career of the measure, Henry Suzzallo, the president of the Carnegie Foundation, wrote of the Carnegie unit, "None recognizes more clearly than the foundation that these standards have served their pur-pose. . . . They should give place to more flexible, more individual, more exact and revealing standards of performance as rapidly as these may be achieved."[30] Now that we have passed the eightieth anniversary of that observation, we should not be surprised that change has not been achieved very rapidly. But Carnegie's 2015 review of the measure concludes that "reliance on the Carnegie Unit is indeed an impediment to some of the solutions sought by today's reformers. Most notably, the federal government's requirement that students must spend federal financial aid at colleges and universities measuring student progress with the Carnegie Unit is a barrier to the spread of flexible delivery models in higher education."[31]

In mid-2015, the Council of Regional Accrediting Commissions (C-RAC), presented a common framework for approving competency-based programs that seems quite balanced and reasonable.[32] The federal government, through either congressional or executive action, should establish standards comparable to C-RAC's, to give institutions some confidence that they can safely experiment in good faith with substantive measures of learning as criteria of student progress rather than vacuous measures of time.

I have suggested already that institutions should maintain an outcomes transcript on every student and that such transcripts should provide feedback to students and to the institution as to individual and collective accomplishment. Such a transcript, designed to illustrate the institution's curricular enactment of the DQP, would be an outline and assessment of learning progress. And if such a transcript were well grounded in actual student performances and products of student learning, it would also be a more meaningful index of real student learning than the transcript of grades. I am suggesting that developing student learning outcomes and developing assessment of competencies go hand in hand, and our goal should be to replace the transcript of grades with the transcript of learning. But even before that is done, institutions can begin to create a counterbalance to the record of credit hours that now defines a college degree. And they should do so.

MAKING A MARKET THROUGH TRANSPARENCY

The federal government today plays an enormous role in higher education not just through regulation of the accreditors but through its role in promoting better information for the higher education market. The White House and the Department of Education have attempted to promote more coherent competition in a variety of ways. In the Bush administration, the Spellings Commission bemoaned, "Our complex, decentralized postsecondary education system has no comprehensive strategy, particularly for undergraduate programs, to provide either adequate internal accountability systems or effective public information. Too many decisions about higher education—

from those made by policymakers to those made by students and families—rely heavily on reputation and rankings derived to a large extent from inputs such as financial resources rather than outcomes."[33]

The commission pointed out that "despite increased attention to student learning results by colleges and universities and accreditation agencies, parents and students have no solid evidence, comparable across institutions, of how much students learn in colleges or whether they learn more at one college than another."[34] To this end, they proposed "the creation of a consumer-friendly information database on higher education with useful, reliable information on institutions, coupled with a search engine to enable students, parents, policymakers and others to weigh and rank comparative institutional performance."[35]

The Obama administration pursued this project in various forms. Of course, a great deal of information about colleges is available to those who know how to access it from the Department of Education website, especially the Integrated Postsecondary Education Data System (IPEDS).[36] But it is not easy for a layperson coming to this source for the first time to see even what to look for. The Obama administration in 2013 announced a plan to provide ratings of cost-effectiveness for colleges, but in 2015 it abandoned the idea.[37] Certainly one reason for the reversal was virulent opposition from many colleges and universities. But another, and a basis for much of the opposition, was that the available evidence of educational outcomes is indirect, spotty, and of frankly dubious value. Similar difficulties will almost certainly face any effort of accrediting agencies to rate or grade institutions. What the government has produced is the *College Scorecard*, a website that can generate information about colleges, individually and comparatively, about graduation rates, programs and degrees offered, tuition, size, and financial aid.[38] It is a useful resource in many ways, and a template that could be expanded. However, it lacks much of what the Spellings Commission called for, especially any direct information on "how much students learn in colleges."

If the government and the accrediting agencies are to change the quality of the market in higher education they must move colleges toward more transparency concerning their teaching and learning practices and their results. If how colleges teach students and how well students learn were public information, it would put a priority on effective innovation and make the market less isomorphic. The variations among different institutions' definitions of learning outcomes and standards for assessing them contribute to the ambiguity of goals and the confusion of means and ends that makes higher education an isomorphic market. If accreditation could move institutions toward common standards, they could help create genuine competition in a market informed by educational value.

Almost all the information available to students and parents is information about the inputs to higher education—faculty education and research, resources, facilities—or very indirect outcomes of student learning such as grades, graduation rates, job placement, and salaries. Indeed, many in Congress and the Trump administration seem to think that job placement and salary are the only relevant outcomes of college. Schneider of the AAC&U warns that "in part because current quality assurance practices now provide no definition of expected learning outcomes whatsoever, we stand in real danger of creating a new regime that assesses quality *only in terms of specific majors'* job placement rates, salaries, loan payment status, and other narrowly focused [return-on-investment] data."[39] One reason for this pressure for measuring indirect and long-term outcomes of college is that the things that colleges *do* measure, or sort of measure, do not easily translate to those outcomes.

Conventional "success" in college is only very loosely correlated with the indirect outcomes that many seek to improve. Certainly, college graduates tend to get better jobs than those who didn't complete college. And there is a modest relationship between college grades and salary. (Of course, in many highly paid professional fields the college credential is a prerequisite for employment, so some of the value of the credential is an artifact of the system, not evidence that college graduates are more able or talented.) Overall, however, the relationship between college success and career success is slight, at best. After reviewing a number of meta-analyses of the relationship between college grades and career success done in the 1990s, Pascarella and Terenzini concluded that "across all studies undergraduate grades accounted for about 2.6 percent of the variance in job success."[40] That is, note, not 2.6 percent of job success, but 2.6 percent of the *variance* in success between the total number of college graduates.

As we saw in chapter 15, those outside the academy, and many in it, regard the transcript with skepticism and fail to find in it persuasive evidence of much anything. If this were not the case, the whole drive for accountability, now well into its third decade, would be pointless. We would see instead a widespread drive to raise grades. But we know better. We have already raised grades, but at the same time seen nearly every other indicator of the effectiveness of higher education decline. So legislators and Education Department officials alike are pushing for some measurement of college effectiveness outside of grades, outside of the secret space protected by the privacy of teaching. The transcript of grades and credit hours remains the defining criterion of "success" in college, but neither public officials nor private employers take it seriously anymore.

The challenge that the accreditors face is to move institutions toward greater transparency. The tools we have already discussed can certainly do that: the teaching inventory and the outcomes transcript and portfolio. Employers show much more interest in a portfolio of student work than in a transcript of grades as evidence to use in hiring. The teaching inventory and outcomes transcript, if made public, could provide much more substantive information about the real learning experience of students in college than anything available today. And the DQP provides an outstanding framework for presenting both teaching and learning data to the public.

If the results of the general teaching inventory were truly public—that is, published for anyone who cared to look at them—then they would become data that could be used to compare different colleges, to form a profile of general faculty practice. Indeed, if such data were widely available they would instantly become more valuable than almost any other public information about colleges, in terms of the quality and nature of undergraduate education. The data would begin to answer the important questions: How would a student who attended this college learn? What would a student do in classes? Today, these questions are unanswerable at most colleges. The answer isn't being hidden; it doesn't exist. Nobody knows.

What we know of outcomes tells us that institutions are much more alike than they are different, that between-college differences tend to be trivial. This pervasive sameness both reinforces and is reinforced by the isomorphic market that offers students and parents no substantive basis for choosing one college over another. If information about teaching practices and learning outcomes were public, it would allow institutions to differentiate themselves, to show themselves to be substantively innovative. It would create a market for change and for the first time reward real productivity.

The student or parent who asks a candidate college what proportion of the faculty lectures, how much they rely on multiple-choice tests, how often students will write papers, and such questions will get no credible answers.

These are the kinds of questions that parents and students should be asking of their prospective colleges. Yet most have no answers today that rise higher than the level of gossip and anecdote wrenched into advertising copy. The anecdotes strongly imply that colleges, at least their enrollment departments, believe that the way faculty teach matters. If anecdotes are important, why are not general patterns of practice more important? Of course they are. Those few colleges and universities that can tell prospective students what kind of learning experience they might expect deserve to be taken much more seriously than the run-of-the-mill institution that relies on dopey and manipulative graphics (laughing students sitting on the lawn or walking to class against a backdrop of ivy-covered brick) to cover a dearth of self-knowledge.

Today, colleges essentially imitate other colleges because they have no clear evidence that they are meeting their own objectives—indeed, they may not be able to even articulate their own objectives in any way that could be tested or confirmed. The accrediting agencies have pushed institutions to articulate their objectives, the learning they want their students to achieve, and to make those objectives public. Still, the evidence of performance on those objectives, if it exists, is hidden or invisible.

Those who rate colleges—*U.S. News* and the dozens of other publications that produce ratings of colleges and universities—are providing their customers what they think they want. But in an isomorphic market where institutions do not provide information that informs, they target the ritual classifications and inputs, many of which are simply irrelevant to the quality of undergraduate education. These ratings in turn serve as feedback to the institutions, which attempt to maximize their evaluations by the standards of the evaluators and increasingly invest in things that distract from rather than contribute to their educational mission.

Those institutions that do well in the rankings have a vested interest in perpetuating their reputational advantage. Thus they resist bringing new data into the mix. (No Ivy League college administers the NSSE.) The challenge for governments and accreditors is to move institutions toward more transparency while not triggering the nearly reflexive resistance to "top-down" mandates. Just waiting for institutions to get religion is no more likely to be successful than it has been in the past.

We should keep in mind that for many students, there is no real competition among colleges; many students just go to the institution that is closest that will accept them. That is certainly true of community colleges and is often true of regional public four-year colleges as well. Among other things, living at home and commuting to college is much less expensive for most students. But regional public institutions depend on enrollment as well, and so must maintain at least a credible stance of being comparable to higher prestige institutions. These institutions are competing for students as well, though sometimes in a different way. But raising standards for the most competitive institutions will also create both pressure and opportunity for regional institutions to improve their situation. In the long run, competition based on genuine, outcomes-based innovation will improve quality across the board.

We need answers to questions of quality: the quality of the curriculum, the quality of the pedagogy, and the quality of the learning. Open information about how students are taught, about the distribution of faculty practices, will go a long way. But in the end, we will also need information about whether and what students are learning. As Robert Zemsky puts it, "The only way to avoid enshrining seat time as the test of a valid undergraduate education is to bite the bullet and define what we expect undergraduates to be able to do when they graduate. Doing so means defining in very practical—and yes, measurable—terms the skills and competencies we want them to acquire as well and the values and learning attitudes we expect them to be able to demonstrate. . . . I am proposing the development of competency-based curricula that explicitly substitute demonstrable competencies for recorded seat time and a passing grade."[41]

18 · LEVERS FOR CHANGE

A New Accountability

For many decades critics in and out of higher education have observed, documented, and called attention to the failures of the system. Yet what has changed has changed because of budgetary pressures or technological shifts, not—with few exceptions—according to any systematic design for improvement. The faculty have changed as contingent teachers have increasingly replaced those on the tenure track. Far from planning this shift, institutional leaders cannot even describe it credibly: most keep no consistent records of who teaches whom and how. Technological innovation has brought computers, the Internet, and now the smartphone into the classroom. But most institutions have shoehorned the conventional curriculum and traditional pedagogy into these new media with as little alteration as possible. That institutions have no very clear idea how these subterranean shifts in the landscape affect student learning should go without saying because institutions have only a fuzzy idea at best of how most of what they do affects student learning. At the same time as these massive shifts have taken place, many organizations and individuals have proposed ways to clarify and advance the real and important goal of colleges: supporting and advancing student learning.

Yet those proposals have not found traction in the academy. From changing pedagogy for individual teachers to better ways to design learning environments and the global systems of framing the work of colleges such as the DQP, changes that offer a real shift in the underlying paradigm governing these institutions have bounced like so many tennis balls off their ivied walls. This is not to say that nothing has changed for the better. Most campuses have enclaves of innovation and academic skunk works that seek to finesse change and sneak new thinking past the myth keepers and shamans who guard the old ways. Many individual faculty members have improved their teaching and come to understand the job better. Some win small victories, some larger ones; some innovations even survive. Yet in only a handful of institutions do those innovations amount to transformation. For the most part, innovation is an institutional pet, kept in a cage and let out on its leash for show, but never allowed to get on the furniture.

The burden of my argument is that colleges and universities as currently configured will never put students first, will never adopt student learning as a functional imperative, because they are configured to do something else. They will keep offering classes without paying much serious attention to whether the classes are bad or good, well or ill designed, functional for the long-term needs of students. The essence of the instruction myth is that colleges exist to offer classes. That is what they are currently designed to do. The reward system and the mythology that frames the work of faculty explicitly and extravagantly reward doing things in the same way and punish those who would make fundamental change. People are naturally loss averse, and the structure of colleges makes paying serious attention to student learning inherently risky, vividly dangerous. This has nothing to do with the personalities or natural proclivities or abilities of the people who work in higher education—nothing whatever, and I really cannot emphasize this too much. It is not at all the case that teachers don't care about students or don't care about learning. As we have seen, most teachers want to teach and would rather be rewarded for the quality of their teaching. But if they are not hypocrites, neither are they fools. They can read the handwriting on the wall, especially when it is written in block letters across the walls of every classroom.

A few of them are heroically brave, and swim upstream for years, trying valiantly to wrench small victories from an unforgiving system. I have known some of these and continue to be inspired by them. But after a while they come to realize that when a new president or provost comes along, or even a new department chair, or a new configuration in the faculty senate, all their efforts can be erased in a stroke. It has happened to me and to many others I could name. Even if they are not trained as statisticians they come to see that in the real world of higher education, upward trends do not persist, as we might naïvely hope, but regress to the mean. And the mean, in higher education, is the Instruction Paradigm. So even the heroic and inspiring champions of student learning eventually come to see that the things truly worth doing cannot be done here.

Given the enormous barriers to change, is there any hope for saving higher education from itself? Or is it a tightly closed system set to maintain itself in stasis indefinitely? This last prospect is not encouraging; in today's world systems that maintain and do not adapt face dim prospects. There is hope, but only if we understand the reasons why designed change is so hard, the reasons why colleges deflect such change so consistently and unerringly. We have explored those reasons in as much detail as the reader might be expected to tolerate. To simplify, this is the situation: Those who control our undergraduate colleges and universities—administrators and tenure-track faculty alike—see it in their interest, both financial and professional, to consent at least tacitly to the Instruction Paradigm mythology. Why? The welfare of everyone depends upon the information available in the system, and the information available in the system cannot be used to fundamentally question the conventional operations of the system because it is generated through those conventional operations. The available information—grades, transcripts, graduation rates—consists almost entirely of measuring gross institutional processes and measuring ritual classifications. This information cannot be used to fundamentally question the instruction myth because the design of the system that generates it is based on the instruction myth. So long as this is the case, change will be dauntingly risky, and even if the system is failing dramatically at its core function this will be invisible because none of the information available relates to its core function.

The only way of breaking this logjam is to introduce new information into the system, information about fundamental functions that is not available today. It is precisely to do this that reformers and accreditors have pushed so hard for learning outcomes assessment. Those who have called for accountability in higher education have been asking for evidence of cost-effectiveness, of good educational performance. The problem with such a concept is that it assumes the existence of credible evidence of performance, and in general we don't have any. The instruction myth thrives in the absence of evidence. The information that does exist has been locked in departmental files or limited to selective generalizations that fail to guide action. Even when institutions gather potentially valuable information they do not channel it where it would need to go to guide organizational learning.

Robert Zemsky, in his 2009 book *Making Reform Work*, argues that "because a catalog of problems and solutions won't yield the desired change, required, instead, is a kind of *dislodging event* of sufficient force that the academy writ large begins to consider changes that no one institution on its own will likely pursue."[1] He suggests several possibilities for dislodging events: a radical change in the financing of student aid, a three-year degree, and other ideas.

While these ideas are worth pursuing, I doubt that any of them would succeed in disrupting the fundamental mythology that holds colleges in stasis in terms of student learning. Many events would be disturbing and stressful for colleges but would still allow them to fall back on the Instruction Paradigm mythology as a framework for reflection and decision. What we need is a paradigm shift, and that would require an event or series of events that would dislodge the myths themselves from their status as the conventional wisdom at colleges and universities. That can be achieved only by shining a light on what is now dark, by making truly transparent what is now concealed by the opaque curtain around the classroom. We need to make the teaching and the learning visible.

But who is *we* here? That is a crucial question because of the unusual nature of the higher education market. To this point, becoming more transparent about teaching and learning has not helped institutions to compete for students. Because the isomorphic market rewards imitation of high-prestige organizations, the high-prestige organizations themselves have no incentive to undermine the instruction myth; it would not be to their advantage to do so (though it would be to the advantage of their students). When less prestigious institutions try to become more transparent, they correspondingly become less like the high-prestige market leaders. Thus, they take a serious risk of damaging their own relative standing. Transparency does not break down the mythology unless it is across the board, unless it provides a body of information that undermines or replaces the instruction myth at many or most institutions, in the academy writ large. To provide a body of information about teaching and learning that could be used to recalibrate the market based not on Instruction Paradigm prestige but on real evidence of educational performance would be the kind of disruptive event that could change the risk calculation for educational innovation. It could undermine the status quo bias in institutional decisions by introducing the chance of reward based on productive innovation—both to individuals and to the institution.

The question has often been framed as one of bottom-up or top-down, of whether change should emerge from within the institutions or should be imposed by outside parties. I think this is not a productive way of framing the issue. It is clear that institutions are not likely to initiate large-scale changes on their own, for all the reasons we have discussed. But it is equally clear that no outside body has either the knowledge or the perspective to impose some preformatted way of doing things better on such large and complex institutions. And we have seen that the competitive marketplace really doesn't work for higher education right now, for the same reasons that faculty and others within the institutions are inhibited: the market doesn't have reliable information about what works and what doesn't. The role of outside authorities should be to mandate a new information flow for the institutions, to create information about what institutions really do and really achieve in the realm of teaching and learning. Given that information, both those within the institutions and those outside will be able to recognize and reward real progress toward real educational goals.

How to do this? We have seen how in the last few chapters. If teaching practices and learning outcomes were visible to everyone, it would begin to create a real market for higher education and to provide a means to reward, rather than punish, innovation that improves learning.

Therefore, accrediting associations should mandate that every institution report publicly, at an institutional level, how teachers teach and what students learn. The apparatus for doing this is not complicated, and in fact the technology and the rubrics for doing it already exist at many institutions. Ultimately, institutions that can conceal teaching and learning behind a curtain of mythic obfuscations, that can conceal the products of their work even from themselves, can never improve reliably because they can never know whether they are improving, and neither can anyone else.

MAKING TEACHING VISIBLE

If the way teachers teach were public knowledge, improving the quality of pedagogy would become an essential mission for colleges and universities.

Most college teachers are now unable to set meaningful goals for teaching better. Even those who have reached the contemplation stage in movement toward new teaching practices are often deterred by the fact that any activities they might undertake would be invisible to the outside world and unmeasurable in their results. As Carl Wieman notes, "The biggest barrier to improving the teaching at research universities is that they are so ineffective at measuring and rewarding effective teaching."[2]

Many institutions promote and invest in professional development to improve the quality of teaching. But participation in such programs is almost always left to the initiative of the teachers themselves, and their results are often unknown even to those who conduct the programs. Crucially, teachers rarely benefit from improving their teaching other than by the satisfaction of a job well done. That is no small thing, and that is why many teachers do work hard at their jobs and seek to improve. But the teacher's endowment, in terms of both money and prestige, is disconnected from teaching results. The public, visible aspects of the professional role will rarely be improved by better teaching. And the results of improved teaching are unobserved and unmonitored.

In most cases, teachers receive feedback on their own performance only when they elicit such feedback themselves. Student evaluations rarely if ever generate meaningful feedback that teachers could use to improve. But a Teaching Inventory would do so. It would first, on the model of the TPI or the PIPS, identify superior teaching practices derived from good research. It would then provide data on how an individual's practices compare with those common in the field and those that have the best results. If practiced widely, it would itself become a tool for further research to test what practices have the best results. It would be a tool that would do more to break down the mythology and reveal the reality of teaching practice than any other reform.

For these reasons, the accrediting agencies should move quickly to require that every institution make its teaching practices public by conducting a Teaching Inventory and making the statistical results openly available. This would not, of course, require revealing information about individual teachers. However, institutions would be well advised to begin integrating this data into their teacher evaluation systems. It would allow every teacher to see what he or she is doing in a framework where improvement has a clear, public meaning.

If information about teaching were public and consequential, it would facilitate, indeed I would say very much encourage, the development of a Teaching Quality Framework (TQF), the structure for genuine peer review we disused in chapter 13, supported by Teaching Improvement Portfolios, William Massy's idea that we discussed in chapter 14. Departments and colleges should begin to build departmental databases for moving beyond student evaluations in hiring and promotion. The TQF would also provide a framework for tracking teaching practices over time, so that departments could set real goals for teaching and could base promotion decisions on evidence of accomplishment. Massy has advocated the portfolio as a means of supporting Academic Quality Work, a process of collecting and using data to improve learning. He has pointed out how it would make departmental practice different from what we are accustomed to: "What's foreign is the notion that educational improvement activities should be systematic rather than situational, that they should go beyond curriculum and personal teaching prowess, and that departments bear collective responsibility for quality assurance."[3] The concept of Academic Quality Work applies to research as well as teaching, and would certainly help to rationalize the research programs in many departments. But as we have seen, the greatest need in most departments for coherence and quality assurance is in teaching. And that is something that the Teaching Inventory supported by the Departmental Teaching Improvement Portfolio could provide. It would also facilitate the accreditation process by making quality control for teaching an ongoing process and not an intermittent burst of activity before the accreditation site visit.

Making information about teaching public would have two added advantages. First, it would give potential students and their parents information about the educational experience at the college that would be more reliable and informative by orders of magnitude than anything available to them today. Unlike the current *U.S. News*–type ratings, it would provide information based not on the experience of students who did not attend the college but on the experience of those who did. If parents and students could see for themselves which colleges, and which departments at colleges, rely exclusively on lecture and which engage in active learning pedagogies, they could see where learning is more likely and where it is not. Thus it would, first gradually and then rapidly, alter the market for college. Today all parties are essentially locked into the instruction myth, which is what makes the college market isomorphic and based essentially on cost and selectivity: the default assumption, for which there is no credible evidence, is that the more expensive colleges are better than the less expensive. The myth of unity allows institutions to play bait and switch with the public and students and substitute evidence of faculty research for evidence of undergraduate student learning, as if the two were interchangeable. If the public has access to the statistical report of the Teaching Inventory, it would be able to see not just how much the classes cost, but what they are worth. It would not by itself be sufficient to rank colleges as to the quality of the undergraduate experience, but it would be better evidence by far than is available to anyone today.

Second, if real data on pedagogical practices were generated not just in rare, one-off studies but at least annually on a regular basis, they would reveal the trends in teaching at the institution. It would be possible to assess and further explore the progress or delay in moving toward better pedagogy. The data would enable institutions to set real goals for teaching and to create incentives to reward their accomplishment. If faculty and administrators could look at a common body of evidence on departmental teaching practices, departments would see evidence of educational quality that would disable many of the defensive routines that they have conventionally used to deflect scrutiny and protect familiar practices. Just a common framework for describing and assessing teaching practice would enable individual teachers to set clear, measurable goals for improvement, so would it do this for entire universities, schools, colleges, and departments. It would be an index of organizational learning.

The objections to mandating such a system are foreseeable. The first and most predictable would be that revealing to the world how teachers are teaching would infringe on the academic freedom of the faculty. We have already discussed the myth of academic freedom and found it without basis in this context. Those who would object to making pedagogy transparent are essentially claiming that academic freedom protects the right to teach badly. None of the questions on the surveys we have discussed have anything to do with the political or social or religious views of the professors or their stands on controversial issues. They have to do with how the teachers teach, not what they teach. Furthermore, I am not suggesting here that any given mode of teaching should be mandated, only that the faculty members' choices should be revealed for what they are.

A second objection would be, "What about faculty research?" Would transparency about teaching damage research? It is hard to imagine why making classroom practices public would directly affect the objects or methods of faculty research. If the system works, some faculty would spend less time on research because they could be rewarded and promoted based on credible evidence of good teaching. We should devoutly hope that this is what happens, that institutions create genuine career paths for teaching that reward and promote excellent teachers. Of course, if some faculty spend more time on teaching they will correspondingly spend less time on research. But we have no reason to believe that this would harm the quality of academic research overall. Indeed, freeing those who would rather teach from the ritual obligation of disciplinary publication would seem to improve the distribution of labor across the board.

The current mindset that more resources for research—for everyone, all the time—is the only route to advancement is based not on any careful analysis of research needs but on the lack of an alternative. When research is the only path to faculty advancement, the research magnet draws all the energy and resources of the academy to it. And one result is that many faculty members write what they do because they must write something, and many of the resulting publications have little or no impact on either the discipline or the world at large. Important research is hardly ever done because the author needs to check a box on the tenure form. The argument that important research would go undone because teaching is visible and rewarded is rooted entirely in the mythology we have been debunking. If institutions valued and attended to teaching, faculty would probably do less and better research.

The essential act that should be required of each institution as a condition of accreditation is that it credibly report how its teachers teach, all of them in every field, and make that report public.

MAKING LEARNING VISIBLE

The transcript as a report of letter grades allocated by credit hours is the institutional embodiment of the instruction myth. It buries the learning experience of students under layers of indefinable abstractions that can never be clarified and can never serve as feedback for improvement to teachers, students, or the institution. This is why calls for learning outcomes have been so persistent. But we have discovered that if institutions devise and collect information about learning outcomes but essentially keep that information limited or secret, it can never change the system. As long as grades are mandatory and learning outcomes optional, as long as grades are a necessary and sufficient condition for granting the degree and learning outcomes a marginal and voluntary add-on, learning outcomes will never change the system. The only way to change the system is to make outcomes public, uniformly collected and reported. If publicly reporting the aggregate results of learning outcomes were a condition of accreditation, then they would very quickly become important evidence of institutional performance.

Again, there is nothing complicated about this. Almost every accredited institution *claims* to have existing rubrics of learning outcomes and to be collecting evidence on them. The AAC&U VALUE rubrics are widely used and universally available as a template of tested standards that could be either adopted directly or revised to meet the needs of a given institution. The software for recording and preserving them is readily available, and already in use at many institutions. Reports of undergraduate learning outcomes would be a step toward real accountability.

The credibility and value of learning outcomes depend on three things: whether the outcomes are intrinsically well designed, whether the student performances that demonstrate those outcomes are credible and substantial, and whether the performances are reasonably assessed. The DQP addresses these matters. It provides a framework and template for organizing outcomes in a way that constitutes a credible description of a liberal education, and it calls for authentic assessment of student work. It is an obvious choice for a default template for describing and assessing student learning outcomes across a curriculum. The DQP itself, of course, is a flexible document, right now being used, tested, and revised. And if any institution has a better idea, it should be encouraged to articulate and develop it. But there needs to be an overall design, not just a basket of miscellaneous outcomes. Just as there should be a curriculum, not—as is sadly often the case today—just a basket of miscellaneous classes.

In the realm of assessment, one of the perennial bogeymen has been standardized tests. Disturbed by the sometimes test-centric efforts at reform in K–12 education, some college teachers and administrators have argued that "assessment" is code for "standardized tests" and that the whole project is a covert effort to hand over higher education to the large testing companies and to reduce education to simplistic testing. This is nonsense. And the argument is especially dubious coming from those who have no idea, and no apparent interest in finding out, how students are currently being assessed in their separate classrooms. Multiple-choice tests are no better an assessment tool because they are administered by a single teacher in the privacy of a classroom instead of a larger group outside the classroom. And to say that a test is standardized is just to report that it has been used with a large group of students to see if the results are consistent across groups and over time. The problem isn't standardization; it is the trivialization and reductionism inherent in simplistic and incomplete methods of assessment. The DQP ends the controversy by making clear that the standard of assessment should be substantial and meaningful student performances. The DQP calls upon students to do work that shows their knowledge and skills and describes that work consistently not in terms of categories of knowledge or ability but in terms of what students do: Students *define, explain, demonstrate, evaluate, clarify, frame, construct, elucidate, assess, articulate, supply, produce, investigate, and translate.* They don't check boxes or select from a, b, c, and d. This is not to say, of course, that there would be no more tests at an institution that adopted the DQP. It is to say that learning would not stop with and be defined by testing, certainly not testing of the reductive sort that students most commonly experience today. Another way of saying the same thing is that assessments under the DQP would consistently produce learning artifacts that could be preserved in a portfolio of student work to provide direct evidence of student performance. Something like such a portfolio would be a necessary accompaniment for a credible transcript of learning outcomes.

It would take a few years for some institutions to implement the Outcomes Transcript and Portfolio, hardly any time at all for others.

LEARNING TO CHANGE

The design of a transcript of learning outcomes that reflects a coherent vision, like the DQP, would be easy for most institutions to implement but hard to assimilate. That is, it would probably call attention to the incoherence of the curriculum and the weakness of pedagogy. It would reveal that at many institutions the grab bag of miscellaneous courses that goes under the name "general education" often fails to achieve, and in no way ensures, the learning outcomes that the institution claims its students achieve. As we have seen, 120 credit hours with a C or better fails to lead to anything in particular in the way of educational outcomes. If the normal flow of information in the organization made this consistently clear, institutions would have to respond. It would be a teachable moment for colleges and universities.

We learn from our failures, but only when we come to recognize them as failures and when we seek and find ways of correcting them. The apparatus of myths that sustains the Instruction Paradigm perpetuates failure by camouflaging or obscuring it. Making teaching and learning transparent would reveal some of the failures of colleges and universities, and so allow them to learn from those failures. Institutions could learn to change for the better if feedback on the outcomes of their actions came to them in the normal course of their work.

Making institutions reveal publicly their teaching practices and learning outcomes would indeed be a disruptive event at most campuses. It would also change the terms of discussion about policy because it would largely move that discussion from the realm of myth to the realm of testable claims.

Institutions that are serious about demonstrably improving student learning will embark on the serious peer review of teaching and the creation of a career track for advancement in teaching. If an institution could claim with credible evidence that their faculty were engaged in scholarly teaching, it would make that institution more attractive to students and their parents than institutions that could not support such a claim.

That would involve, of course, the support for a second-order environment around teaching and learning to balance against the disciplinary community manifested in the academic departments. The prospect of advancement as a faculty member can no longer reside completely in the disciplinary community that exists to nurture and support research. If the faculty member's endowment falls under the exclusive authority of the research apparatus, faculty will have little incentive to move from the contemplation to the action stage in improving their teaching. But if the interests of the institution are linked to raising the quality of teaching, then there are several ways that the endowment can be enriched.

Many departments would welcome the introduction of solid and reliable information into their decision making about teaching and learning. And the college or university would have a means to engage in real quality work with departments. All institutions have processes, at least on paper, for program review or oversight. And often these processes are helpful in terms of keeping budgets balanced and resources distributed where they are needed. But rarely does an institution exercise any meaningful oversight of the teaching and learning process. That is because, beyond enrollment statistics and grade point averages, there is simply no evidence of quality one way or the other. Departmental planning usually takes the form of planning to offer so many sections of which classes in the next year.

The Departmental Teaching Improvement Portfolio, especially if embedded in an institutional Teaching Quality Framework, would let departments plan to raise the quality of student learning and provide evidence of problems or progress. And faculty members who were active in cross-departmental work on teaching would bring added value to departmental planning for improving teaching. In today's environment, departments can preserve their control by maintaining privacy and secrecy because there is little or no public evidence of either practices or results. If such evidence were available, departments would profit from focusing on results, and would thus be more open to collaboration that could lead to better approaches. Departments would be more likely to learn from each other if secrecy were not an option. The Departmental Teaching Improvement Portfolio would also reinforce the departments in hiring the best teachers and providing career ladders based on teaching improvement. It would link the quality of teaching to the faculty member's endowment.

DESIRABLE DIFFICULTIES ON THE PATH TO LEARNING

Breaking down the ruling myths would not instantly transform colleges and universities. But it would create feedback that institutions, and others, could use to assess their performance. Departments locked in groupthink would not suddenly become open forums for evidence-based reflection on curriculum and pedagogy. But the infusion of new information and new responsibilities will begin to change the conversations.

One of the foundational insights about teaching and learning that we must accept to improve education is that teachers have to start where the students are. Brief reflection will reveal that there is no alternative. The same principle applies to efforts to change faculties and colleges. They start from where they are—just because they are there.

But an equally important insight for the teacher that applies as well to the educational reformer is that you can't leave them where they are. You need to get them moving to somewhere else, or you are wasting your time. As I tell my writing students, good prose moves; it doesn't just sit there. And as I tell all my students, engaged students move, they see new sights, hear new sounds, make discoveries. Learning is change; it starts where you are, but doesn't let you stay there.

We serve our students poorly when we flatter them, cater to them, and protect them from the rigors of the work that discovery entails. We serve them poorly when we offer ease and effortless reward. To serve our students is to support them in facing challenges that they may not readily welcome. We serve them best when we support them in surmounting barriers higher than they have surmounted before, facing trials harsher than they have overcome before. Likewise, we serve our faculty and our institutions poorly when we protect them from inconvenient evidence of problems, when we let them hide behind the myth of quality from the reality of their problems and create a false boosterism to camouflage their failures.

UCLA psychologist Robert A. Bjork, whose research has greatly advanced our understanding of memory and how it works, coined the term *desirable difficulties* to identify experiences that "appear *during* the learning process to impede learning," but that after the fact are found to have enhanced the learning.[4] For example, if we introduce enough challenges into a passage to make it harder, but not impossible, to read, then students are more likely to remember its content. If you want to get better at something—whether it's playing tennis, solving sudoku puzzles, or writing essays—you'll never do it simply by repeating familiar formulas. You need to face new challenges to learn to do things better. Fill-in tests are harder than multiple-choice tests, but students who take fill-in tests remember more of what they were tested on, all other things being equal, than students who take multiple-choice tests. It is harder to write an argument than a narrative, but students who write arguments become capable of new kinds of persuasion and analysis that those who stop with narrative cannot handle. A desirable difficulty is one that the student can cope with from where she is right now, but with effort, not by simply applying a formula or plugging in a routine. The task must be difficult to be desirable for learning. We encountered essentially the same concept earlier when we noted that gaining mastery consists of learning to perform in System 1 tasks that we learn in System 2. System 2 is by definition effortful, demanding. Tasks don't become easy until you have first done them hard.

As we think of how colleges and universities might change, we should not think of some global idea of the perfect university, some College of Utopia that will provide a blueprint for the ideal education. Rather, we should think of those difficult tasks for today's faculties and institutions that will help them to learn. We should recognize that paradigm shifts are always difficult and seek to emphasize those difficulties that will be desirable for learning.

The teacher who poses a problem for students and then has them discuss their solutions with one another to compare them is quite self-consciously creating difficulties for those students; she knows that if the problems are too easy they will not lead to learning. She seeks to formulate problems that will make students struggle with their prior assumptions, that will make it hard for them to fall back on easy algorithms. But she knows as well that if the problem is just unmanageable, leaves the students without recourse or a method of approach, that will also be fatal to learning. She seeks to find and frame problems that present challenges that students can meet, but only by making some mistakes first and learning how to correct them. She seeks to create desirable difficulties. The same thing is going on for the teacher who poses a challenge in interpreting a historical event, predicting the outcome of a chemical interaction, finding the weaknesses in an economic theory, or developing an argument in an essay. Teaching at its best is the creation of desirable difficulties, hard tasks that are doable with the support and interaction available at the time and in the place where you ask students to do them.

By creating desirable difficulties for our colleges and universities, we will allow them to set goals and measure their progress. Transparency, collaboration, and a changed reward system will not be a panacea. There are no panaceas; they are as imaginary as unicorns. The work that colleges and universities are trying to do is inherently hard and will never be easy. The evidence indicates that it is going to get harder, not easier. But by undermining the myths that currently prevent institutions from learning to change, we would channel their effort toward those hard tasks that could lead to learning and growth.

We can take the risks that learning entails when we see the clear prospect of reward. Of course, there are several kinds and levels of rewards in life. There is the payment in money we get for doing a job and the respect and recognition we receive from colleagues and others for doing the job well. And there is the most powerful of all rewards, the satisfaction of knowing that we have accomplished something worth doing, that we have made something or helped someone or planted a seed that will grow, that we have altered the trajectory toward the future in a way that will bear fruit. That reward, the reward of getting it right, of making a difference, is the most fundamental motivation we can experience. When the internal desire to accomplish something that counts and the external reward for doing a job reinforce each other, then an individual is poised for inspiration and accomplishment, set up to thrive and to succeed.

I am biased, of course. But I suspect that many others will see the justice in my claim that one of those life tasks that offers, potentially, the greatest intrinsic rewards, the greatest sense of accomplishment, is teaching. I think I speak quite objectively and from the best evidence when I say that, measured by every measure of real consequence, teaching makes an enormous difference, for better or for worse, in the way the world goes. Every teacher, every day, in every classroom and seminar and email and conference and marking session, bends the trajectory of the future one way or another, up or down, for better or for worse, for the students he or she touches. And most teachers, I am convinced, feel the weight of the task, the potential force of it. The vast majority of teachers choose this line of work because at some level they know that it counts, it really matters. At any rate, they know that at the beginning of their careers.

But today, for most college and university faculty and administrators, the internal drive to teach is not reinforced by the external system. The place where teaching happens is not friendly to teaching; the people in charge don't give it a lot of serious attention. The teacher in higher education is confronted with a plethora of difficulties that are not desirable for learning, because they contain no feedback on learning and no reward for correcting mistakes, for growing in the work. They work in the closed classroom, by themselves, largely in the dark.

What I said of colleges and universities in the introduction to this book is frequently true of the teachers who do the core work of those institutions: they don't know what they are doing. Not in the sense that they are incompetent or negligent, but in the sense that they do not see the consequences of their work, and so are never fully aware of what they have accomplished.

But they could be. They don't need to work in the darkness. The mythic infrastructure of colleges is completely artificial and insubstantial. If exposed to the light it will deteriorate rapidly.

I do not suggest that the rather simple and rudimentary apparatus for measuring teaching and learning that I have suggested here is comprehensive or adequate. The point is that if the apparatus for measuring teaching and learning is made central to the work of colleges, then they will begin to cast more light on what is important. It will change the difficulties that teachers and administrators face. Grappling with the outcomes of learning experiences, arguing about what really counts as an index of learning, seeking to better measure the effects of a learning experience, these are difficult tasks. Teaching in a way that leads to learning is not a problem that will ever be solved. It is a difficulty that will be managed only to arise again in a new form. And it is a desirable difficulty, because we will always learn something valuable from grappling with it and will grow from the struggle.

What is a teacher? What is a student? Many students think that what defines their role is that they attend classes and take tests. And for most colleges and universities today, what defines the role of a teacher is that they meet classes and assign grades. Is it any wonder that, for many of them, it often seems aimless drudgery? Who, after all, cares about these things? And why should they? The difficulties they face, slogging through the lectures and the tests, are instrumental, trivial, and rarely memorable.

Both teachers and students could trade the trivial difficulties of testing and grading for the desirable difficulties of learning and growing. And the ways they can do that are very similar. Students studying alone for a test, memorizing what seems the minutiae of their subject or practicing the algorithms or formulas that will let them push the right button or check the right box, are working for pay. Students engaged in trying to persuade other students that the problem works this way, engaging with the objections that others raise, and trying to see how others came at things differently, are learning for understanding. Likewise, the teacher who tells students what they need to know and then tries to devise a test to see whether they know it, is working for pay. As in the student's case, this teacher will devote as little time to the task as is necessary to accomplish it. The teacher who is seeking to find out what students think that creates paths and barriers to new knowledge, who is engaged in a conversation with those students, adjusting to them as they adjust to her, is teaching for understanding. Both tasks are hard, but the nature of their hardness is completely different. One is hard as growing is hard, as tilling the soil for planting is hard, as shaping the bowl on the wheel or the tool at the forge is hard. The other is hard as breaking rocks on a chain gang is hard.

If teachers can become learners, can grow in their work, can talk with other teachers about how to do the work better, can look at evidence of their accomplishment and weigh it on an ongoing basis, they will become better teachers and students will become better students. If we can replace the trivializing difficulties of the Instruction Paradigm with the empowering difficulties of the Learning Paradigm, colleges will get better and students will learn more, and they will thrive in the process.

As I said at the beginning, change for the sake of change is a fool's errand. To change wisely and well we need to first understand why we are changing. If we have a place to stand, we can move the world. To find that place, we need to ask who we are and what we want to do. Some argue that colleges and universities are cybernetic systems impervious to fundamental change; teachers and students are cogs in the machine that moves people through classes, interminably, with periodic adjustments and curricular blips. Moving people through classes is what they do. They are the process they carry out. If that is who we are, then change is indeed beyond our ken or reach.

Colleges and universities have changed vastly over the centuries. They are not set in a pattern, impervious to alteration. And they are human institutions. People run them and make their rules. They are failing us today because they are set in their ways and deflecting the evidence they could use to improve. This is not inevitable. They are not machines, they are groups of people with free will. If they seek and pay attention to the right kinds of information, they can learn. If they can learn to change, they can change to learn.

We know this: there are a lot of students and potential students out there, all around us, who need to learn how to understand the world better and to live their lives better and to do their jobs better. It is only a perfectly bland and factual observation that the future of the world depends on how well those students and potential students learn and grow. But the whole project of modern civilization embarks from the premise that these students are not bound to repeat the lives of their parents but have the possibility of doing new, different, and better things. The whole project of civilization, the idea of democracy, and the concept of progress depend on the belief that a student can learn in more than trivial ways, in transformative ways. We believe that the son or daughter of a farmworker or a housekeeper can come to understand things and do things in ways that are so different from what he or she has known before as to accomplish things unknown to his or her ancestors. We believe that human capital can be built through the workings of the human mind. We believe in learning. Stop to think about it. We, we in the United States of America especially, have staked everything on this belief. Everything.

So in the end the quintessential idea behind our hope for the future is that the daughter of a day laborer and a housekeeper can study and learn and as a result of studying and learning can become competent and skilled at doing things her parents could never do, can earn more and contribute greatly, can change. We believe that people can change, and our whole history proves that it is true. Colleges and universities especially must believe that their students can change because that is their only rationale for existing. Education is transformation.

So this is what it comes down to. Can we believe that the first-generation student entering the halls of one of our great universities can become transformed, can grow in knowledge and abilities and capacities, but that the great university that she is about to enter cannot?

Sadly, that is the state of affairs today. These institutions, the very existence of which is premised on their mission to change their students, have insulated themselves against learning, against change. The very institutions in which we have invested the great responsibility to define what knowledge matters and what challenges must be met have become accustomed to camouflaging knowledge of their own actions and deflecting the challenges that they face. The institutions that we trust with the preparation of students young and old for serious and important work have become accustomed to shirking their own work. It is time for the colleges to learn from their students how to learn and how to change.

ACKNOWLEDGMENTS

This book has been underway, in one form or another, for a long time. And hence it is a product of conversations with more people than I could easily recount, or in some cases even recall. At a deep level, it emerged from the felt struggles of people at dozens of campuses who were trying to grapple with the intransigence of the system, often thinking it was just them, or just their institution that was the barrier. I am deeply grateful to all those good folks for their candor, their good will, and their unfailing efforts.

Some of those conversations proved to be recurrent, or at least very long. I want to express special gratitude to Russell Edgerton, whose example of persistence and creativity in the face of daunting obstacles has been an inspiration and whose thinking has been a touchstone; Peter Ewell, who perhaps knows more than anyone about higher education and yet addresses its recurrent problems with a freshness and alacrity that cannot but inspire; Ralph Wolff, who understands things deeply, yet has the special skill of engaging in a productive way those who do not understand at all; Robert Barr, the originator of the Learning Paradigm and sometime coauthor, who has provided ongoing conversation and grounding over the years; David Shupe, long a champion for ideas that work, even in the face of an intransigent and often unappreciative system; Anton Tolman, who introduced me to a whole new way of thinking about change, and was kind enough to review the relevant chapters in progress; Jeff King, who has been able to spare time from a very productive schedule to provide a sounding board and feedback on the ideas in genesis and the text in progress; Pat Schwerdtfeger, whose conversations over many years have kept me grounded in the reality of the way colleges work; Daniel Bernstein, whose work inspired much of the thinking behind this work and who was kind enough to provide feedback and ongoing updates.

In addition, I greatly appreciate the assistance of those who provided feedback and information on specific issues. These individuals include, but are not limited to, Simon Bates, Lisa Berry, Joel Dubois, Deborah Clark, and Jessica Winston.

My thanks to Kimberly Guinta, who welcomed the manuscript at Rutgers University Press, and Lisa Banning, who guided it through the review and editorial processes.

Finally, thanks to my wife, Marilee, who was the sole breadwinner during the roughly five years that I was writing this book, and to my son Dylan, now a college student himself, who helped to get the manuscript in shape for publication.

Portions of chapters 3, 5, and 14 were originally published in "Venture Colleges: Charters for Change in Higher Education," *Change: The Magazine of Higher Learning* (January/February 2005): 35–43, and "Why Does the Faculty Resist Change?," *Change: The Magazine of Higher Learning* (January/February 2012): 6–15.

NOTES

INTRODUCTION

1. Barr and Tagg, "From Teaching to Learning."
2. Eliade, *Myth and Reality*, 1.

CHAPTER 1   THE CHRONIC CRISIS

1. Barr, "From Teaching to Learning."
2. Blaich and Wise, "Moving from Assessment to Institutional Improvement," 77.
3. Keeling and Hersh, *We're Losing Our Minds*, 14.
4. Ochoa, "Guidance to Institutions and Accrediting Agencies."
5. Ibid., 20.
6. Astin, *Are You Smart Enough?*, 1.
7. Brewer and Tierney, "Barriers to Innovation," 16.
8. Mazur, *Peer Instruction*, 4.
9. Cuban, *How Scholars Trumped Teachers*.
10. Study Group, "Involvement in Learning," 15.
11. Ibid., 21.
12. Association of American Colleges, "Integrity in the College Curriculum," 1.
13. Ibid., 4.
14. Robert Zemsky, *Structure and Coherence: Measuring the Undergraduate Curriculum* (Washington, DC: Association of American Colleges, 1989), quoted in Robert Zemsky, *Checklist for Change*, 8.
15. Pascarella and Terenzini, *How College Affects Students*, 592.
16. Dale and Krueger, "Estimating the Payoff," 1523.
17. Ibid., 1523.
18. Astin, *What Matters in College?*, 434.
19. Ibid., 435.
20. Pascarella and Terenzini, *How College Affects Students, Volume 2*, 641.
21. National Assessment of Adult Literacy, "Literacy in Everyday Life," 36.
22. Astin, *Are You Smart Enough?*, 39.
23. Zemsky, *Checklist for Change*, 93.
24. National Survey of Student Engagement, "NSSE 2000," 33.
25. Blaich and Wise, "Moving from Assessment to Institutional Improvement."
26. Shavelson, *Measuring College Learning Responsibly*, 50.
27. Arum and Roksa, *Academically Adrift*, 36.
28. Arum and Roksa, *Aspiring Adults Adrift*, 118.

29. Ibid., 38.

30. Ibid., 44.

31. Arum and Roksa, *Academically Adrift*, 121.

32. Pascarella et al., "How Robust Are the Findings of *Academically Adrift*?," 23.

33. Zemsky, *Checklist for Change*, 201.

34. Babcock and Marks, "Falling Time Cost of College," 468.

35. Baier et al., "College Students' Textbook Reading, or Not!"

36. Rojstaczer and Healy, "Where A Is Ordinary."

37. Rojstaczer and Healy, "Grading in American Colleges and Universities."

38. Rojstaczer and Healy, "Where A Is Ordinary."

39. Halpern and Hakel, "Applying the Science of Learning," 4.

40. Hersh and Keeling, "Changing Institutional Culture," 5.

41. Astin, *Are You Smart Enough?*, 25.

42. Tough, "Who Gets to Graduate?"

43. Baum, Ma, and Payea, *Education Pays*, 42.

44. Ma and Baum, "Trends in Community Colleges," 20.

45. Astin, *Are You Smart Enough?*, 63.

46. Strauss, "Connection between Education, Income Inequality, and Unemployment."

47. Bailey, Jaggars, and Jenkins, *Redesigning America's Community Colleges*, 2, italics in original.

48. Hanushek and Woessmann, "How Much Do Educational Outcomes Matter in OECD Countries?," 10.

49. Ibid., table 7.

50. Ibid.

51. Astin, *Are You Smart Enough?*, 62.

52. Ewell, "Assessment, Accountability, and Improvement," 16.

53. Freeman et al., "Active Learning Increases Student Performance," 8412.

54. Ibid., 8412.

55. Ibid., 8413.

56. Ibid., 8413.

57. Stains et al., "Anatomy of STEM Teaching in North American Universities," 1469.

58. Ibid., 1469.

59. Zemsky, *Making Reform Work*, 121.

CHAPTER 2 HOW DID IT GET THIS WAY?

1. Quoted in Morison, *Founding of Harvard College*, 93.

2. Rudolph, *Curriculum*, 3.

3. Ibid., 31–32.

4. Ibid., 47.

5. Quoted in ibid., 61–62.

6. Quoted in Hawkins, *Between Harvard and America*, 66.

7. Fallon, *German University*, 6.
8. Quoted in ibid., 25.
9. Quoted in ibid., 20.
10. Ibid., 52.
11. Quoted in Smith, *Killing the Spirit*, 45.
12. Hawkins, *Between Harvard and America*, 65.
13. Quoted in Lucas, *American Higher Education*, 172.
14. Quoted in ibid., 173.
15. Quoted in ibid., 173.
16. Quoted in Cuban, *How Scholars Trumped Teachers*, 19.
17. Rudolph, *American College and University*, 271–272.
18. Quoted in Veysey, *Emergence of the American University*, 160.
19. Quoted in ibid., 93.
20. Lewis, *Excellence without a Soul*, 34.
21. Quoted in ibid., 165.
22. Ibid., 34.
23. Cuban, *How Scholars Trumped Teachers*, 55.
24. Lewis, *Excellence without a Soul*, 40.
25. Cuban, *How Scholars Trumped Teachers*, 53.
26. Shedd, "History of the Student Credit Hour," 7.
27. Ibid., 8.
28. Quoted in ibid., 8.
29. Quoted in ibid., 7.
30. Rudolph, *Curriculum*, 196.
31. Veysey, *Emergence of the American University*, 144–145.
32. Lewis, *Excellence without a Soul*, 39.
33. Veysey, *Emergence of the American University*, 176–177.
34. Rudolph, *Curriculum*, 18.
35. Ibid., 58.
36. Menand, *Marketplace of Ideas*, 64–65.
37. Ibid., 76.
38. Ibid., 76.
39. Ibid., 76–77.
40. Kerr, *Uses of the University*, 49.
41. Damrosch, *We Scholars*, 18.

CHAPTER 3   THE STATUS QUO BIAS

1. *Oxford English Dictionary*, s.v. "bias."
2. Quoted in Plous, *Psychology of Judgment and Decision Making*, 80.
3. Ibid.
4. Ibid., 64.

5. Ibid., 67–68.

6. Harris, "Answering Questions."

7. Loftus, *Eyewitness Testimony*, 157.

8. Kahneman and Tversky, "Choices, Values, and Frames," 1.

9. Kahneman, *Thinking, Fast and Slow*, 273.

10. Ibid., 275.

11. Ibid., 275.

12. Kahneman and Tversky, "Choices, Values, and Frames," 4–5.

13. Ibid., 5.

14. Ibid., 6.

15. Thaler, *Misbehaving*, 34.

16. Ibid., 153.

17. Ibid., 154.

18. Ariely, *Predictably Irrational*, 132–133.

19. Ibid., 135.

20. Kahneman, Ritov, and Schkade, "Economic Preferences or Attitude Expressions?," 666.

21. Ibid., 665–666, italics in original.

22. Loftus, *Eyewitness Testimony*, 156–157.

23. Ariely, *Predictably Irrational*, 28.

24. Kahneman, Ritov, and Schkade, "Economic Preferences or Attitude Expressions?"; Plous, *Psychology of Judgment and Decision Making*.

25. Ariely, *Predictably Irrational*, 36.

26. Thaler, *Misbehaving*, 61.

27. Kahneman and Tversky, "Choices, Values, and Frames," 13.

28. Samuelson and Zeckhauser, "Status Quo Bias in Decision Making," 41.

29. Ibid., 40.

30. Ibid., 31.

31. Ibid., 31–32.

32. Ibid., 33.

33. Ibid., 33.

34. Kahneman, *Thinking, Fast and Slow*, 305.

35. Thaler, *Misbehaving*, 64.

36. Thaler, "Toward a Positive Theory of Consumer Choice," 47.

37. Festinger, Riecken, and Schachter, *When Prophecy Fails*; Festinger, *Theory of Cognitive Dissonance*.

38. Samuelson and Zeckhauser, "Status Quo Bias in Decision Making," 39.

CHAPTER 4   HOW THE STATUS QUO BIAS DEFENDS ITSELF IN ORGANIZATIONS

1. Argyris, *Overcoming Organizational Defenses*, 10.

2. Argyris, Putnam, and Smith, *Action Science*, 81–82.

3. Rice and Sorcinelli, "Can the Tenure Process Be Improved?," 106.
4. Barr and Tagg, "From Teaching to Learning"; and Tagg, *Learning Paradigm College.*
5. Argyris, *Reasoning, Learning, and Action,* 85.
6. Argyris and Schön, *Organizational Learning II,* 99–100.
7. Hornstein, *Managerial Courage,* 82.
8. Ibid., 82–83.
9. Ibid., 12.
10. Argyris and Schön, *Organizational Learning II,* 100.
11. Ibid., 100.
12. Ibid., 100.
13. Ibid., 102.
14. Zemsky, *Checklist for Change,* 174.
15. Argyris, *Overcoming Organizational Defenses,* 46.
16. Argyris, *Reasons and Rationalizations,* 11.
17. Kahneman, *Thinking, Fast and Slow,* 20–21.

CHAPTER 5   THE DESIGN OF COLLEGES AND THE MYTHS OF QUALITY

1. Kuh and Ikenberry, "More Than You Think," 24.
2. Kerr, *Uses of the University,* 118.
3. Ibid., 15–16.
4. Bok, *Our Underachieving Colleges,* 334.
5. Muscatine, *Fixing College Education,* 35, italics in original.
6. Bok, *Our Underachieving Colleges,* 50.
7. Burgan, *What Ever Happened to the Faculty?,* 20.
8. Ibid., 28.
9. Muscatine, *Fixing College Education,* 97.
10. Ibid., 97.
11. Foertsch et al., "Persuading Professors," 22.
12. Ibid., 22.
13. Institute for Research on Higher Education, "Why Is Research the Rule?," 54.
14. Fairweather, *Faculty Work and Public Trust,* 67.
15. Ibid., 46.
16. Ibid., 199.
17. Taylor, *Crisis on Campus,* 58.
18. Schuster and Finkelstein, *American Faculty,* 129.
19. Seymour and Hewitt, *Talking about Leaving,* 147.
20. Schuster and Finkelstein, *American Faculty,* 87.
21. Weick, "Contradictions in a Community of Scholars."
22. Meyer and Rowan, "Structure of Educational Organizations," 62.
23. Tagg, *Learning Paradigm College.*

24. Hattie, *Visible Learning*, 22.
25. Pascarella and Terenzini, *How College Affects Students, Volume 2*, 641–642.
26. Meyer and Rowan, "Structure of Educational Organizations," 66.
27. Seymour and Hewitt, *Talking about Leaving*, 145.
28. Ibid., 154.
29. Ibid., 155.
30. Ibid., 156.
31. Meyer and Rowan, "Structure of Educational Organizations," 62.
32. Weick, "Contradictions in a Community of Scholars," 16.
33. Ibid., 17.
34. Lutz, "Tightening Loose Coupling," 668.

CHAPTER 6 FRAMING THE FACULTY ROLE

1. MLA Task Force, 7.
2. Walker et al., *Formation of Scholars*, 5.
3. Prewitt, "*Who* Should Do *What*," 23.
4. Walker et al., *Formation of Scholars*, 33.
5. Ibid., 34.
6. Damrosch, "Vectors of Change," 34.
7. Walker et al., *Formation of Scholars*, 67.
8. Newport, "Teaching Tips for Graduate Students."
9. Prewitt, "*Who* Should Do *What*," 26.
10. Walker et al., *Formation of Scholars*, 90.
11. Beyer, Taylor, and Gillmore, *Inside the Undergraduate Teaching Experience*, 6.
12. Golde and Dore, "At Cross Purposes."
13. Beyer, Taylor, and Gillmore, *Inside the Undergraduate Teaching Experience*, 20.
14. Austin, "Preparing the Next Generation of Faculty," 108.
15. Quoted in ibid., 110.
16. Tobin, "Couldn't Teach a Dog to Sit."
17. Boice, "New Faculty as Teachers," 155.
18. Ibid., 155.
19. Ibid., 171.
20. Lombardi, *How Universities Work*, 4.
21. Fairweather, *Faculty Work and Public Trust*, 105.
22. Ibid., 104.
23. Schuster and Finkelstein, *American Faculty*, 105.
24. Levine, *Why Innovation Fails*, 162.
25. Bok, *Our Underachieving Colleges*, 49.
26. Zemsky, *Checklist for Change*, 27–28.
27. Keith Sawyer, a psychologist at Washington University in St. Louis, puts it this way in *Group Genius*, 71: "A long research tradition shows that when solving complex, non-

routine problems, groups are more effective when they're composed of people who have a variety of skills, knowledge, and perspective."

28. Janis, *Groupthink*, 9.
29. Ibid., 11–12.
30. Ibid., 175.
31. Ibid., 175.
32. Quoted in ibid., 38, italics in original.
33. Sunstein, *Going to Extremes*, 10.
34. Damrosch, *We Scholars*, 71.
35. Ceci, Williams, and Mueller-Johnson, "Is Tenure Justified?," 568.
36. Ceci and Williams, "Does Tenure Really Work?"
37. Ibid.
38. Janis, *Groupthink*, 175.
39. Lutz, "Tightening Loose Coupling," 668.
40. Bok, *Our Underachieving Colleges*, 316.
41. Grubb et al., *Honored but Invisible*, 49.

CHAPTER 7   THE MYTH OF UNITY AND THE PARADOX OF EFFORT

1. Jencks and Riesman, *Academic Revolution*, 532.
2. Duderstadt, *University for the 21st Century*, 80.
3. Fairweather, *Faculty Work and Public Trust*, 111.
4. Hattie and Marsh, "Relationship between Research and Teaching," 530.
5. Ibid., 529.
6. Hattie and Marsh, "Relation between Research Productivity and Teaching Effectiveness," 630.
7. Ibid., 635.
8. Figlio and Schapiro, "Are Great Teachers Poor Scholars?" 4.
9. Ibid., 6.
10. Hattie and Marsh, "Relationship between Research and Teaching," 511.
11. Ibid., 512.
12. Newman, *Idea of a University*, 10.
13. Fairweather, *Faculty Work and Public Trust*, 113.
14. Ibid., 114.
15. Wieman, *Improving How Universities Teach Science*, 137–138.
16. Seymour and Hewitt, *Talking about Leaving*, 146.
17. Ibid., 146–147.
18. Barnett, "Teaching and Research Are Inescapably Incompatible."
19. Fairweather, "Mythologies of Faculty Productivity," 43.
20. Ibid., 43.
21. Barnett, "Teaching and Research Are Inescapably Incompatible."

22. Barnett, "Linking Teaching and Research," 631.

23. Hattie and Marsh, "Relation between Research Productivity and Teaching Effectiveness," 634.

24. Ibid., 634.

25. Ibid., 634.

26. Kluger and DeNisi, "Effects of Feedback Interventions on Performance."

CHAPTER 8   FACULTY EXPERTISE AND THE MYTH OF TEACHER PROFESSIONALISM

1. Elmore, *School Reform from the Inside Out*, 108–109.

2. Argyris, *Reasons and Rationalizations*, 11.

3. Ericsson, "Influence of Experience and Deliberate Practice," 684.

4. The ten-thousand-hour rule was advanced by Malcolm Gladwell in his 2008 book *Outliers*. He probably erred in taking a mean for a minimum and counting performance as practice in some domains. At best, it should be taken as a very rough rule of thumb.

5. Ericsson, "Influence of Experience and Deliberate Practice, 694.

6. Ibid., 692.

7. Bereiter and Scardamalia, *Surpassing Ourselves*, 11, italics in original.

8. Elmore, *School Reform from the Inside Out*, 109.

9. Bereiter and Scardamalia, *Surpassing Ourselves*, 89.

10. Ibid., 93.

11. Tetlock, *Expert Political Judgment*, 239.

12. Ibid., 233.

13. Ibid., 2.

14. Berlin, *Hedgehog and the Fox*, 7.

15. Ibid., 7–8.

16. Ibid., 11.

17. Ibid., 9.

18. Tetlock, *Expert Political Judgement*, 117.

19. Ibid., 81.

20. Ibid., 81.

21. Ibid., 119.

22. Zemsky, Wegner, and Massy, *Remaking the American University*, 142.

23. Weimer, *Enhancing Scholarly Work on Teaching and Learning*, 10.

24. Bereiter and Scardamalia, *Surpassing Ourselves*, 106.

25. Ibid., 106.

26. Connolly, "Helping Future Faculty 'Come Out' as Teachers."

27. Ibid.

28. Ibid.

29. Baker and Zey-Ferrell, "Local and Cosmopolitan Orientations of Faculty," 97.

30. Ibid., 99.

31. Ibid., 100.
32. Edgerton, "Education White Paper," 46–47.
33. Ibid., 47.

CHAPTER 9   TRIAL RUN

1. Gumport, "Strategic Thinking in Higher Education Research," 19.
2. Marcy, "Why Foundations Have Cut Back in Higher Education."
3. Ibid.
4. Chambliss and Takacs, *How College Works*, 169.
5. Lumina Foundation, "Degree Qualifications Profile," 1.
6. Ibid., 1.
7. Ibid., 1.
8. Ibid., 5.
9. Ibid., 11.
10. Ibid., 11.
11. Ibid., 10.
12. Ewell, "Lumina Degree Qualifications Profile," 8.
13. Ibid., 8.
14. Ibid., 12.
15. Ibid., 18.
16. Tagg, "Changing Minds in Higher Education."
17. Ewell, "Lumina Degree Qualifications Profile," 17.
18. Lumina Foundation, "Degree Qualifications Profile," 4.
19. Ewell, "Lumina Degree Qualifications Profile," 17.
20. Banta, "Editor's Notes," 3.
21. Ibid., 4.
22. Lumina Foundation, "Degree Qualifications Profile," 1.
23. Schneider, afterword, 23.
24. Ewell, "Lumina Degree Qualifications Profile," 11.
25. Schneider, afterword, 24.
26. Ibid., 26–27.
27. Ibid., 27.

CHAPTER 10   SEEDS OF CHANGE

1. Hurtado et al., "Undergraduate Teaching Faculty," 31.
2. Ibid., 31.
3. Golde and Dore, "At Cross Purposes," 20.
4. National Center for Education Statistics, "National Study of Postsecondary Faculty," table 19.
5. Leslie, "Resolving the Dispute," 56–57.
6. Hurtado et al., "Undergraduate Teaching Faculty," 10.

7. Leslie, "Resolving the Dispute," 68.

8. Schuster and Finkelstein, *American Faculty*, 184.

9. Ibid.

10. Leslie, "Resolving the Dispute," 69.

11. Austin, "Preparing the Next Generation of Faculty," 105.

12. Leslie, "Resolving the Dispute," 70.

CHAPTER 11   HOW DO PEOPLE LEARN TO CHANGE?

1. Chambliss and Takacs, *How College Works*, 168.

2. Ibid., 169.

3. Ibid., 268.

4. Prochaska, Norcross, and DiClemente, *Changing for Good*, 204.

5. See Prochaska and Norcross, *Systems of Psychotherapy*, and Prochaska, Norcross, and DiClemente, *Changing for Good*.

6. Tolman, "TMM Teaching Survey."

7. Prochaska, Norcross, and DiClemente, *Changing for Good*, 40.

8. Prochaska, DiClemente, and Norcross, "In Search of How People Change," 1103.

9. Ibid., 1103.

10. Prochaska, Norcross, and DiClemente, *Changing for Good*, 78.

11. Tolman, "TMM Teaching Survey."

12. Ibid.

13. Prochaska, Norcross, and DiClemente, *Changing for Good*, 77.

14. Prochaska, DiClemente, and Norcross, "In Search of How People Change," 1103.

15. Ibid., 1104.

16. Tolman, "TMM Teaching Survey."

17. Prochaska, Norcross, and DiClemente, *Changing for Good*, 110.

18. Tolman, "TMM Teaching Survey."

19. Prochaska, DiClemente, and Norcross, "In Search of How People Change," 1104.

20. Ibid., 1104.

21. Tolman, "TMM Teaching Survey."

22. Prochaska, DiClemente, and Norcross, "In Search of How People Change," 1104.

23. Ibid., 1104.

24. Finkel, *Teaching with Your Mouth Shut*.

25. Prochaska, DiClemente, and Norcross, "In Search of How People Change," 1104.

26. Ibid., 1105.

27. Ibid., 1105.

28. Ibid., 1106.

29. Ibid., 1110.

30. Prochaska and Norcross, *Systems of Psychotherapy*, 530.

31. Dweck, *Mindset*.

32. Anton Tolman, email message to the author, August 29, 2013.

CHAPTER 12   DIFFUSING INNOVATION BY MAKING PEER GROUPS

1. Rogers, *Diffusion of Innovations*, 233.
2. Ibid., 254.
3. Ibid., 426.
4. Ibid., 19.
5. Brownell and Tanner, "Barriers to Faculty Pedagogical Change," 339.
6. Ibid., 341.
7. Ibid., 341.
8. Ibid., 342.
9. Ibid., 342.
10. Ibid., 343.
11. Baker and Zey-Ferrell, "Local and Cosmopolitan Orientations of Faculty," 101.
12. Ibid., 101.
13. Cox, "Introduction to Faculty Learning Communities," 9.
14. Richlin and Essington, "Overview of Faculty Learning Communities."
15. Cox, "Introduction to Faculty Learning Communities," 18.
16. Ibid., 18.
17. Mentkowski and Associates, *Learning That Lasts*, 269.
18. Ibid., 270.

CHAPTER 13   PROMOTING INNOVATION THROUGH SCHOLARLY TEACHING

1. Bernstein, "Peer Review," 48.
2. Remler and Pema, "Why Do Institutions of Higher Education Reward Research while Selling Education?," 6.
3. Ibid., 21, italics in original.
4. Delbanco, *College*, 155.
5. Cross and Goldenberg, *Off-Track Profs*, 125.
6. Spooren, Brockx, and Mortelmans, "On the Validity of Student Evaluation of Teaching," 5.
7. Ibid., 6.
8. Ibid., 5.
9. Ibid., 26.
10. Ibid., 32.
11. Cross and Goldenberg, *Off-Track Profs*, 123.
12. Stark, "What Exactly Do Student Evaluations Measure?"
13. Uttl, White, and Gonzalez, "Meta-analysis of Faculty's Teaching Effectiveness," 19.
14. Ibid., 19.
15. Ibid., 19.
16. Wieman, *Improving How Universities Teach Science*, 20.
17. Stark, "What Exactly Do Student Evaluations Measure?"

18. Uttl, White, and Gonzalez, "Meta-Analysis of Faculty's Teaching Effectiveness."

19. Stark, "What Exactly Do Student Evaluations Measure?"

20. Daniel Bernstein, email message to the author, January 25, 2014.

21. Handal, "Consultation Using Critical Friends," 59.

22. Ibid., 60.

23. Ibid., 60.

24. Hativa, *Teaching for Effective Learning*, 19.

25. Ibid., 19.

26. Shulman, *Wisdom of Practice*, 393.

27. Ibid., 393.

28. Ibid., 394.

29. Ibid., 394.

30. Ibid., 394.

31. Edgerton, Hutchings, and Quinlan, *Teaching Portfolio*, 5.

32. Ibid., 6.

33. Huber, *Balancing Acts*.

34. Quoted in ibid., 50.

35. "Peer Review of Teaching Project."

36. Bernstein et al., *Making Teaching and Learning Visible*, 8.

37. Ibid., 8–9.

38. Finkelstein et al., "Evaluating Teaching in a Scholarly Manner," 3.

39. Daniel Bernstein, email message to the author, January 25, 2014.

40. Rojstaczer and Healy, "Where A Is Ordinary."

CHAPTER 14   THE TEACHING INVENTORY AND PORTFOLIO

1. Ramsden and Martin, "Recognition of Good University Teaching."

2. Ibid.

3. Kruger and Dunning, "Unskilled and Unaware of It," 1127.

4. Ibid., 1124.

5. Ibid., 1131.

6. Ibid., 1131.

7. Tagg, "Dispelling the Fog of Learning through SoTL."

8. Wieman and Gilbert, "Teaching Practices Inventory," 552.

9. Ibid.

10. Ibid. The entire inventory appears as an appendix to this article and is available on the website of the Carl Wieman Science Education Initiative at the University of British Columbia: http://www.cwsei.ubc.ca/resources/TeachingPracticesInventory .htm.

11. Walter et al., "Introducing the Postsecondary Instructional Practices Survey (PIPS)."

12. Ibid., supplementary material.

13. Massy, *Reengineering the University*, 103.

CHAPTER 15   THE OUTCOMES TRANSCRIPT AND PORTFOLIO

1. Wergin, *Departments That Work*, 86.
2. Milton, Pollio, and Eison, *Making Sense of College Grades*, 212.
3. Astin, *Are You Smart Enough?*, 41.
4. Ewell, "Lumina Degree Qualifications Profile," 18.
5. Astin, *Are You Smart Enough?*, 38.
6. eLumen.
7. Hart Research Associates, "Falling Short?," 13.
8. Peet et al., "Fostering Integrative Knowledge and Lifelong Learning," 15.
9. Ibid., 16.
10. Jeff King, email message to the author, January 5, 2017.
11. Jeff King, email message to the author, January 17, 1017.

CHAPTER 16   CHANGING THE FACULTY ENDOWMENT

1. Massy, *Honoring the Trust*, 105.
2. Ehrenberg, "Rethinking the Professoriate," 105.
3. Ibid., 108.
4. Walker et al., *Formation of Scholars*, 142.
5. Ibid.
6. Chandler, "Graduate and Professional Student Development," 80.
7. Von Hoene, "Graduate Student Teaching Certificates."
8. MLA Task Force, 23.
9. Jessica Winston, personal communication with the author, September 12, 2014.
10. Department of English and Philosophy, "English Ph.D. Program Handbook."
11. Schuster and Finkelstein, *American Faculty*, 175–176.
12. Cross and Goldenberg, *Off-Track Profs*, 22.
13. Ibid., 22–23.
14. Ibid., 3.
15. Ibid., 128.
16. Hamilton, "Proactively Justifying the Academic Profession's Social Contract," 2.
17. Ibid., 4.
18. Ibid., 4.
19. Ibid., 3.
20. Ibid., 8.
21. Leslie, "Redefining Tenure," 675.
22. Ibid., 673.
23. Ibid., 673.
24. University of British Columbia, "Guidelines for Promotion to Professor of Teaching," 1.
25. Ibid., 1.

26. Simon Bates, personal communication with the author, September 17, 2014.
27. Weimer, "Positioning Scholarly Work on Teaching and Learning," 3.
28. Ibid., 1.

CHAPTER 17   CREATING A MARKET FOR EDUCATION

1. DiMaggio and Powell, "Iron Cage Revisited," 149.
2. Ibid., 152.
3. Toma, "Institutional Strategy," 120.
4. Ibid., 119.
5. Ibid., 118.
6. Ibid., 129.
7. Ibid., 147.
8. Zemsky, Wegner, and Massy, *Remaking the American University*, 40.
9. Monks and Ehrenberg, "Impact of *U.S. News & World Report* College Rankings," 10.
10. Wieman, *Improving How Universities Teach Science*, 20.
11. Gaston, *Higher Education Accreditation*, 132.
12. Schneider, "Policy Priorities for Accreditation."
13. Ibid.
14. Kelly and Hess, *Beyond Retrofitting*, 25, italics in original.
15. Ochoa, "Guidance to Institutions and Accrediting Agencies."
16. Laitinen, "Cracking the Credit Hour," 7.
17. Ibid., 8
18. Ibid., 7–8.
19. Ibid., 9.
20. "Department of Education: Program Integrity Issues; Final Rule," 34872.
21. Brint and Cantwell, "Undergraduate Time Use and Educational Outcomes," 3.
22. NSSE, "NSSE 2015 U.S. Summary Means and Standard Deviations."
23. "Department of Education: Program Integrity Issues; Final Rule," 34872.
24. Ibid., 34872, italics added.
25. McCormick, "It's about Time," 38.
26. Ibid., 39.
27. Ochoa, "Guidance to Institutions and Accrediting Agencies."
28. Ibid.
29. Silva, White, and Toch, "Carnegie Unit," 25.
30. Quoted in ibid., 10.
31. Ibid., 11.
32. C-RAC, "Regional Accreditors Announce Common Framework."
33. U.S. Department of Education, "Test of Leadership," 14.
34. Ibid., 14.
35. Ibid., 21.
36. U.S. Department of Education, "IPEDS."

37. Anderson, "Obama Administration Retreats from Federal College Rating Plan."

38. U.S. Department of Education, *College Scorecard.*

39. Schneider, "Policy Priorities for Accreditation."

40. Pascarella and Terenzini, *How College Affects Students, Volume 2,* 511.

41. Zemsky, *Checklist for Change,* 189.

CHAPTER 18   LEVERS FOR CHANGE

1. Zemsky, *Making Reform Work,* 210–211, italics in original.

2. Wieman, *Improving How Universities Teach Science,* 21.

3. Massy, *Reengineering the University,* 107.

4. Bjork, "On the Symbiosis of Remembering, Forgetting, and Learning," 8.

BIBLIOGRAPHY

Anderson, Nick. "Obama Asministration Retreats from Federal College Rating Plan." *Washington Post*, June 25, 2015. https://www.washingtonpost.com/news/grade-point /wp/2015/06/25/obama-administration-retreats-from-federal-college-rating-plan/ ?utm_term=.b2f6f77a4419

Argyris, Chris. *Flawed Advice and the Management Trap: How Managers Can Know When They're Getting Good Advice and When They're Not*. New York: Oxford University Press, 2000.

———. *Overcoming Organizational Defenses: Facilitating Organizational Learning*. Upper Saddle River, NJ: Prentice Hall, 1990.

———. *Reasoning, Learning, and Action: Individual and Organizational*. San Francisco: Jossey-Bass, 1982.

———. *Reasons and Rationalizations: The Limits to Organizational Knowledge*. New York: Oxford University Press, 2004.

Argyris, Chris, Robert Putnam, and Diana McLain Smith. *Action Science*. San Francisco: Jossey-Bass, 1985.

Argyris, Chris, and Donald Schön. *Organizational Learning II: Theory, Method, and Practice*. Reading, MA: Addison-Wesley, 1996.

Ariely, Dan. *Predictably Irrational: The Hidden Forces That Shape Our Decisions*. New York: HarperCollins, 2008.

Arum, Richard, and Josipa Roksa. *Academically Adrift: Limited Learning on College Campuses*. Chicago: University of Chicago Press, 2011.

———. *Aspiring Adults Adrift: Tentative Transitions of College Graduates*. Chicago: University of Chicago Press, 2014.

Association of American Colleges. "Integrity in the College Curriculum: A Report to the Academic Community." Washington, DC: Association of American Colleges, 1985.

Astin, Alexander W. *Are You Smart Enough? How Colleges' Obsession with Smartness Shortchanges Students*. Sterling, VA: Stylus, 2016.

———. *What Matters in College? Four Critical Years Revisited*. San Francisco: Jossey-Bass, 1993.

Austin, Ann E. "Preparing the Next Generation of Faculty: Graduate School as Socialization to the Academic Career." *Journal of Higher Education* 73, no. 1 (January–February 2002): 94–122.

Babcock, Philip, and Mindy Marks. "The Falling Time Cost of College: Evidence from Half a Century of Time Use Data." *Review of Economics and Statistics* 93, no. 2 (May 2011): 468–478.

Bahrick, Harry P., and Lynda K. Hall. "Lifetime Maintenance of High School Mathematics Content." *Journal of Experimental Psychology: General* 120, no. 1 (1991): 20–33.

Baier, Kylie, Cindy Hendricks, Kiesha Warren Gorden, James E. Hendricks, and Lessie Cochran. "College Students' Textbook Reading, or Not!" *American Reading Forum Annual Yearbook* 31 (2011). http://americanreadingforum.org/yearbook/11_yearbook /documents/BAIER%20ET%20AL%20PAPER.pdf.

Bailey, Thomas R., Shanna Smith Jaggars, and Davis Jenkins. *Redesigning America's Community Colleges.* Cambridge, MA: Harvard University Press, 2015.

Baker, Paul J., and Mary Zey-Ferrell. "Local and Cosmopolitan Orientations of Faculty: Implications for Teaching." *Teaching Sociology* 12, no. 1 (October 1984): 82–106.

Banta, Trudy. "Editor's Notes: A Surprising Reaction." *Assessment Update* 24, no. 1 (January–February 2012): 3–4.

Barber, Brad M., and Terrance Odean. "Trading Is Hazardous to Your Wealth: The Common Stock Investment Performance of Individual Investors." *Journal of Finance* 55, no. 2 (April 2000): 773–806.

Barnett, Bryan. "Teaching and Research Are Inescapably Incompatible." *Chronicle of Higher Education,* June 3, 1992. http://chronicle.com/article/TeachingResearch-Are /79455/.

Barnett, Ronald. "Linking Teaching and Research: A Critical Inquiry." *Journal of Higher Education* 63, no. 6 (November–December 1992): 619–636.

Barr, Robert B. "From Teaching to Learning: A New Reality for Community Colleges." *Leadership Abstracts* 8 (1995): 3.

Barr, Robert B., and John Tagg. "From Teaching to Learning: A New Paradigm for Undergraduate Education." *Change,* November–December 1995, 12–25.

Basken, Paul. "Crusader for Science Teaching Finds Colleges Slow to Change." *Chronicle of Higher Education,* June 17, 2013. http://chronicle.com/article/Crusader-for -Better-Science/139849/.

Baum, Sandy, Jennifer Ma, and Kathleen Payea. *Education Pays: The Benefits of Higher Education for Individuals and Society.* New York: College Board, 2013.

Bender, David S., and Maryellen Weimer. "The Phenomenology of Change: How Do Individual Faculty Manage the Instructional Change Process?" Paper presented at the Annual Meeting of the American Educational Research Association, Montreal, April 2005.

Bereiter, Carl, and Marlene Scardamalia. *Surpassing Ourselves: An Inquiry into the Nature and Implications of Expertise.* Chicago: Open Court, 1993.

Berlin, Isaiah. *The Hedgehog and the Fox: An Essay on Tolstoy's View of History.* New York: Mentor, 1957.

Bernstein, Daniel J. "Peer Review and the Evaluation of the Intellectual Work of Teaching." *Change,* March–April 2008, 48–51.

Bernstein, Daniel J., Amy Nelson Burnett, Amy Goodburn, and Paul Savory. *Making Teaching and Learning Visible: Course Portfolios and the Peer Review of Teaching.* Bolton, MA: Anker, 2006.

Beyer, Catherine Hoffman, Edward Taylor, and Gerald M. Gillmore. *Inside the Undergraduate Teaching Experience: The University of Washington's Growth in Faculty Teaching Study.* Albany: State University of New York Press, 2013.

Biggs, John. *Teaching for Quality Learning at University: What the Student Does*. Philadelphia: Society for Research into Higher Education and Open University Press, 1999.

Bjork, Robert A. "On the Symbiosis of Remembering, Forgetting, and Learning." In *Successful Remembering and Successful Forgetting: A Festschrift in Honor of Robert A. Bjork*, edited by Aaron S. Benjamin, 1-22. New York: Psychology Press, 2011.

Blaich, Charles F., and Kathleen S. Wise. "Moving from Assessment to Institutional Improvement." In *Longitudinal Assessment for Student Improvement*, edited by Tricia A. Seifert. *New Directions for Institutional Research: Assessment Supplement 2010* (2010): 67–78.

Blumenstyk, Goldie. *American Higher Education in Crisis? What Everyone Needs to Know*. New York: Oxford University Press, 2015.

Boice, Robert. "New Faculty as Teachers." *Journal of Higher Education* 62, no. 2 (March–April 1991): 150–173.

Bok, Derek. *Higher Education in America*. Princeton, NJ: Princeton University Press, 2013.

———. *Our Underachieving Colleges: A Candid Look at How Much Students Learn and Why They Should Be Learning More*. Princeton, NJ: Princeton University Press, 2006.

———. "We Must Prepare Ph.D. Students for the Complicated Art of Teaching." *Chronicle of Higher Education*, November 11, 2013. http://chronicle.com/article/We-Must-Prepare-PhD-Students/142893/?cid=at&utm_source=at&utm_medium=en.

Boud, David, and Elizabeth Molloy. "Rethinking Models of Feedback for Learning: The Challenge of Design." *Assessment & Evaluation in Higher Education* 38, no. 6 (2013): 698–712.

Bowen, William G., and Michael S. McPherson. *Lesson Plan: An Agenda for change in American Higher Education*. Princeton, NJ: Princeton University Press, 2016.

Boyer, Ernest L. *Scholarship Reconsidered: Priorities of the Professoriate*. San Francisco: Carnegie Foundation for the Advancement of Teaching/Jossey Bass, 1990.

Bradley, Martin J., Robert H. Seidman, and Steven R. Painchaud. *Saving Higher Education: The Integrated, Competency-Based Three-Year Bachelor's Degree Program*. San Francisco: Jossey-Bass, 2012.

Brewer, Dominic J., and William G. Tierney. "Barriers to Innovation in U.S. Higher Education." In *Reinventing Higher Education: The Promise of Innovation*, edited by Ben Wildavsky, Andrew P. Kelly, and Kevin Carey, 11–40. Cambridge, MA: Harvard Education Press, 2011.

Brint, Steven, and Allison M. Cantwell. "Undergraduate Time Use and Educational Outcomes: Results from the UCUES 2006." Research and Occasional Paper Series CHE.14.08, Center for Studies in Higher Education, University of California, Berkeley, October 2008. http://cshe.berkeley.edu/.

Brownell, Sara E., and Kimberly D. Tanner. "Barriers to Faculty Pedagogical Change: Lack of Training, Time, Incentives and . . . Tensions with Professional Identity?" *Life Sciences Education* 11 (Winter 2012): 339–346.

Bryant, Adam. "In Head-Hunting, Big Data May Not Be Such a Big Deal" (interview with Laszlo Bock). *New York Times*, June 19, 2013, F6. http://www.nytimes.com/2013/06/20/business/in-head-hunting-big-data-may-not-be-such-a-big-deal.html.

Burgan, Mary. *What Ever Happened to the Faculty? Drift and Decision in Higher Education.* Baltimore: Johns Hopkins University Press, 2006.

Carey, Kevin. *The End of College: Creating the Future of Learning and the University of Everywhere.* New York: Riverhead Books, 2015.

———. "That Old College Lie: Are Our Colleges Teaching Students Well? No. But Here's How to Make Them." *Democracy: A Journal of Ideas* 15 (Winter 2010). http://democracyjournal.org/magazine/15/that-old-college-lie/.

Ceci, Stephen J., and Wendy M. Williams. "Does Tenure Really Work?" *Chronicle of Higher Education,* March 9, 2007. http://chronicle.com/article/Does-Tenure-Really-Work-/25565/.

Ceci, Stephen J., Wendy M. Williams, and Katrin Mueller-Johnson. "Is Tenure Justified? An Experimental Study of Faculty Beliefs about Tenure, Promotion, and Academic Freedom." *Behavioral and Brain Sciences* 29 (2006): 553–594.

Chambliss, Daniel F., and Christopher G. Takacs. *How College Works.* Cambridge, MA: Harvard University Press, 2014.

Chandler, Elizabeth O'Connor. "Graduate and Professional Student Development: The Role of the Pedagogy Course." In *Mapping the Range of Graduate Student Professional Development,* edited by Laura L. B. Border, 69–86. Stillwater, OK: New Forums Press, 2011.

Connolly, Mark R. "Helping Future Faculty 'Come Out' as Teachers." *Toward the Best in the Academy* 22, no. 6 (2010–11). http://www.podnetwork.org/publications/teaching excellenc e/10-11/V22_N6_Connolly.pdf.

Cook, Bryan J. "The American College President Study: Key Findings and Takeaways." *Presidency: Special Supplement* (2012): 2–5. http://www.acenet.edu/the-presidency/columns-and-features/Pages/The-American-College-President-Study.aspx.

Cornford, F. M. *Microcosmographia Academica: Being a Guide for the Young Academic Politician.* London: Bowes & Bowes, 1908.

Council of Regional Accrediting Commissions (C-RAC). "Regional Accreditation and Student Learning: Principles for Good Practices." http://www.accjc.org/wp-content/uploads/2013/08/C-RAC_Regional_Accreditation__Student_Learning_Principles_of_Good_Practice.pdf.

———. "Regional Accreditors Announce Common Framework for Defining and Approving Competency-Based Education Programs." June 2, 2015, http://www.nwccu.org/Pubs%20Forms%20and%20Updates/Publications/C-RAC%20CBE%20Statement%20Press%20Release%206_2.pdf.

Covey, Stephen R. *The Seven Habits of Highly Effective People: Restoring the Character Ethic.* New York: Simon & Schuster, 1989.

Cox, Milton D. "Introduction to Faculty Learning Communities." In *Building Faculty Learning Communities,* edited by Milton D. Cox and Laurie Richlin. *New Directions for Teaching and Learning* 97 (Spring 2004): 5–23.

———. "Phases in the Development of a Change Model: Communities of Practice as Change Agents in Higher Education." In *The Realities of Change in Higher Education:*

Interventions to Promote Learning and Teaching, edited by Lynne Hunt, Adrian Bromage, and Bland Tomkinson, 91–100. New York: Routledge, 2006.

Cross, John G., and Edie N. Goldenberg. *Off-Track Profs: Nontenured Teachers in Higher Education*. Cambridge, MA: MIT Press, 2009.

Cuban, Larry. *How Scholars Trumped Teachers: Change without Reform in University Curriculum, Teaching, and Research, 1890–1990*. New York: Teachers College Press, 1999.

Dale, Stacy Berg, and Alan B. Krueger. "Estimating the Payoff to Attending a More Selective College: An Application of Selection on Observables and Unobservables." *Quarterly Journal of Economics* 117 (November 2002): 1491–1527.

Damrosch, David. "Vectors of Change." In *Envisioning the Future of Doctoral Education: Preparing Stewards of the Discipline*, edited by Chris M. Golde, George E. Walker, and Associates, 34–45. San Francisco: Jossey-Bass, 2006.

———. *We Scholars: Changing the Culture of the University*. Cambridge, MA: Harvard University Press, 1995.

Dancy, Melissa H., and Charles Henderson. "Beyond the Individual Instructor: Systemic Constraints in the Implementation of Research-Informed Practices." Paper presented at the Physics Education Research Conference, Sacramento, CA, August 2005.

———. "Pedagogical Practices of Physics Faculty in the USA." Paper presented at the Physics Education Research Conference, Ann Arbor, MI, August 2009.

DeAngelo, Linda, Sylvia Hurtado, John H. Pryor, Kimberly R. Kelly, José Luis Santos, and William S. Korn. *The American College Teacher: National Norms for the 2007–2008 HERI Faculty Survey*. Los Angeles: Higher Education Research Institute, UCLA, 2009.

Delbanco, Andrew. *College: What It Was, Is, and Should Be*. Princeton, NJ: Princeton University Press, 2012.

"Department of Education: Program Integrity Issues; Final Rule." 75 *Federal Register* 117 (June 18, 2010): 66832–66975.

Department of English and Philosophy, Idaho State University. "English Ph.D. Program Handbook." Pocatello: Idaho State University, 2012. http://www.isu.edu/english/DeptDocs/PhD_Program_Handbook.pdf.

DiMaggio, Paul J., and Walter W. Powell. "The Iron Cage Revisited: Institutional Isomorphism and Collective Rationality in Organizational Fields." *American Sociological Review* 48 (April 1983): 147–160.

Duderstadt, James J. *A University for the 21st Century*. Ann Arbor: University of Michigan Press, 2000.

Dweck, Carol S. *Mindset: The New Psychology of Success*. New York: Random House, 2006.

———. *Self-Theories: Their Role in Motivation, Personality, and Development*. Philadelphia: Psychology Press, 2000.

Eagan, Kevin, Ellen Bara Stolzenberg, Jennifer Berden Lozano, Melissa C. Aragon, Maria Ramirez Suchard, and Sylvia Hurtado. *Undergraduate Teaching Faculty: The 2013–2014 HERI Faculty Survey*. Los Angeles: Higher Education Research Institute, UCLA, 2014.

Edgerton, Russell. "Education White Paper." Washington, DC: Pew Charitable Trusts, 1997.

Edgerton, Russell, Patricia Hutchings, and Kathleen Quinlan. *The Teaching Portfolio: Capturing the Scholarship in Teaching*. Washington, DC: American Association for Higher Education, 1991.

Ehrenberg, Ronald G. "Rethinking the Professoriate." In *Reinventing Higher Education: The Promise of Innovation*, edited by Ben Wildavsky, Andrew P. Kelly, and Kevin Carey, 101–128. Cambridge, MA: Harvard Education Press, 2011.

Eisenhower, Dwight D. "Address at the Second Assembly of the World Council of Churches." Santa Barbara: University of California, Santa Barbara, American Presidency Project, 2015. http://www.presidency.ucsb.edu/ws/?pid=9991.

Eliade, Mircea. *Myth and Reality*. Translated by Willard R. Trask. New York: Harper & Row, 1963.

Elmore, Richard F. *School Reform from the Inside Out: Policy, Practice and Performance*. Cambridge, MA: Harvard Education Press, 2004.

eLumen. "eLumen: The Platform for Student Outcomes." http://elumen.info/.

Ericsson, K. Anders. "The Influence of Experience and Deliberate Practice on the Development of Superior Expert Performance." In *The Cambridge Handbook of Expertise and Expert Performance*, edited by K. Anders Ericsson, Neil Charness, Paul J. Feltovich, and Robert R. Hoffman, 683–703. New York: Cambridge University Press, 2006.

Ewell, Peter T. "Assessment, Accountability, and Improvement: Revisiting the Tension." NILOA Occasional Paper 1, University of Illinois and Indiana University, National Institute of Learning Outcomes Assessment, November 2009. http://learningoutcomesassessment.org/documents/PeterEwell_005.pdf.

———. "The Lumina Degree Qualifications Profile (DQP): Implications for Assessment." NILOA Occasional Paper 16, University of Illinois and Indiana University, National Institute of Learning Outcomes Assessment, January 2013. http://www.learningoutcomesassessment.org/documents/EwellDQPop1.pdf.

Ewert, Stephanie, and Robert Kominski. "Measuring Alternative Education Credentials: 2012." U.S. Census Bureau, U.S. Department of Commerce, January 2014. http://www.census.gov/hhes/socdemo/education/data/files/p70-138.pdf.

Fairweather, James S. *Faculty Work and Public Trust: Restoring the Value of Teaching and Public Service in American Academic Life*. Boston: Allyn & Bacon, 1996.

———. "Linking Evidence and Promising Practices in Science, Technology, Engineering and Mathematics (STEM) Undergraduate Education." Washington, DC: National Academies. http://sites.nationalacademies.org/cs/groups/dbassesite/documents/webpage/dbasse_072637.pdf.

———. "The Mythologies of Faculty Productivity: Implications for Institutional Policy and Decision Making." *Journal of Higher Education* 73, no. 1 (January–February 2002): 26–48.

Fallon, Daniel. *The German University: A Heroic Ideal in Conflict with the Modern World*. Boulder: Colorado Associated University Press, 1980.

Festinger, Leon. *A Theory of Cognitive Dissonance*. Stanford, CA: Stanford University Press, 1967.

Festinger, Leon, Henry W. Riecken, and Stanley Schachter. *When Prophecy Fails: A Social and Psychological Study of a Modern Group That Predicted the Destruction of the World.* New York: Harper & Row, 1956.

Figlio, David N., and Morton Schapiro. "Are Great Teachers Poor Scholars?" Evidence Speaks Reports, vol. 2, no. 6. Washington, DC: Brookings Institution, 2017. https://www.brookings.edu/research/are-great-teachers-poor-scholars/.

Fink, L. Dee. *Creating Significant Learning Experiences: An Integrated Approach to Designing College Courses.* San Francisco: Jossey-Bass, 2003.

Finkel, Donald L. *Teaching with Your Mouth Shut.* Portsmouth, NH: Heinemann, 2000.

Finkelstein, Noah, Joel C. Corbo, Daniel L. Reinholz, Mark Gammon, and Jessica Keating. "Evaluating Teaching in a Scholarly Manner: A Model and Call for an Evidence-Based, Departmentally-Defined Approach to Enhance Teaching Evaluation for CU Boulder." Boulder: Colorado University Boulder, n.d.

Foertsch, Julie, Susan B. Millar, Lynn Squire, and Ramona Gunter. "Persuading Professors: A Study of the Dissemination of Educational Reform in Research Institutions." Madison: LEAD Center, University of Wisconsin–Madison, June 1997.

Fogg, Piper. "For These Professors, 'Practice' Is Perfect." *Chronicle of Higher Education,* April 16, 2004. http://chronicle.com/article/For-These-Professors/31149/.

Freeman, Scott, Sarah L. Eddy, Miles McDonough, Michelle K. Smith, Nnadozie Okoroafor, Hannah Jordt, and Mary Pat Wenderoth. "Active Learning Increases Student Performance in Science, Engineering, and Mathematics." *Proceedings of the National Academy of Science USA* 111, no. 23 (2014): 8410–8415. http://www.pnas.org/content/111/23/8410.full.

Friedman, Thomas L. "How to Get a Job at Google." *New York Times,* February 22, 2014. http://www.nytimes.com/2014/02/23/opinion/sunday/friedman-how-to-get-a-job-at-google.html?partner=rssnyt&emc=rss.

Garvin, David A. "Building a Learning Organization." *Harvard Business Review* 71, no. 4 (July–August 1993): 78–91.

Gaston, Paul. *The Challenge of Bologna: What United States Higher Education Has to Learn from Europe, and Why It Matters That We Learn It.* Sterling, VA: Stylus, 2010.

———. *Higher Education Accreditation: How It's Changing, Why It Must.* Sterling, VA: Stylus, 2014.

Ginder, Scott A., Janice E. Kelley-Reid, and Farrah B. Mann. "Postsecondary Institutions and Cost of Attendance in 2015–16; Degrees and Other Awards Conferred, 2014–15; and 12–Month Enrollment, 2014–15." National Center for Education Statistics, U.S. Department of Education, July 2016. http://nces.ed.gov/pubs2016/2016112.pdf.

Gladwell, Malcolm. *Outliers: The Story of Success.* New York: Little, Brown, 2008.

Glassick, Charles E., Mary Taylor Huber, and Gene I Maeroff. *Scholarship Assessed: Evaluation of the Professoriate.* San Francisco: Jossey-Bass, 1997.

Gobet, Fernand, and Neil Charness. "Expertise in Chess." In *The Cambridge Handbook of Expertise and Expert Performance,* edited by K. Anders Ericsson, Neil Charness, Paul J. Feltovich, and Robert R. Hoffman, 523–538. New York: Cambridge University Press, 2006.

Golde, Chris M., and Timothy M. Dore. "At Cross Purposes: What the Experience of Today's Doctoral Students Reveals about Doctoral Education." Madison: University of Wisconsin–Madison, 2002.

Golde, Chris M., George E. Walker, and Associates, eds. *Envisioning the Future of Doctoral Education: Preparing Stewards of the Discipline.* San Francisco: Jossey-Bass, 2006.

Grubb, W. Norton (with Helena Worthen, Barbara Byrd, Elnora Webb, Norena Badway, Chester Case, Stanford Goto, and Jennifer Curry Villeneuve). *Honored but Invisible: An Inside Look at Teaching in Community Colleges.* New York: Routledge, 1999.

Gumport, Patricia J. "Strategic Thinking in Higher Education Research." In *The Organization of Higher Education: Managing Colleges for a New Era,* edited by Michael N. Bastedo, 18–44. Baltimore: Johns Hopkins University Press, 2012.

Halloun, Ibrahim Abou, and David Hestenes. "The Initial Knowledge State of College Physics Students." *American Journal of Physics* 53, no. 11 (1985): 1043–1055.

Halpern, Diane F., and Milton Hakel. "Applying the Science of Learning to the University and Beyond: Teaching for Long-Term Retention and Transfer." *Change,* July–August 2003, 36–41.

Hamilton, Neil W. "Proactively Justifying the Academic Profession's Social Contract." In *The Future of the Professoriate: Academic Freedom, Peer Review, and Shared Governance,* edited by Neil W. Hamilton and Jerry G. Gaff, 1–18. Washington, DC: Association of American Colleges and Universities, 2009.

Handal, Gunnar. "Consultation Using Critical Friends." In *Using Consultants to Improve Teaching,* edited by Christopher Knapper and Sergio Piccinin. *New Directions for Teaching and Learning* 79 (Fall 1999): 59–70.

Hanushek, Eric A., and Ludger Woessmann. "How Much Do Educational Outcomes Matter in OECD Countries?" Working Paper 16515, National Bureau of Economic Research, 2010. http://www.nber.org/papers/w16515.

Harris, Richard J. "Answering Questions Containing Marked and Unmarked Adjectives and Adverbs." *Journal of Experimental Psychology* 97 (1973): 399–401.

Hart Research Associates. "Falling Short? College Learning and Career Success." Washington, DC: Hart Research Associates, 2015. http://www.aacu.org/sites/default/files/files/LEAP/2015employerstudentsurvey.pdf.

Hativa, Nira. *Teaching for Effective Learning in Higher Education.* Boston: Kluwer, 2000.

Hattie, John. *Visible Learning: A Synthesis of over 800 Meta-analyses Relating to Achievement.* New York: Routledge, 2009.

Hattie, John, and Herbert W. Marsh. "The Relation between Research Productivity and Teaching Effectiveness: Complementary, Antagonistic, or Independent Constructs?" *Journal of Higher Education* 73, no. 5 (September–October 2002): 603–641.

———. "The Relationship between Research and Teaching: A Meta-analysis." *Review of Educational Research* 66, no. 4 (Winter 1996): 507–542.

Hawkins, Hugh. *Between Harvard and America: The Educational Leadership of Charles W. Eliot.* New York: Oxford University Press, 1972.

Heller, Donald E. "The End of College? Not So Fast." *Chronicle of Higher Education,* March 30, 2015. http://www.chronicle.com/article/The-End-of-College-Not-So /228937.

Hersh, Richard H., and Richard P. Keeling. "Changing Institutional Culture to Promote Assessment of Higher Learning." NILOA Occasional Paper 17, University of Illinois and Indiana University, National Institute of Learning Outcomes Assessment, February 2013. http://learningoutcomesassessment.org/documents/occasionalpaperseven teen.pdf.

Holloway, Perry A. "Is Fundamental Change Really 'Inevitable'?" *Inside Higher Ed,* December 6, 2010. http://www.insidehighered.com/views/2010/12/06/holloway.

Hornstein, Harvey. *Managerial Courage.* New York: John Wiley, 1986.

Huber, Mary Taylor. *Balancing Acts: The Scholarship of Teaching and Learning in Academic Careers.* Sterling, VA: Stylus, 2004.

Huber, Mary Taylor, and Pat Hutchings. *The Advancement of Learning: Building the Teaching Commons.* San Francisco: Jossey-Bass, 2005.

Hurtado, Sylvia, Kevin Eagan, John H. Pryor, Hannah Whang, and Serge Tran. "Undergraduate Teaching Faculty: The 2010–2011 HERI Faculty Survey." Los Angeles: Higher Education Research Institute, UCLA, 2012.

Hutchings, Pat. "Opening Doors to Faculty Involvement in Assessment." NILOA Occasional Paper 4, University of Illinois and Indiana University, National Institute of Learning Outcomes Assessment, April 2010. http://learningoutcomesassessment.org /documents/PatHutchings.pdf.

"IMPACT Annual Report 2014." West Lafayette, IN: Purdue University, 2014. http:// www.purdue.edu/impact/program-effectiveness.php.

Institute for Research on Higher Education. "Why Is Research the Rule? The Impact of Incentive Systems on Faculty Behavior." *Change,* March–April 2000, 53–56.

Institute-Wide Task Force on the Future of MIT Education. "Final Report." Cambridge, MA: MIT. http://web.mit.edu/future-report/TaskForceFinal_July28.pdf.

Janis, Irving L. *Groupthink: Psychological Studies of Policy Decisions and Fiascoes.* Boston: Houghton Mifflin, 1983.

Jencks, Christopher, and David Riesman. *The Academic Revolution.* Chicago: University of Chicago Press, 1969.

Jones, Elizabeth A. "Is a Core Curriculum Best for Everybody?" In *Assessment and Curriculum Reform,* edited by James L. Ratcliff. *New Directions for Higher Education* 80 (1992): 37–46.

Kahneman, Daniel. *Thinking, Fast and Slow.* New York: Farrar, Straus and Giroux, 2011.

Kahneman, Daniel, Ilana Ritov, and David Schkade. "Economic Preferences or Attitude Expressions? An Analysis of Dollar Responses to Public Issues." In *Choices, Values, and Frames,* edited by Daniel Kahneman and Amos Tversky, 642–671. New York: Russell Sage Foundation/Cambridge University Press, 2000.

Kahneman, Daniel, and Amos Tversky. "Choices, Values, and Frames." In *Choices, Values, and Frames,* edited by Daniel Kahneman and Amos Tversky, 1–16. New York: Russell Sage Foundation/Cambridge University Press, 2000.

———. "Prospect Theory: An Analysis of Decision under Risk." In *Choices, Values, and Frames*, edited by Daniel Kahneman and Amos Tversky, 17–43. New York: Russell Sage Foundation/Cambridge University Press, 2000.

Keeling, Richard P., and Richard H. Hersh. *We're Losing Our Minds: Rethinking American Higher Education*. New York: Palgrave Macmillan, 2012.

Keller, George. *Transforming a College: The Story of a Little-Known College's Strategic Climb to National Distinction*. Baltimore: Johns Hopkins University Press, 2004.

Kelly, Andrew P., and Frederick M. Hess. *Beyond Retrofitting: Innovation in Higher Education*. Washington, DC: Hudson Institute, June 2013.

Kerr, Clark. *The Uses of the University*. 5th ed. Cambridge, MA: Harvard University Press, 2001.

Kinzie, Jillian. "Perspective from Campus Leaders on the Current State of Student Learning Outcomes Assessment: NILOA Focus Group Summary 2009–2010." Urbana, IL: University of Illinois and Indiana University, National Institute of Learning Outcomes Assessment, October 2010. http://learningoutcomesassessment.org/documents/FocusGroUniversity PressFinal.pdf.

Kluger, Avraham N., and Angelo DeNisi. "The Effects of Feedback Interventions on Performance: A Historical Review, a Meta-analysis, and a Preliminary Feedback Intervention Theory." *Psychological Bulletin* 119, no. 2 (1996): 254–284.

Krueger, Alan, and Stacy Berg Dale. "Estimating the Payoff to Attending a More Selective College: An Application of Selection on Observables and Unobservables." Working Paper 7322, National Bureau of Economic Research, August 1999. http://www.nber.org/papers/w7322.pdf.

Kruger, Justin, and David Dunning. "Unskilled and Unaware of It: How Difficulties in Recognizing One's Own Incompetence Lead to Inflated Self-Assessments." *Journal of Personality and Social Psychology* 77, no. 6 (1999): 1121–1134.

Kuh, George D. "How Are We Doing? Tracking the Quality of the Undergraduate Experience, 1960s to the Present." *Review of Higher Education* 22, no. 2 (1999): 99–120.

Kuh, George, and Stanley Ikenberry. "More Than You Think, Less Than We Need: Learning Outcomes Assessment in American Higher Education." Urbana, IL: University of Illinois and Indiana University, National Institute for Learning Outcomes Assessment, October 2009. http://learningoutcomesassessment.org/NILOAsurvey results09.htm.

Kwiram, Alvin L. "Time for Reform?" In *Envisioning the Future of Doctoral Education: Preparing Stewards of the Discipline*, edited by Chris M. Golde, George E. Walker, and Associates, 141–166. San Francisco: Jossey-Bass, 2006.

Laitinen, Amy. "Cracking the Credit Hour." New America Foundation and Education Sector, September 2012. https://static.newamerica.org/attachments/2334–cracking -the-credit-hour/Cracking_the_Credit_Hour_Sept5_0.ab0048b12824428cba568c a359017ba9.pdf.

Leslie, David W. "Redefining Tenure: Traditional verses the New Political Economy in Higher Education." *American Behavioral Scientist* 41, no. 5 (February 1998): 652–679.

———. "Resolving the Dispute: Teaching Is Academe's Core Value." *Journal of Higher Education* 73, no. 1 (January–February 2002): 49–73.

Levine, Arthur. *Why Innovation Fails.* Albany: State University of New York Press, 1980.

Lewis, Harry R. *Excellence without a Soul: Does Liberal Education Have a Future?* New York: Public Affairs, 2006.

Light, Richard J. *Making the Most of College: Students Speak Their Minds.* Cambridge, MA: Harvard University Press, 2001.

Liu, Yujia, and David B. Grusky. "The Payoff to Skill in the Third Industrial Revolution." *American Journal of Sociology* 118, no. 5 (March 2013): 1330–1374.

Loftus, Elizabeth F. *Eyewitness Testimony.* Cambridge, MA: Harvard University Press, 1979.

Lombardi, John V. *How Universities Work.* Baltimore: Johns Hopkins University Press, 2013.

Lucas, Christopher J. *American Higher Education: A History.* New York: St. Martin's Griffin, 1994.

Lumina Foundation. "The Degree Qualifications Profile." Indianapolis: Lumina Foundation, 2011.

Lutz, Frank W. "Tightening Loose Coupling in Organizations of Higher Education." *Administrative Science Quarterly* 27, no. 4 (1982): 653–669.

Ma, Jennifer, and Sandy Baum. "Trends in Community Colleges: Enrollment, Prices, Student Debt, and Completion." College Board Research Brief, April 2016.

Marcy, Mary B. "Why Foundations Have Cut Back in Higher Education." *Chronicle of Higher Education,* July 25, 2003. http://chronicle.com/article/Why-Foundations -Have-Cut-Back/10925/.

Massy, William F. *Honoring the Trust: Quality and Cost Containment in Higher Education.* Bolton, MA: Anker, 2003.

———. *Reengineering the University: How to Be Mission Centered, Market Smart, and Margin Conscious.* Baltimore: Johns Hopkins University Press, 2016.

Mazur, Eric. *Peer Instruction: A User's Manual.* Upper Saddle River, NJ: Prentice Hall, 1997.

McCormick, Alexander C. "It's about Time: What to Make of Reported Declines in How Much College Students Study." *Liberal Education* 97 (Winter 2011): 30–39.

Meiklejohn, Alexander. *The Experimental College.* Edited and abridged by John Walker Powell. 1932. Reprint, Washington, DC: Seven Locks Press, 1981.

Menand, Louis. *The Marketplace of Ideas: Reform and Resistance in the American University.* New York: Norton, 2010.

Mentkowski, Marcia, and Associates. *Learning That Lasts: Integrating Learning, Development, and Performance in College and Beyond.* San Francisco: Jossey-Bass, 2000.

Mervis, Jeffrey. "Transformation Is Possible if a University Really Cares." *Science* 340 (April 19, 2013): 292–296.

Meyer, John, and Brian Rowan. "The Structure of Educational Organizations." In *The Dynamics of Organizational Change in Education,* edited by J. Victor Baldridge and Terrence Deal, 60–87. Berkeley, CA: McCutchan, 1983.

Milton, Ohmer, Howard R. Pollio, and James A. Eison. *Making Sense of College Grades*. San Francisco: Jossey-Bass, 1986.

MLA Task Force on Doctoral Study in Modern Language and Literature. "Report of the MLA Task Force on Doctoral Study in Modern Language and Literature." New York: Modern Language Association, 2014. http://www.mla.org/pdf/taskforcedocstudy 2014.pdf.

Monks, James, and Ronald G. Ehrenberg. "The Impact of *U.S. News & World Report* College Rankings on Admissions Outcomes and Pricing Policies at Selective Private Institutions." Working Paper 7227, National Bureau of Economic Research, July 1999. http://www.nber.org/papers/w7227.

Morison, Samuel Eliot. *The Founding of Harvard College*. Cambridge, MA: Harvard University Press, 1935.

Muscatine, Charles. *Fixing College Education: A New Curriculum for the Twenty-First Century*. Charlottesville: University of Virginia Press, 2009.

National Assessment of Adult Literacy. "Literacy in Everyday Life: Results from the 2003 National Assessment of Adult Literacy." National Center for Education Statistics, U.S. Department of Education, NCES-480, April 2007.

National Center for Education Statistics. "National Study of Postsecondary Faculty: 2004." U.S. Department of Education. https://nces.ed.gov/surveys/nsopf/nedrc.as.

National Institute for Learning Outcomes Assessment (NILOA). "Higher Education Quality: Why Documenting Learning Matters. A Policy Statement from the National Institute for Learning Outcomes Assessment." Urbana, IL: University of Illinois and Indiana University, National Institute for Learning Outcomes Assessment, May 2016. http://www.learningoutcomesassessment.org/documents/NILOA_policy _statement.pdf.

National Survey of Student Engagement. "Bringing the Institution into Focus: Annual Results 2014." Bloomington, IN: Center for Postsecondary Research, 2014.

———. "The NSSE 2000 Annual Report: National Benchmarks and Effective Educational Practice." Bloomington: Indiana University Center for Postsecondary Research and Planning, 2000.

———. "NSSE 2015 U.S. Summary Means and Standard Deviations." http://nsse .indiana.edu/2015_institutional_report/pdf/Means/Mean%20-%20SR%20by%20 Carn.pdf.

———. "Summary Tables." 2014. http://nsse.iub.edu/html/summary_tables.cfm.

Newman, John Henry Cardinal. *The Idea of a University*. New York: Doubleday, Image, 1959.

Newport, Melanie. "Teaching Tips for Graduate Students." *Chronicle of Higher Education*, September 27, 2016. https://chroniclevitae.com/news/1558-teaching-tips-for -graduate-students?cid=at&utm_source=at&utm_medium=en&elqTrackId=e9c9 59c504cd4171a6d4276f77aeead5&elq=1ea84b9262374940bc891c8317ab2b38&elqaid =10848&elqat=1&elqCampaignId=4124.

Ochoa, Eduardo M. "Guidance to Institutions and Accrediting Agencies Regarding a Credit Hour as Defined in the final Regulations Published on October 29, 2010." U.S.

Department of Education, March 18, 2011. https://ifap.ed.gov/dpcletters/GEN1106 .html.

Pace, David. "The Amateur in the Operating Room: History and the Scholarship of Teaching and Learning." *American Historical Review* 109 (October 2004): 1171–1192.

Palmer, Michael S. "Graduate Student Professional Development: A Decade after Calls for National Reform." In *Mapping the Range of Graduate Student Professional Development*, edited by Laura L. B. Border, 1–17. Stillwater, OK: New Forums Press, 2011.

Pascarella, Ernest, Charles Blaich, Georgianna L. Martin, and Jana M. Hanson. "How Robust Are the Findings of *Academically Adrift*?" *Change*, May–June 2011, 20–24.

Pascarella, Ernest T., and Patrick T. Terenzini. *How College Affects Students: Findings and Insights from Twenty Years of Research*. San Francisco: Jossey-Bass, 1991.

———. *How College Affects Students, Volume 2: A Third Decade of Research*. San Francisco: Jossey-Bass, 2005.

"Peer Review of Teaching Project." University of Nebraska. http://www.courseportfolio .org/peer/pages/index.jsp.

Peet, Melissa R., Laura Reynolds-Keefer, Patricia Gurin, and Steve Lonn. "Fostering Integrative Knowledge and Lifelong Learning." *Peer Review*, Fall 2011/Winter 2012, 15–17.

Plous, Scott. *The Psychology of Judgment and Decision Making*. New York: McGraw-Hill, 1993.

President's Council of Advisers on Science and Technology, Executive Office of the President. "Engage to Excel: Producing One Million Additional College Graduates with Degrees in Science, Technology, Engineering, and Mathematics." February 2012. http://www.whitehouse.gov/sites/default/files/microsites/ostp/pcast-engage-to -excel-final_2-25-12.pdf.

Prewitt, K. "*Who* Should Do *What*: Implications of Institutional and National Leaders." In *Envisioning the Future of Doctoral Education: Preparing Stewards of the Discipline*, edited by Chris M. Golde, George E. Walker, and Associates, 23–33. San Francisco: Jossey-Bass, 2006.

Prochaska, James O., Carlo C. DiClemente, and John C. Norcross. "In Search of How People Change: Applications to Addictive Behaviors." *American Psychologist* 47 (September 1992): 1102–1114.

Prochaska, James O., and John C. Norcross. *Systems of Psychotherapy: A Transtheoretical Analysis*. Belmont, CA: Brooks-Cole, 2006.

Prochaska, James O., John C. Norcross, and Carlo C. DiClemente. *Changing for Good*. New York: Harper, 1994.

Prochaska, James O., and Janice M. Prochaska. "Why Don't Continents Move? Why Don't People Change?" *Journal of Psychotherapy Integration* 9, no. 1 (1999): 83–102.

Provezis, Staci. "Regional Accreditation and Student Learning Outcomes: Mapping the Territory." Urbana, IL: University of Illinois and Indiana University, National Institute for Learning Outcomes Assessment, October 2010. http://www .learningoutcomeassessment.org/documents/OccasionalPaper6.pdf.

Quinn, Jennifer Woods. "If It Catches My Eye: A Report of Faculty Pedagogical Reading Habits." *Innovative Higher Education* 19, no. 1 (Fall 1994): 53–66.

Ramsden, Paul, and Elaine Martin. "Recognition of Good University Teaching: Policies from an Australian Study." *Studies in Higher Education* 21, no. 3 (October 1996): 299–315. http://web.a.ebscohost.com.prozy.palomar.edu/.

Ratcliff, James L. "What We Can Learn from Coursework Patterns about Improving the Undergraduate Curriculum." In *Assessment and Curriculum Reform*, edited by James L. Ratcliff. *New Directions for Higher Education* 80 (1992): 5–22.

Ratcliff, James L., and Associates. *Realizing the Potential: Improving Postsecondary Teaching, Learning, and Assessment*. University Park, PA: National Center on Postsecondary Teaching, Learning, and Assessment, 1995.

Remler, Dahlia K., and Elda Pema. "Why Do Institutions of Higher Education Reward Research while Selling Education?" Working Paper 14974, National Bureau of Economic Research, May 2009.

Rice, R. Eugene, and Mary Deane Sorcinelli. "Can the Tenure Process Be Improved?" In *The Questions of Tenure*, edited by Richard P. Chait, 101–124. Cambridge, MA: Harvard University Press, 2002.

Richlin, Laurie, and Amy Essington. "Overview of Faculty Learning Communities." In *Building Faculty Learning Communities*, edited by Milton D. Cox and Laurie Richlin. *New Directions for Teaching and Learning* 97 (2004): 25–39.

Rogers, Everett M. *Diffusion of Innovations*. 5th ed. New York: Free Press, 2003.

Rojstaczer, Stuart, and Christopher Healy. "Grading in American Colleges and Universities." *Teachers College Record*, March 4, 2010. http://www.tcrecord.org/content.asp?contentid=15928.

———. "Where A Is Ordinary: The Evolution of American College and University Grading, 1940–2009." *Teachers College Record* 114, no. 7 (2012). http://www.tcrecord.org/content.asp?contentid=16473.

Rothwell, Jonathan. "No Recovery: An Analysis of Long-Term U.S. Productivity Decline." Washington, DC: Gallup, 2016. http://www.gallup.com/reports/198776/no-recovery-analysis-long-term-productivity-decline.aspx.

Rudolph, Frederick. *The American College and University: A History*. Athens: University of Georgia Press, 1962.

———. *Curriculum: A History of the American Undergraduate Course of Study since 1636*. San Francisco: Jossey-Bass, 1977.

Russell, Thomas. *The Search for a Common Learning: General Education, 1800–1960*. New York: McGraw-Hill, 1962.

Samuelson, William, and Richard Zeckhauser. "Status Quo Bias in Decision Making." *Journal of Risk and Uncertainty* 1 (1988): 7–59.

Sawyer, Keith. *Group Genius: The Creative Power of Collaboration*. New York: Basic Books, 2007.

Schneider, Carol Geary. Afterword to "The Lumina Degree Qualifications Profile (DQP): Implications for Assessment," by Peter T. Ewell. NILOA Occasional Paper 16, University of Illinois and Indiana University, National Institute of Learning Outcomes Assessment, January 2013. http://www.learningoutcomesassessment.org/documents/EwellDQPop1.pdf.

———. "Policy Priorities for Accreditation Put Quality College Learning at Risk: A Message from AAC&U President Carol Geary Schneider." Washington, DC: Association of American Colleges & Universities, December 2, 2015. http://www.aacu.org/about/statements/2015/accreditation.

Schuster, Jack H., and Martin J. Finkelstein. *The American Faculty: The Restructuring of Academic Work and Careers*. Baltimore: Johns Hopkins University Press, 2006.

Scorcinelli, Mary Deane, Ann E. Austin, Pamela L. Eddy, and Andrea L. Beach. *Creating the Future of Faculty Development: Learning from the Past, Understanding the Present*. San Francisco: Jossey-Bass, 2006.

Seymour, Elaine, and Nancy M. Hewitt. *Talking about Leaving: Why Undergraduates Leave the Sciences*. Boulder, CO: Westview, 1997.

Shapiro, Fred R. *The Yale Book of Quotations*. New Haven, CT: Yale University Press, 2006.

Shapiro, Howard N. "Promotion & Tenure & the Scholarship of Teaching & Learning." *Change*, March–April 2006, 38–43.

Shavelson, Richard J. *Measuring College Learning Responsibly: Accountability in a New Era*. Stanford, CA: Stanford University Press, 2010.

Shear, Michael D. "Colleges Rattled as Obama Seeks Rating System." *New York Times*, May 25, 2014. http://www.nytimes.com/2014/05/26/us/colleges-rattled-as-obama-presses-rating-system.html?ref=us&_r=0.

Shedd, Jessica M. "The History of the Student Credit Hour." In *How the Student Credit Hour Shapes Higher Education: The Tie That Binds*, edited by Jane V. Wellman and Thomas Ehrlich. *New Directions for Higher Education* 122 (Summer 2003): 5–12.

Shulman, Lee S. *The Wisdom of Practice: Essays on Teaching, Learning, and Learning to Teach*. San Francisco: Carnegie Foundation for the Advancement of Teaching/Jossey-Bass, 2004.

Silva, Elena, Taylor White, and Thomas Toch. "The Carnegie Unit: A Century-Old Standard in a Changing Educational Landscape." Stanford, CA: Carnegie Foundation for the Advancement of Teaching, January 2015. http://cdn.carnegiefoundation.org/wp-content/uploads/2015/01/Carnegie_Unit_Report.pdf.

Smallwood, Mary Lovett. *An Historical Study of Examinations and Grading Systems in Early American Universities*. Cambridge, MA: Harvard University Press, 1935.

Smith, Page. *Killing the Spirit: Higher Education in America*. New York: Viking, 1990.

Spooren, Pieter, Bert Brockx, and Dimitri Mortelmans. "On the Validity of Student Evaluation of Teaching: The State of the Art." *Review of Educational Research* 20, no. 10 (2013): 1–45.

Stains, M., J. Harshman, M. K. Barker, S. V. Chasteen, R. Cole, S. E. DeChenne-Peters, et al. "Anatomy of STEM Teaching in North American Universities." *Science* 359, no. 6383 (March 30, 2018): 1468–1470.

Stark, Philip. "What Exactly Do Student Evaluations Measure?" *Berkeley Blog*, October 21, 2013. http://blogs.berkeley.edu/2013/10/21/what-exactly-do-student-evaluations-measure/.

Strauss, Steven. "The Connection between Education, Income Inequality, and Unemployment." *Huffington Post*, November 2, 2011. http://www.huffingtonpost.com
/steven-strauss/the-connection-between-ed_b_1066401.html.

Struck, Peter T. "Report to the Teagle Foundation on a Listening on Assessment." Teagle
Foundation, 2007. http://www.teaglefoundation.org/teagle/media/library/documents
/resources/20070201_struck.pdf.

Study Group on the Conditions of Excellence in American Higher Education. "Involvement in Learning: Realizing the Potential of American Higher Education." Washington, DC: National Institute of Education, 1984. (ERIC ED 246 833)

Sunstein, Cass R. *Going to Extremes: How Like Minds Unite and Divide.* New York: Oxford
University Press, 2009.

Tagg, John. "Changing Minds in Higher Education: Students Change, So Why Can't Colleges?" *Planning for Higher Education*, October–December 2008, 13–20.

———. "Dispelling the Fog of Learning through SoTL." *International Journal for the
Scholarship of Teaching and Learning* 4, no. 2 (July 2010). http://w3.georgiasouthern
.edu/ijsotl/v4n2/invited_essays/PDFs/_Tagg.pdf.

———. *The Learning Paradigm College.* San Francisco: Jossey-Bass, 2003.

Taylor, Mark C. *Crisis on Campus: A Bold Plan for Reforming Our Colleges and Universities.* New York: Knopf, 2010.

Tetlock, Philip E. *Expert Political Judgment: How Good Is It? How Can We Know?* Princeton, NJ: Princeton University Press, 2005.

Thadani, Vandana, William Breland, and Jacqueline Dewar. "College Instructors' Implicit
Theories about Teaching Skills and Their Relationship to Professional Development
Choices." *Journal on Excellence in College Teaching* 21, no. 2 (2010): 113–131.

Thaler, Richard H. *Misbehaving: The Making of Behavioral Economics.* New York: Norton,
2015.

———. "Toward a Positive Theory of Consumer Choice." *Journal of Economic Behavior
and Organization* 1 (1980): 39–60.

Thaler, Richard, and Cass R. Sunstein. *Nudge: Improving Decisions about Health, Wealth,
and Happiness.* New Haven, CT: Yale University Press, 2008.

Tobin, Anna. "Couldn't Teach a Dog to Sit." *Times Higher Education Supplement*, July 29,
1996. http://www.timeshighereducation.co.uk/news/couldnt-teach-a-dog-to-sit
/99805.article.

Tolman, Anton. "TMM Teaching Survey." Orem: Utah Valley University, 2010.

Toma, J. Douglas. "Institutional Strategy: Positioning for Prestige." In *The Organization
of Higher Education: Managing Colleges for a New Era*, edited by Michael N. Bastedo,
118–159. Baltimore: Johns Hopkins University Press, 2012.

Tough, Paul. "Who Gets to Graduate?" *New York Times Magazine*, May 15, 2014. https://
www.nytimes.com/2014/05/18/magazine/who-gets-to-graduate.html?_r=0

University of British Columbia. "Guidelines for Promotion to Professor of Teaching."
University of British Columbia, June 28, 2011. http://www.hr.ubc.ca/faculty-relations
/files/Guidelines-for-Promotion-to-Professor-of-Teaching.pdf.

U.S. Department of Education. *College Scorecard.* https://collegescorecard.ed.gov/.

———. "IPEDS." Institute of Education Sciences, National Center for Educational Statistics, n.d. http://nces.ed.gov/ipeds/?src=ft.

———. "A Test of Leadership: Charting the Future of Higher Education." Washington, DC, 2006.

Uttl, Bob, Carmela A. White, and Daniela Wong Gonzalez. "Meta-analysis of Faculty's Teaching Effectiveness: Student Evaluation of Teaching Ratings and Student Learning Are Not Related." *Studies in Educational Evaluation* 54 (2017): 22–42. http://dx.doi.org/10.1016/j.stueduc.2016.08.007.

Veysey, Laurence R. *The Emergence of the American University*. Chicago: University of Chicago Press, 1965.

von Hoene, Linda. "Graduate Student Teaching Certificates: Survey of Current Programs." In *Mapping the Range of Graduate Student Professional Development*, edited by Laura L. B. Border, 101–124. Stillwater, OK: New Forums Press, 2011.

Walker, George E., Chris M. Golde, Laura Jones, Andrea Conklin Bueschel, and Pat Hutchings. *The Formation of Scholars: Rethinking Doctoral Education for the Twenty-First Century*. San Francisco: Jossey-Bass, 2008.

Walter, Emily M., Charles R. Henderson, Andrea L. Beach, and Cody T. Williams. "Introducing the Postsecondary Instructional Practices Survey (PIPS): A Concise, Interdisciplinary, and Easy-to-Score Survey." *CBE-Life Sciences Education* 15, no. 4 (2016): ar53. http://www.lifescied.org.

Weick, Karl E. "Contradictions in a Community of Scholars: The Cohesion-Accuracy Tradeoff." In *College and University Organization: Insights from the Behavioral Sciences*, edited by James L. Bess, 15–29. New York: New York University Press, 1984.

Weimer, Maryellen. *Enhancing Scholarly Work on Teaching and Learning: Professional Literature That Makes a Difference*. San Francisco: Jossey-Bass, 2006.

———. "Positioning Scholarly Work on Teaching and Learning." *International Journal for the Scholarship of Teaching and Learning* 2, no. 1 (January 2008). https://digitalcommons.georgiasouthern.edu/ij-sotl/vol2/iss1/4/

Wellman, Jane V., and Thomas Ehrlich, eds. *How the Student Credit Hour Shapes Higher Education: The Tie That Binds. New Directions for Higher Education* 122 (Summer 2003).

Wergin, Jon F. *Departments That Work: Building and Sustaining Cultures of Excellence in Academic Programs*. Bolton, MA: Anker, 2003.

Whitehead, Alfred North. *The Aims of Education and Other Essays*. New York: Free Press, 1929.

Wieman, Carl. "Applying New Research to Improve Science Education." *Issues in Science and Technology*, Fall 2012, 25–32.

———. "A Better Way to Evaluate Undergraduate Teaching." *Change*, January–February 2015, 6–15.

———. *Improving How Universities Teach Science: Lessons from the Science Education Initiative*. Cambridge, MA: Harvard University Press, 2017.

———. "Large Scale Comparison of Science Teaching Methods Sends Clear Message." *Proceedings of the National Academy of Sciences* 111, no. 23 (June 10, 2014): 8319–8320. http://www.pnas.org/content/111/23/8319.full.pdf+html.

———. "A New Model for Post-secondary Education, the Optimized University." University of British Columbia, n.d. http://www.cwsei.ubc.ca/resources/files/BC_Campus2020_Wieman_think_piece.pdf.

———. "Science Education for the 21st Century; A Scientific Approach to Science Education." Paper presented at Atomic Physics 20, Innsbruck, July 2006.

———. "Why Not Try a Scientific Approach to Science Education?" *Change,* September–October, 2007, 9–15.

Wieman, Carl, and Sarah Gilbert. "The Teaching Practices Inventory: A New Tool for Characterizing College and University Teaching in Mathematics and Science." *CBE-Life Science Education* 13 (2014): 552–569.

Zemsky, Robert. *Checklist for Change: Making American Higher Education a Sustainable Enterprise.* New Brunswick, NJ: Rutgers University Press, 2013.

———. *Making Reform Work: The Case for Transforming American Higher Education.* New Brunswick, NJ: Rutgers University Press, 2009.

Zemsky, Robert, and Joni Finney. "Changing the Subject: Costs, Graduation Rates and the Importance of Rethinking the Undergraduate Curriculum." *National Cross Talk,* May 2010. http://www.highereducation.org/crosstalk/ct0510/voices0510–zemfin.shtml.

Zemsky, Robert, Gregory R. Wegner, and William F. Massy. *Remaking the American University: Market-Smart and Mission-Centered.* New Brunswick, NJ: Rutgers University Press, 2005.

INDEX

ABOUT THE AUTHOR

JOHN TAGG is author of *The Learning Paradigm College* (Jossey-Bass, 2003) and professor emeritus of English at Palomar College. He has been an advocate for the Learning Paradigm since the 1995 publication, with Robert Barr, of the seminal article "From Teaching to Learning: A New Paradigm for Undergraduate Education." He has published widely in educational periodicals and has made presentations at hundreds of colleges and universities and professional conferences.